INTELLIGENT DESIGN

William A. Dembski *& Michael Ruse *in Dialogue*

Robert B. Stewart, editor

Fortress Press
Minneapolis

INTELLIGENT DESIGN
William A. Dembski and Michael Ruse in Dialogue

Cover design: Kevin Van der Leek
Book design: Christy J. P. Barker and Douglas Schmitz

Library of Congress Cataloging-in-Publication Data
Intelligent design : William A. Dembski and Michael Ruse in dialogue /
Robert B. Stewart, editor.
    p. cm.
 Includes bibliographical references and index.
 ISBN 978-0-8006-6218-9 (alk. paper)
1. Intelligent design (Teleology) 2. Religion and science.
3. Creationism—Philosophy. I. Stewart, Robert B., 1957–
BL263.I58 2007
231.7'652—dc22   2007027505

Manufactured in the U.S.A.

11   10   09   08   2   3   4   5   6   7   8   9   10

For Marilyn

My best friend,
The love of my life,
And my favorite science instructor

Contents

Contributors

Francis J. Beckwith is associate professor of church-state studies at Baylor University, where he teaches in the departments of philosophy and political science, as well as in the Institute of Church-State Studies. A graduate of Fordham University (Ph.D., philosophy) and the Washington University School of Law, St. Louis (Master of Juridical Studies), his over one dozen books include *Defending Life: A Moral and Legal Case Against Abortion Choice* (Cambridge University Press, 2007), *To Everyone An Answer: A Case for the Christian Worldview* (InterVarsity, 2004), *Law, Darwinism, and Public Education* (Rowman & Littlefield, 2003), and *Relativism: Feet Firmly Planted in Mid-Air* (Baker, 1998). His areas of academic interest include jurisprudence, politics, philosophy of religion, philosophy of science, and constitutional law.

William Lane Craig is a research professor at Talbot School of Theology in La Mirada, California. He earned a doctorate in philosophy at the University of Birmingham, England, before taking a doctorate in theology from the Ludwig Maximilians Universität-München, Germany, where for two years he was a Fellow of the Alexander von Humboldt-Stiftung, writing on the historicity of the resurrection of Jesus. He spent seven years at the Katholike Universiteit Leuven, Belgium, before taking his post at Talbot in 1994. Among the many books he has authored or edited are *The Kalam Cosmological Argument* (Macmillan, 1979), *God? A Debate between a Christian and an Atheist* (Oxford University Press, 2003), *Does God Exist?*, ed. S. Wallace (Ashgate, 2003). He currently lives in Atlanta with his wife, Jan; they have two children, Charity and John.

William A. Dembski (M.Div., Ph.D. mathematics, Ph.D philosophy) is research professor in philosophy at Southwestern Seminary in addition to serving as the executive director of the International Society for Complexity, Information, and Design and a Senior Fellow with Discovery Institute's Center for Science and Culture. He has taught at the Southern Baptist Theological Seminary, Baylor University, Northwestern University, the University of Notre Dame, and the University of Dallas. He has held National Science Foundation graduate and postgraduate fellowships. In addition to publishing articles in mathematics, philosophy, and theological journals, he has authored or edited numerous books, including *The Design Inference: Eliminating Chance through Small Probabilities* (Cambridge University Press, 1998), *No Free Lunch: Why Specified Complexity Cannot Be Purchased without Intelligence* (Rowman & Littlefield, 2002), *The Design Revolution: Answering the Toughest Questions about Intelligent Design* (InterVarsity, 2004), and, with Michael Ruse, *Debating Design: From Darwin to DNA* (Cambridge University Press, 2004).

Wesley R. Elsberry (B.S., M.S.C.S., Ph.D.) is visiting research associate at Michigan State University investigating the evolution of intelligent behavior using evolutionary computation. He previously served as information project director for the National Center for Science Education. His work experience includes anesthesiology research, veterinary research, software design and production for military aircraft and logistics, and programming, electronics design, and data analysis in behavioral research. His area of research is dolphin biosonar sound production and bioenergetics. He is a coauthor of peer-reviewed papers in the *Journal of Experimental Biology* and in *Biology and Philosophy*. He received the Society for Marine Mammalogy's Fairfield Memorial Award for Innovation in Marine Mammal Research in 2001.

Martinez Hewlett is an emeritus professor in the department of molecular and cellular biology at the University of Arizona in Tucson. He has published thirty scientific papers and a novel, *Divine Blood* (Ballantine, 1994). He is a founding member of the St. Albert the Great Forum on Theology and the Sciences at the University of Arizona. He serves as an adjunct professor at the Dominican School of Philosophy and Theology at the Graduate Theological Union, Berkeley. Along with Ted Peters, he is coauthor of *Evolution from Creation to New Creation* (Abingdon, 2003) and *Can We Believe in God and Evolution?* (Abingdon, 2006).

Ken Keathley is senior associate dean and professor of theology at Southeastern Baptist Theological Seminary in Wake Forest, North Carolina. He graduated from Southeastern with a Master of Divinity and a Ph.D. in theology. His research focuses on the history of the doctrine of creation and its relationship to science, with a particular emphasis on how science relates to biblical interpretation. He lives with his wife, Penny, and their two children in the Wake Forest area.

John C. Lennox (M.A., D.Phil., D.Sc.) is a research fellow in mathematics at Green College and the Mathematical Institute, Oxford, and a senior fellow of the Whitfield Institute. He is author or coauthor of a number of books including: *The Theory of Infinite Soluble Groups* (Oxford University Press, 2004), *Subnormal Subgroups of Groups* (Oxford University Press, 1987), *Christianity: Opium or Truth?* (Gospel Folio, 1997). He has been a Senior Alexander von Humboldt Fellow at the Universities of Wuerzburg and Freiburg in Germany and a visiting professor at the Universities of Vienna, Alberta, and Bar Ilan. He has lectured in many universities abroad, including in the former Soviet Union (Moscow, St. Petersburg, Novosibirsk, Kiev, Minsk, and others) as an invitee of the Academy of Sciences.

Nicholas Matzke is a public information project director at the National Center for Science Education. He has a double B.S. in biology and chemistry from Valparaiso University and a master's degree in geography from the University of California at Santa Barbara. He specializes in making the scientific literature related to evolution accessible and understandable to the public. During the landmark case *Kitzmiller v. Dover*, he spent a year working for the plaintiff's legal team, providing scientific advice and researching the creationist origins of the ID movement. He intends to enter a Ph.D. program where he can work on the integration of bioinformatics, biogeography, and large-scale evolution.

Alister McGrath is professor of historical theology at Oxford University and senior research fellow at Harris Manchester College, Oxford. He holds Oxford doctorates in both molecular biophysics and Christian theology. His research focuses on the relation of science and Christianity, especially in relation to the biological sciences. Among the many books that he has authored are the three-volume *A Scientific Theology, The Twilight of Atheism: The Rise and Fall of Disbelief in the Modern World* and *Dawkins' God: Genes, Memes, and the Meaning of Life*, the first book-length assessment of the religious ideas of the Oxford atheist writer Richard Dawkins.

J. P. Moreland is distinguished professor of philosophy at Talbot School of Theology, Biola University. He has authored, edited, or contributed to thirty-five books, including *Does God Exist?* (Prometheus, 1993), *Philosophy of*

Religion (Oxford University Press, 1996), *Naturalism: A Critical Analysis* (Routledge, 2000), *Body & Soul* (InterVarsity, 2000), *Universals* (McGill-Queens, 2001), *Philosophy of Religion: A Reader and Guide* (Edinburgh University Press, 2002), and *Blackwell Companion to Natural Theology* (forthcoming). He has also published over sixty articles in professional journals, including *American Philosophical Quarterly*, *Australasian Journal of Philosophy*, *MetaPhilosophy*, *Philosophy and Phenomenological Research*, *Religious Studies*, and *Faith and Philosophy*.

Nancey Murphy is professor of philosophy at Fuller Seminary, Pasadena. She received her Ph.D. from U. C. Berkeley and her Th.D. from the Graduate Theological Union. Her first book, *Theology in the Age of Scientific Reasoning*, won the American Academy of Religion award for excellence. She is the author of seven other books and coeditor of eight. Her most recent, with Warren Brown, is *Did My Neurons Make Me Do It? Philosophical and Neurobiological Perspectives on Moral Responsibility and Free Will* (Oxford University Press, 2007). Her research focuses on the role of modern and postmodern philosophy in shaping Christian theology, on relations between theology and science, and on neuroscience and philosophy of mind.

Hal N. Ostrander is chair of the religion and philosophy division and the Barney Averitt Associate Professor of Christian Studies, Brewton-Parker College, Mount Vernon, Georgia. He received his M.Div. and Ph.D. degrees from Southwestern Baptist Theological Seminary. He is the author of several articles on theology and faith/science matters appearing in *Baptist Press*, *SBC Life*, *The Christian Index*, *Journal of Christian Apologetics*, and *The Southern Baptist Journal of Theology*. His research interests include Christian apologetics, theology, and science and their integrative relations. In addition, he regularly conducts Christian apologetics and intelligent design seminars for ministerial students in the United States, Belarus, and Russia.

Wolfhart Pannenberg (Th.D., University of Heidelberg) is author of several books on the relationship of science and theology. Among these are *Theology and the Philosophy of Science* (Westminster, 1976) and *Toward a Theology of Nature: Essays on Science and Faith* (Westminster, 1993). In addition, both his three-volume *Systematic Theology* (Eerdmans, 1991, 1995, 1997) and his *Jesus—God and Man* (Westminster, 1968) are widely hailed as being among the most significant theological works of the last half of the twentieth century. The belief that theology must be informed by the best science available has marked his work from the beginning.

Sir John Polkinghorne is a fellow of the Royal Society, a fellow (and former president) of Queens' College, Cambridge, and canon theologian of Liverpool Cathedral. The founding president of the International Society for Science and Religion, he was awarded the Templeton Prize for Science and Religion in 2002. After teaching physics in the United Kingdom for over twenty years (Edinburgh and Cambridge), he resigned his professorship to train for the Anglican priesthood. Besides writing many books and articles on the relationship between Christianity and science, he was one of the founders of the Society of Ordained Scientists, a dispersed preaching Order of the Anglican Communion.

Michael Ruse is Lucyle T. Werkmeister professor of philosophy at Florida State University and is also director of the program in history and philosophy of science. He has held John Simon Guggenheim and Isaak Walton Killam Fellowships and is a fellow of the Royal Society of Canada and the American Association for the Advancement of Science. He was a Herbert Spencer lecturer at Oxford University in 1995, a Gifford lecturer at Glasgow University in 2001, and a Herbert Jennings lecturer at Baylor University in 2003. He was the founding editor of the journal *Biology and Philosophy* and is the editor of the University of Cambridge Press Series in the Philosophy of Biology. His many books include *The Darwinian Revolution: Science Red in Tooth and Claw* (University of Chicago Press, 1999), *Can a Darwinian Be a Christian?* (Cambridge University Press, 2001), and *The Evolution-Creation Struggle* (Harvard Univeristy Press, 2005).

Robert B. Stewart is associate professor of philosophy and theology at New Orleans Baptist Theological Seminary, where he is Greer-Heard Professor of Faith and Culture. He is editor of *The Resurrection of Jesus: John Dominic Crossan and N. T. Wright in Dialogue* (Fortress Press, 2005) and author of *The Quest of the Hermeneutical Jesus: The Impact of Hermeneutics on the Jesus Research of John Dominic Crossan and N. T. Wright* (University Press of America, forthcoming). A contributor to the *Cambridge Dictionary of Christianity* and the *Revised Holman Bible Dictionary*, he has published articles and book reviews in numerous journals.

Preface

Early Monday morning, August 29, 2005, Hurricane Katrina struck the New Orleans area. The flooding in New Orleans began around 4:30 A.M., and by midmorning numerous levees in the greater New Orleans area had either failed or been topped. Roughly 80 percent of the city was flooded as a result.[1] The campus of New Orleans Baptist Theological Seminary (NOBTS), the host institution for the Greer-Heard Point-Counterpoint Forum in Faith and Culture, was almost entirely underwater.

As I sat in my sister-in-law's house in Texas, watching it all on television, my mind was far from thoughts of the second Greer-Heard Point-Counterpoint Forum in Faith and Culture, and even further still from thinking about intelligent design, a controversial theory recently embraced by many evangelical Christians (plus a few non-Christians and even some nontheists). The forum is a five-year pilot program made possible by a gracious financial gift from William L. Heard Jr. and his wife, Carolyn (née Greer) to provide a forum for an evangelical and a nonevangelical scholar to come together for dialogue on a particular issue of religious or cultural significance. As the director of the Greer-Heard Forum, it was my responsibility to organize and lead in implementing the event each year. But when you are wondering if your home has been flooded, if your office has been flooded—or looted—if your library and computer files have been destroyed, things like conferences that are still over five months into a suddenly very uncertain future do not readily come to mind. (For the record, my home was severely flooded—as a family, we lost nearly 90 percent of our material possessions—my office was neither flooded nor looted, and thus most of my library and work was safe. What really matters is that my family was safe.)

Our chief administrators and staff relocated to the NOBTS extension center site in Decatur, Georgia, and immediately began putting together a plan to save our school. Their efforts were, as our president, Chuck Kelley, likes to say, the stuff of legend. By early October, most courses had been redesigned to be offered via the Internet and the majority of our students continued with their studies; all this while virtually everyone—students, staff, and faculty—had to make decisions concerning the future, such as where to live, where to send their children to school, what to replace first, as well as dealing with the Federal Emergency Management Agency (FEMA), the Red Cross, insurance (for those fortunate enough to have flood insurance), replacing automobiles, finding new employment, and a hundred other mundane things that one never really thinks about until faced with an unimaginable situation like Katrina.

When I finally did get around to thinking about the 2006 Greer-Heard Forum, I assumed that there would be no such event that year. In a phone conversation with our provost, Steve Lemke, I mentioned this and was surprised to hear him say not to rule it out too quickly. He suggested considering a large church as the site for the event, and that if we were able to pull it off, it would make a statement that NOBTS was still alive and making a difference. Frankly, I thought he was suffering from post-traumatic stress syndrome. But the longer I thought about it the more the idea made sense. We already had lined up William Dembski and Michael Ruse to headline the dialogue on intelligent design. But would our agreed-upon dates still work? Where could we do it? And how could we put all the pieces together in such a brief amount of time—especially given that we had students, staff, and faculty spread all around the nation? It was hard enough doing an event like this in New Orleans, where we had support staff and a familiar on-campus setting.

Initially, my ideas as to places and settings in which to reschedule the event all went up in smoke upon further investigation. Then, providentially, William Lane (Bill) Craig suggested during a phone conversation that we hold the forum at his home church, Johnson Ferry Baptist Church (JFBC) in Marietta, Georgia, a suburb of Atlanta. Bill was good enough to run the idea by his pastor and senior staff and called me back to say that they could host the event—if we could reschedule to the previous weekend. I feared that this necessary change of date would doom the event, but was pleased to learn that not only could Dembski and Ruse reschedule, but three of the four other invited speakers were available on the new dates as well. I greatly appreciated (and still do!) their flexibility and willingness to work around these changes. Bill Craig agreed to take the place of J. P. Moreland, who was already committed on the new dates.

This was good news, but we were still left with a great deal of work needing to be done in a short time. Were it not for the professionalism and graciousness of the staff at JFBC, it would have been an impossible task. They were prepared for every contingency and regularly exceeded my expectations in terms of quality and timeliness. Their core values include excellence in ministry and extra-mile servant ministry—and they embody those ideals. With their help and the support of our NOBTS administration and staff, the event took place February 3–4, 2006, with over 850 people attending. The spirit of the event was friendly and collegial throughout without any participant sacrificing any of their convictions. There was profound disagreement at points, some agreement at other points, and to a person a sense that it was time well spent.

In recent years, intelligent design has been a particularly controversial—and emotional—issue in Cobb County, Georgia, where JFBC is located.[2] The good people of Cobb County were especially appreciative of an event that featured calm rational discussion of such an important issue. They also contributed to the event significantly in that they were an especially well-informed audience.

Our authors who were not present at the meeting in Marietta are world-class scholars eminently qualified to write on the relationship of science and faith. All the contributors bring to the table considerable knowledge and relevant expertise in the areas they address. I know of no other book that brings together such highly qualified authors from such diverse fields to consider this topic.

All in all, Katrina aside, I could not have hoped for a better Greer-Heard Point-Counterpoint Forum in Faith and Culture. I hope that we will have many more such events. I also hope that you are enriched by the differing perspectives you will find in this book.

Acknowledgments

I always have a sense of trepidation when beginning to thank others in public because I fear that I will fail to recognize someone who truly deserves a word of appreciation. But many deserve to be publicly thanked, and even praised, so I must go on. First of all, I must thank Bill and Carolyn Heard for their passion to have a forum where leading scholars can dialogue about important issues in faith and culture in a collegial manner and on a balanced playing field—and their willingness to fund such a project. Without them the Greer-Heard Point-Counterpoint Forum in Faith and Culture would be a dream rather than a reality. Thanks are also due to President Chuck Kelley and Provost Steve Lemke of the New Orleans Baptist Theological Seminary (NOBTS) for their willingness to proceed with the forum after the destruction of hurricane Katrina.

Without the high-quality graphic art and public relations work of Jeff Audirsch and Gary Myers the task would have proven too great. The NOBTS public relations department went from numerous people working out of a suite of offices on campus to two guys working out of a Sunday School classroom on a couple laptop computers. Nevertheless, they performed admirably. Their efforts are much appreciated.

Many people from Johnson Ferry Baptist Church (JFBC) deserve mentioning: first of all, pastor Bryant Wright, who sets the tone for all that happens at JFBC, and whose passion for excellence inspires all his staff. John Herring, assistant pastor of adult ministries at JFBC, led the team of positive-thinking staff in every area. His optimism and patience are exceeded only by his ability as an administrator. His assistant, Marti Davie, did everything asked of her and more, and always with a gracious spirit. Outreach coordinator Lisa Joyner produced first-rate advertisements and other print materials without which we would have been doomed to failure. Her skills are extraordinary. Dottie Poythress ordered materials and organized the conference bookstore flawlessly. Mary Cinibulk, who organized all the volunteer teams, such as greeters, speaker hosts, registration teams, etc. deserves a word of thanks, as do countless JFBC volunteers.

Our conference speakers, William Dembski, Michael Ruse, Francis Beckwith, Martinez Hewlett, Wesley Elsberry, and William Lane Craig must all be thanked. I am so grateful that they could make the required adjustments to their schedules that Katrina necessitated. William Lane Craig also must be thanked not only for speaking at the conference and contributing to this volume but also for seeing that JFBC would be the right place for a conference such as this. In addition, he served on the steering committee that ensured that all the relevant details were addressed.

I am also grateful to our other contributors, Ken Keathley, John Lennox, Alister McGrath, J.P. Moreland, Nancey Murphy, Hal Ostrander, Wolfhart Pannenberg, and John Polkinghorne. I am pleased that they could find their way free to contribute on this important subject.

C. Kelly Salmon must be thanked for his keen editorial eye and ability to format widely different types of articles. I appreciate him not only as a gifted former student and research assistant but as a friend as well. Rhyne Putman, my present research assistant, has also been a great help in preparing this book.

Blaize Stewart (no relation) is without a doubt a genius when it comes to computers—and an invaluable resource for a philosophy professor in his late 40s who knows nothing about website design. Blaize worked tirelessly to see to it that the Greer-Heard website was not only functional but also superior in its look and ease of use. James Walker, Bob Waldrep, Allan McConnell, and Michael Glawson, and the staff of the Birmingham, AL office of Watchman Fellowship deserve a word of public appreciation for their work in making audio recordings and MP3 files of the conference available.

Michael West, editor-in-chief of Fortress Press, must be thanked for his enthusiasm for fair-minded respectful dialogue on important issues and for choosing to publish the fruit of the Greer-Heard forum. Michael's knowledge of contemporary theology coupled with his judicious recommendations significantly strengthened this book. I would be remiss if I failed to thank Susan Johnson for her invaluable work in preparing this book, especially in helping to secure permission to include the work of Wolfhart Pannenberg. Carolyn Banks must also be thanked for her diligent work in getting this book to press.

Finally it would be unforgivable if I did not thank my wife, Marilyn, and my children, Ray, Bethany, and Rebekah, for their patience when I was away from home during the months, weeks, and days leading up to this event. The absence of a husband and a father is difficult on a family in the best of times—but even more so in the aftermath of an event like Katrina. A former high-school physics and chemistry teacher, Marilyn also helped me to grasp certain scientific principles related to the issues addressed in this book. Further, she was my most trusted advisor in the difficult planning that took place prior to the conference; she not only supported what I was doing, but also helped in the planning and promotion leading up to the conference. She has always been there for me. It is to her that I lovingly dedicate this book.

Introduction

What Are We Talking About?

Robert B. Stewart

We live in a day and age in which cultural diversity is trumpeted as a matter of great importance, but far too often cultural differences are communicated in shrill tones. Perhaps never has Western culture been subjected to so many petty and fallacious attacks on individuals and ideas. It seems that both sides on any issue of significance delight in name calling and character assassination, and when called to account for such tactics routinely insist, "They started it." Perhaps nowhere is this sort of discourse more evident than in the ongoing debate over intelligent design (ID). One wonders whether the interested bystander who has yet to decide what to think on the subject will be turned off by the vitriol and the volume level emanating from those writing "informed" works on the subject. One is reminded of a long and protracted war in which each side is dug in in its trenches and occasionally rises up to fire wildly toward an enemy they can't see. At other times, they hunker down to launch a mortar round toward the opposite trench, all the while writing home when the conflict lets up to assure the local folks that they are winning. Surely this is no model for public dialogue.

If there is one thing that everyone writing on ID agrees upon it is that ID is an explosive (no pun intended) idea. Some see it as a powerful new paradigm within which to pursue science fruitfully. Others see it as a poison pill, a cleverly concealed new version of the old creationism that has already been expunged from laboratories by working scientists and from the schools by the courts. Often the charge is heard from both sides of the conflict that those on the other have been blinded by ideological presuppositions, whether of a religious or a secular nature.

One thing is certain—ID is controversial. But what exactly is ID? How did it begin? What are its key ideas? In short, What is all the fuss about? My purpose in this brief introduction is primarily descriptive; that is, to survey highpoints in the brief history of ID, to state its basic premises as well as the most common objections to ID. Recognizing that objectivity is unattainable, I shall endeavor as far as possible to allow the participants to speak for themselves. My goal, for the most part, is to set the stage for the discussion to follow, not to try to settle the issue but to draw a broad outline of the issues to date for the conversation that will follow.

Most observers, both within and without the ID community, recognize University of California at Berkeley law professor Phillip E. Johnson as the father of ID, and his 1991 book, *Darwin on Trial*,[1] as a landmark moment in the history of the movement. Johnson himself, however, credits two earlier books, Richard Dawkins's *The Blind Watchmaker*[2] and Michael Denton's *Evolution: A Theory in Crisis*,[3] with influencing him to see the importance of the issue.[4] Denton, a research professor of human molecular genetics at the University of Otago in New Zealand and a religious agnostic who considers "various forms of teleological theories, extending from Creationist intervention theories to nature mysticism" to be occultist theories,[5] nevertheless questioned the capacity of random mutation coupled with natural selection to account for all that neo-Darwinian theory required of it. Dawkins, Charles Simonyi Professor of the Public Understanding of Science at Oxford University, and an atheist, on the other hand, argued that neo-Darwinian theory could do exactly what Denton thought it could not—account for life and creativity, as well as explaining why life is the way it is. Even though it appears to be designed, it is not!

Challenged by one book, but encouraged by the other, Johnson published *Darwin on Trial*, in which he argues that evolutionary biologists contend for Darwinism not on the basis of overwhelming evidence but because their philosophy of science made it virtually impossible for them to consider any alternative. Johnson, a master attorney, produced in *Darwin on Trial* a rhetorical tour de force. The book garnered immediate attention both from the Christian press and from the scientific community, but had it been Johnson and ID's last word, it would merely have been a blip on the cultural radar screen.

Following the publication of *Darwin on Trial*, Johnson and others sympathetic to his critique of Darwinism met in March 1992 at the Darwinism: Scientific Inference or Philosophical Preference? conference hosted by Southern Methodist University. Among those present at this meeting were

William Dembski, Michael Behe, and Stephen Meyer. Following the SMU conference, Johnson arranged for a several-day meeting of potential ID leaders in Pajaro Dunes, California, in 1993. At Johnson's behest, all agreed to network via a listserv that Johnson would run from Berkeley. Reflecting on these events, Dembski states: "The meeting at Pajara Dunes was critical for getting all of us on the same page. The listserv was critical for keeping us networked and for building momentum."[6] Together, over time, Johnson and company forged a strategy for unseating materialism that would involve three phases: (1) research, writing, and publication; (2) publicity and opinion-making; and (3) cultural confrontation and renewal. This strategy is often spoken of as The Wedge, and there is great debate concerning it. Some tell a story where ID proponents stop just short of resembling something out of *The Da Vinci Code*, secretly conspiring to take modern science education back to the Middle Ages through nefarious means. Others insist that everything has been out in the open from the beginning. The reader can judge where the truth lies on this issue.[7]

Johnson followed the publication of *Darwin on Trial* with *Reason in the Balance: The Case against Naturalism in Science, Law, and Education*.[8] In this book, Johnson examines American culture on several fronts and finds that the fundamental issue is the debate between theism and naturalism—and the central issue in that debate is Darwinian evolution as expressed through methodological naturalism.

The year 1996 was important for three reasons: (1) the establishment by the Discovery Institute of the Center for the Renewal of Science and Culture;[9] (2) the publication of Michael Behe's *Darwin's Black Box: The Biochemical Challenge to Evolution*;[10] and (3) the Mere Creation conference held at Biola University (November 14–17), which brought together over two hundred scientists, philosophers, and theologians to discuss ID and creation.[11]

In *Darwin's Black Box* Behe, a biochemist and professor at Lehigh University, argues that there are numerous examples of biological systems that are irreducibly complex. He writes: "By irreducibly complex I mean a single system composed of several well-matched, interacting parts that contribute to the basic function wherein the removal of any one of the parts causes the system to effectively cease functioning."[12] Behe is not concerned to deny common ancestry or to argue that Darwinism does not indeed answer many biological questions. His main issue is with gradualism, the belief that evolution works directly through numerous small changes via random mutations over time as a result of the mechanism of natural selection to produce new systems serving new functions. This, according to Behe, is extremely improbable.

Behe's preferred analogy is that of a mousetrap. All the parts of a mousetrap are needed to make an effective and functioning mousetrap.

The mousetrap has both a function (to catch mice) and multiple parts, all of which are required for the mousetrap as a system to function. Take away one part of the mousetrap and it cannot function without alteration or addition. It's the same way with many biochemical systems. Behe examines five cellular systems as examples of irreducible complexity. They are the cellular cilium and bacterial flagellum,[13] the blood clotting cascade,[14] the intracellular trafficking system,[15] the immune system,[16] and pathways of intermediary metabolism.[17] In every case, he declares these systems to be irreducibly complex. Behe then concludes that irreducible complexity requires an intelligent designer.

Behe's work has encountered vigorous opposition. Probably the one writer who has most directly and often challenged Behe's position is Brown University professor Kenneth Miller. In *Finding Darwin's God: A Scientist's Search for Common Ground Between God and Evolution*, Miller gives numerous examples from the literature that he believes show that Behe is mistaken. He then concludes:

> Michael Behe's purported biochemical challenge to evolution rests on the assertion that Darwinian mechanisms are simply not adequate to explain the existence of complex biochemical machines. Not only is he wrong, he's wrong in a most spectacular way. The biochemical machines whose origins he finds so mysterious actually provide us with powerful and compelling examples of evolution in action. When we go to the trouble to open that black box, we find out once again that Darwin got it right.[18]

Behe and other ID proponents have responded to Miller and others who criticize the idea of irreducible complexity.[19] Most often, ID proponents argue that what their critics say are rebuttals are either misunderstandings of the concept that fail to address irreducible complexity properly understood, or examples that actually involve intelligent design (generally the intelligence of the scientist in manipulating the conditions of a particular experiment), or simply imagined stories of how irreducibly complex systems might possibly come to be that lack hard data to support any of their stories. One thing seems certain: neither Behe nor Miller, nor their supporters and/or detractors, has yet had the final word on irreducible complexity.

In 1998, William A. Dembski published *The Design Inference: Eliminating Chance through Small Probabilities*.[20] This work, which to my knowledge is the first peer-reviewed ID offering, was published by Cambridge University Press as part of the Cambridge Studies in Probability, Induction, and Decision Theory series. Whereas Johnson simply critiqued the arguments of Darwinists and Behe argued that is was highly improbable that Darwinian mechanisms could result in the irreducibly complex systems biologists encounter, Dembski proposes a model for discerning design from apparent design. How does he do this?

According to Dembski, ID begins with a question: "Might there be natural systems that cannot be explained entirely in terms of natural causes and that exhibit features characteristic of intelligence?"[21] Dembski's answer is an unambiguous yes: "there are natural systems that cannot be adequately explained in terms of undirected natural forces and that exhibit features which in any other circumstance we would attribute to intelligence."[22] But Dembski is not satisfied merely to assert that natural causes cannot explain everything we find in nature; he also insists that design is empirically detectable.

> As a theory of biological origins and development, intelligent design's central claim is that only intelligent causes adequately explain the complex, information-rich structures of biology and that these causes are empirically detectable. To say intelligent causes are empirically detectable is to say there exist well-defined methods that, based on observable features of the world, can reliably distinguish intelligent causes from undirected natural causes. Many special sciences have already developed such methods for drawing this distinction—notably, forensic science, cryptography, archeology and the search for extraterrestrial intelligence (SETI). Essential to all these methods is the ability to eliminate chance and necessity.[23]

Dembski insists that intelligence can be detected via the presence of specified complexity.

> Intelligence leaves behind a characteristic trademark or signature— what I call *specified complexity*. An event exhibits specified complexity if it is contingent and therefore not necessary; if it is complex and therefore not readily repeatable by chance; and if it is specified in the sense of exhibiting an independently given pattern.[24]

He realizes that a judgment of specified complexity must be as objectively given as possible (that is, there must be a system of detection that is not simply imposed on events after the fact, as would be the case, for instance, with an archer firing an arrow into a wall and then painting a target around the arrow).[25] Dembski therefore introduces the concept of an explanatory filter from which design inferences are derived. The filter involves three gates or decision nodes that an event or object must pass through in order for one to draw a proper design inference.

At the first gate the question is asked: Is this a necessary or contingent event, object, or system? For instance, an ice crystal would be an object that might at first glance appear to be contingent but upon closer examination is revealed to be necessary; that is, to be as it is because the laws governing the properties of water and the applicable random external conditions dictate as much.

At the second gate the question is posed: Is this a chance or complex event, object, or system? Given that an improbable event might nevertheless still be the result of chance, how does Dembski distinguish between an event, object, or system that exhibits complexity and one that is merely improbable? His method is mathematical, or more properly, statistical. He insists that any event that exceeds his "universal probability bound" satisfies the condition of complexity. The universal probability bound is arrived at by multiplying the estimated total number of elementary particles in the universe (10^{80}) times the age of the universe in seconds (10^{25}) times (10^{45}), which corresponds to Planck time; that is, the smallest physically meaningful unit of time. The sum of these figures is 10^{150}. Therefore "any specified event of probability less than 1 in 10^{150} will remain improbable even after all conceivable probabilistic resources from the observable universe have been factored in."[26]

Arriving at the third gate the question is asked: Is this event, object, or system the result of chance or is it specified? Not only does the filter require that an event, object, or system be both contingent and complex such that the probability of it occurring or coming to be is less than 1 in 10^{150}, it must be specified; that is, it must have a low probability of being a chance event in that it can be simply, or minimally, defined.[27] In other words, specification requires the presence of a pattern whose character is such as naturally to suggest a role for intelligence in its formation. This is a difficult condition to define. Dembski's favorite example comes from the movie *Contact*, where SETI researchers recognize purportedly extraterrestrial intelligence via a long series of numbers made up entirely of prime numbers.[28] One may not be able to define it but one can recognize it.

An event, object, or system that successfully passed through Dembski's filter would be designated "designed." In this way, Dembski proposes what he considers a valid model to use in the search for empirical evidence of design.

Dembski's work has received much praise and criticism. For example, Branden Fitelson, Christopher Stephens, and Elliott Sober criticize his explanatory filter for being both too hard and too lenient statistically on both chance and design.[29] Dembski has responded to them and others in several places.[30] Other challenges to Demsbki have been less technical. Barbara Forrest and Paul Gross focus on the politics of ID and contend that ID is nothing but the latest brand of antievolution, fundamentalist creationism to come down the path.[31] Others contend that Dembski's work isn't science because it makes no predictions and is not testable, or that if it is testable, it has failed the test.[32] Dembski, on the other hand, insists that ID is testable. If ID theorists are correct, he asserts, then biology should have numerous examples of structures that exhibit specified complexity—and he also responds that Darwinism as practiced is itself not subject to testing; that is, not falsifiable.[33]

But is it possible that ID will prove scientific in this regard? Stuart Kauffman, an adamant critic of ID in general and Dembski in particular, grudgingly admits the possibility. "Nevertheless, there is a core of 'could be' science in intelligent design which must be acknowledged. . . . In short, 'Is it designed or not?' can be a legitimate and deep scientific question."[34] No doubt the debate on this point will rage on for some time. It may be that ID proponents will make some testable predictions that will satisfy all involved. They may not. Time will tell on that count.

Many observers see ID following in the ancient tradition of design arguments for God's existence.[35] Dembski insists that there is a difference between a design *inference* and a design *argument.*

> The design argument is at its heart a philosophical and theological argument. It attempts to establish the existence and attributes of an intelligent cause behind the world based on certain features of the world. By contrast, the design inference is a generic argument for identifying the effects of intelligence regardless of the intelligence's particular characteristics and regardless of where, when, how or why the intelligence acts. (The intelligence can be animal, human, extraterrestrial, singular, plural, immanent or transcendent.) Thus, when an event, object or structure in the world exhibits specified complexity, one infers that an intelligence was responsible for it. In other words, one draws a design inference.[36]

Behe, on the other hand, devotes a significant portion of chapter 10 of *Darwin's Black Box* to defending the design argument as put forward by William Paley.[37] One must remember that the ID movement is not monolithic; there are differences within the ID community. Having said this, it does not appear that whether or not ID is an argument *from* design or *to* design is a determinative factor in ascertaining whether it is good science or not. Further, there is no denying that ID has the feel of a design argument. I suspect this is why it stirs up so many on both sides of the issue. It may not formally be a design argument, but it is a small step from a design inference to a design argument.

ID advocates are adamant that ID is not creationism. Although most (not all) ID proponents are theists,[38] generally evangelical Christian theists, they insist that ID is not to be confused with young-earth creationism and that they are not trying to harmonize ID and a literal reading of the Bible with science, as is the case with creation science. Phillip Johnson forthrightly declares: "I am not a defender of creation-science, and in fact I am not concerned in this book with addressing any conflicts between the Biblical accounts and the scientific evidence."[39] Behe states:

> As commonly understood, creationism involves belief in an earth formed only about ten thousand years ago, an interpretation of the Bible that is still very popular. For the record, I have no reason to doubt that the universe is the billions of years old that physicists say it is. Further, I find the idea of common descent (that all organisms share a common ancestor) fairly convincing, and have no particular reason to doubt it. I greatly respect the work of my colleagues who study the development and behavior of organisms within an evolutionary framework, and I think that evolutionary biologists have contributed enormously to our understanding of the world.[40]

On this point, ID advocates take fire from both sides: from Darwinists, both naturalists and theists who are methodological naturalists on the one hand, and on the other, from young-earth creationists. Darwinists often assert that ID proponents are being disingenuous and have ulterior, strategic reasons for refusing to admit their beliefs—and thus their purpose: to sneak religion into public education through the back door.[41] Young-earth creationists, however, criticize ID advocates for not looking to the Bible to explain things like the problem of evil or the apparent age of the earth. They also object that ID does not logically lead to the biblical God; it could just as easily lead to deism or pantheism.[42]

There have, of course, been several court cases in recent years involving ID. Two of the most recent and significant being the cases in Cobb County, Georgia (the county that is home to Johnson Ferry Baptist Church, where the 2006 Greer-Heard Point-Counterpoint Forum on ID took place), and Dover, Pennsylvania.

On March 28, 2002, the Cobb County Board of Education voted to put stickers in science texts stating: "This textbook contains material on evolution. Evolution is a theory, not a fact, regarding the origin of living things. This material should be approached with an open mind, studied carefully, and critically considered."[43] In January 2005, Judge Clarence Cooper ruled the stickers unconstitutional and ordered them removed from the science textbooks. The stickers were removed later that summer. In 2006, a federal appeals court vacated that decision and ordered the case remanded to a lower court. In January 2006, the case was settled out of court. The school district will not seek to place the same, or similar, stickers in science textbooks in exchange for the plaintiffs dropping the suit. In addition, the school district will pay a portion of the plaintiffs' legal fees.[44]

The most publicized case in recent times has been the *Kitzmiller v. Dover* case in Dover, Pennsylvania. In this highly publicized case, the Dover Area school board of directors passed a resolution by a margin of 6 to 3 stating, "Students will be made aware of gaps/problems in Darwin's theory and of other theories of evolution including, but not limited to, Intelligent Design. Note: Origins of Life is not taught."[45] As a result, science teachers were required to read disclaimers declaring:

> The Pennsylvania Academic Standards require students to learn about Darwin's Theory of Evolution and eventually to take a standardized test of which evolution is a part. Because Darwin's Theory is a theory, it continues to be tested as new evidence is discovered. The Theory is not a fact. Gaps in the Theory exist for which there is no evidence. A theory is defined as a well-tested explanation that unifies a broad range of observations. Intelligent Design is an explanation of the origin of life that differs from Darwin's view. The reference book, *Of Pandas and People*, is available for students who might be interested in gaining an understanding of what Intelligent Design actually involves. With respect to any theory, students are encouraged to keep an open mind. The school leaves the discussion of the Origins of Life to individual students and their families. As a Standards-driven district, class instruction focuses upon preparing students to achieve proficiency on Standards-based assessments.[46]

Once again, the decision led to a court case. In this case, after six weeks of testimony, Judge John E. Jones ruled that the school board decision was unconstitutional and, further, that ID was not science.[47] This case will be further discussed later in the book. Suffice it to say that ID has not succeeded in convincing any court that it is a valid scientific alternative to evolutionary biology. This does not mean that it will not fare better in some future case, or that ID is not a legitimate subject for study in other courses in public schools, such as philosophy or religion courses. Nevertheless, it does set a legal precedent.

So, what does this all mean? It means that we are back where we first started: ID is controversial. How will this controversy play out in the end? Only God knows.

In the interest of full disclosure, I must say a word about myself and my position on this issue. I am a professor of philosophy and theology, specializing in philosophy of religion. In other words, when it comes to science—and particularly to mathematics—I am a layman. My first degree was in music, in part because most of the time one only had to count to four. My next degree was in theology, where so long as one remains an orthodox Christian, one only has to count to three: Father, Son, and Holy Spirit. My doctoral training was in philosophical theology and, nowadays, I often find myself asking, "What are numbers, really?" I am unable to grasp the scientific complexity and nuanced detail with which much of this discussion must take place, but I am not unable to recognize fallacious arguments or unwarranted conclusions at a more basic level. Might it not be the case that there is more evidence for Darwinism, and more fruit from the Darwinian paradigm, than is often admitted by design theorists (particularly by their lay enthusiasts), but at the same time also much less evidence for Darwinism and many more problems with the Darwinian paradigm than is commonly acknowledged by Darwinists who hold to either methodological or metaphysical naturalism? On the latter possibility, note the comment by process theologian David Ray Griffin:

> There are, I am assured, evolutionists who have described how the transitions in question could have occurred. When I ask in which books I can find these discussions, however, I either get no answer or else some titles that, upon examination, do not in fact contain the promised accounts. That such accounts exist seems to be something that is widely known, but I have yet to encounter someone who knows where they exist.[48]

On the former possibility, virtually everyone admits that significant advances have been made predicated on the assumption that Darwin was correct. As cited above, even Michael Behe grants that evolutionary biologists have "contributed enormously to our understanding of the world."[49] In other words, there may be areas of agreement, perhaps quite small (some perhaps larger), upon which most if not all involved in this discussion can agree. If there can be more agreement, then perhaps the level of rhetoric can come down and the level of understanding rise. Theistic evolutionists Ted Peters and Martinez Hewlett state it this way:

> If the scientific research program proposed by Dembski in *No Free Lunch* were allowed to proceed, would it not rise or fall based on its explanatory merits? What is there to fear in this? In the history of science, many alternative proposals have been raised and, with the test of experiment, have either succeeded (quantum theory) or failed (phlogiston). Perhaps some trust in the open process of scientific criticism might be called for here as we search for the most adequate explanation for what we observe in nature.[50]

What is there to fear indeed?

At the end of the day, the crucial issue seems to be one of philosophy of science. Is methodological naturalism *always* the appropriate stance for a scientist to take? ID proponents say no while their critics say yes. Might there not be some middle ground, however, where a scientist could say something like, "We are faced with apparent design. Nevertheless, over and over scientists have found answers as to how seeming impossibilities have naturally come about; therefore we should continue to seek such answers. Yet, one cannot be certain that a naturalistic answer will be forthcoming—ever. Therefore one cannot declare definitively either that God or evolution did it. The safest position is to continue seeking a naturalistic answer while keeping an open mind on the issue until an answer is forthcoming." In this way one would avoid the evolution of the gaps as well as the God of the gaps. Perhaps ID theorists will put forward a body of peer-reviewed research with agreed-upon criteria that will satisfy a significant percentage of the scientific community that ID design is indeed a legitimate approach to science. Perhaps they will not. But this proposed middle-road approach does not prejudge the matter. Accordingly, ID's success is neither certain nor impossible.

I was a Christian before I, or even Phillip Johnson, ever heard of intelligent design. My faith in the Christian doctrine of Creation does not depend solely on a scientific assessment of the nature of life—but neither is science unimportant to my spiritual life. If ID is proved true (using proof in the pragmatic way that a scientist usually does, not the formal way of a logician), then my faith will be strengthened—but if ID is proved false (again in the same way), my faith will not be destroyed. *I hope that ID succeeds in this way.* I also hope that this book will be profitable—but I don't go out and buy a new home and car based on that hope. I check my bank account before I make a large purchase—and I keep my eyes open in other areas of life as well because I believe that God has so ordered his creation in general, and humanity in particular, in such a way as to be rational. (This is in fact a basic Christian idea that has driven much of the history of Western science—including the advances!) I intend to continue studying ID.

The relationship between Christianity and science is an important and complicated one—and well worth studying. Therefore I am pleased to present the discussion that is to follow in this book. I hope you find it informative and useful in your assessment of ID in particular and the relationship of science and theology in general.

1

Intelligent Design: A Dialogue

William A. Dembski and Michael Ruse

Opening Statement
William A. Dembski

I want to begin by thanking Johnson Ferry Baptist Church for making it possible for us to be here. Certainly, a word of appreciation is due to New Orleans Baptist Theological Seminary. The faculty of the seminary has gone through so much that it is amazing that we have this opportunity to be here at all. Frankly, when Katrina hit, I thought we'd be lucky if this event was postponed merely by a year. Yet here we are, right on schedule. And of course I want to thank the Heard family for their generosity in endowing this forum. In addition, I want to thank Michael Ruse. We've done these exchanges now a number of times. He's one of the people on the other side who values open, honest discussion about these issues, and that means so much to me. I think you'll find that also to be the case with the panel here; they are all good guys—not just on my side, but on the other side as well: Marty Hewlett and Wesley Elsberry. I always enjoy meeting them and discussing these issues with them in person.

So, the question I want to start with is, "Why is design back on the table?" To answer that question, let me offer two jokes. One involves a physicist, a chemist, and an economist, and the other a mathematician, an engineer, and a biologist. The first joke: the physicist, chemist, and economist are stranded on an island. They have a can of food, but they need to open it. The physicist says, "Let's drop it from fifty meters; it will hit the ground and spill open." The chemist says, "Let's heat it up to 101° C; that will bring the contents to a boil and burst the can open." The economist says, "Imagine a can opener."

That's one joke. Bear with me for the next one. The other involves a mathematician, an engineer, and a biologist, each seeking to explain the origin of life. The mathematician looks at the problem and says, "The chances of this are just too unlikely; I don't believe it could happen." The engineer says, "The engineering problems involved here are daunting." The biologist says, "Imagine an evolutionary pathway." The first joke is apocryphal. The second one actually happened. It happened in 1967 at a symposium sponsored by the Wistar Institute. You had mathematicians, Stan Ulam and Marcel Schützenberger, who said, "The odds are against this happening." Murray Eden, the M.I.T. engineer, said, "The problems are daunting—they require amazing feats of engineering." Ernst Mayr and Richard Lewontin, Harvard biologists, said, "Hey, but we're here. Evolution must have happened." I'm paraphrasing, but that's the gist.

I want to explore the Harvard biologists' response. Evolutionary pathways—are we just imagining them? How can we get a handle on whether these pathways really exist? And not just exist, but happened the way the evolutionary community tells us they happened. I think here we need to be very clear what we are talking about with evolutionary theory. We're not talking about a guided form of evolution in which God or some intelligence was controlling the process in some substantive way where we can see clear, empirically detectable marks of that intelligence. What is meant by evolution is a process that, for all our scientific investigation can reveal, did not require any intelligence. Francisco Ayala, for instance, describes what he calls "Darwin's Greatest Achievement" as showing how you get the organization of living forms apart from any design or creative intelligence.

So that's the great selling point of evolutionary theory, that you can get the amazingly complex organization of life without any need for design. This was really brought home to me in a debate that I did three or four years ago. It was a tag-team debate: Michael Behe and me versus Kenneth Miller and Robert Pennock. It was at the American Museum of Natural History in Manhattan. As with most debates, there was an actual question on the table to be debated. The original question that was posed when I got an e-mail inviting me to take part in the debate was, "Blind Evolution or Intelligent Design?" But when I showed up at the auditorium and the programs were handed out, the word "blind" was omitted. It now read, "Evolution or Intelligent Design?" So we're talking about a form of evolution, which, if God had anything to do with it, makes him a master of stealth. There is nothing taking place in the evolution-ary process that would point us, in a scientific way, toward intelligence. Ken-neth Miller, in his book, *Finding Darwin's God*, says that design is "scientifically undetectable."

Are biologists merely imagining evolutionary pathways? Darwin addressed this point in a backhanded way. In his *Origin of the Species* he remarked that if it could be demonstrated that any complex organ existed which could not possibly have been formed except through numerous suc-cessive slight modifications, his theory would absolutely break down. He then immediately added, "But I can find out no such case." Now I want to focus on this phrase, "numerous successive, slight modifications." Once intelligence is out of the picture, evolution, as Darwin notes here, has to be gradual. You can't just magically materialize completely new structures out of nowhere. There has to be a path-dependence. You have to get there by some gradual route from something that already exists.

But there's more to it than just describing, if you will, "the fact of evolu-tion." There is also a mechanism that is supposed to drive this evolutionary process. This mechanism is supposed to accumulate complexity in a way that does not require any intelligence. So, what you have are incidental changes, or random errors, that are the source of novelty. And then these get sifted through a mechanism of natural selection, which in turn gets carried over one generation to the next. This mechanism of selection and variation is supposed to drive the evolutionary process without any need for intelligence.

Darwin, in proposing that his theory would break down if some complex biological system could be shown not to arise by numerous successive slight modifications, was ostensibly proposing a test of this theory. But it was really no test at all. To see this, let's turn his test around. Imagine if a theist were to claim: "If it could be demonstrated that any organ could not possibly have been formed by God, my God-theory would absolutely break down." Now, when you put it that way, the challenge becomes highly implausible. Darwin is offering what appears to be a sweeping concession, but in fact he is proposing an impossible test. Of course, no one would allow a comparable test for divine activity. And yet for material forces, it seems that the scientific community is willing to cut Darwin unlimited slack. Indeed, "numerous successive slight modifications" is so vague and ill-defined, how could anything convincingly serve as a counterexample?

The real point at issue is not what could not possibly happen, but what could reasonably be expected to happen. What is the positive evidence for evolutionary theory? What is the positive evidence for intelligent design? Many evolutionary biologists seem to think that if you can merely imagine a material force or process that could bring about some biological structure, then it's immediately going to trump intelligent design. But is there actual evidence for the creative power of these material forces? Or is the more compelling evidence on the side of intelligent design? It seems to me that really is where the issue should be.

Now, to illustrate what's at stake in these evidential questions, I would like to consider an example that is well known to many of you who have studied the evolution-design controversy. There was an experiment that was very popular in the 1950s. It was called the Miller/Urey experiment. It was an experiment not so much about biological evolution as what is called chemical or prebiotic evolution. The question was: How do you get the chemicals that were present before life to organize themselves in a way that will then bring about living forms? The Miller/Urey experiment was a primitive earth atmospheric simulation experiment. Miller and Urey took gases such as methane and ammonia, placed them in an apparatus, shot some sparks into it, and discovered that some amino acids were produced—in other words, the experiment yielded some of the basic building blocks of life.

This experiment was immediately touted as though the origin-of-life problem had virtually been solved—that the solution was right around the corner. That optimism has since faded. Yes, we're able to get these basic building blocks. But then putting them together into biomacromolecules— more complicated assemblages that are needed for life to exist at all—has been much more difficult. Getting that sort of organization to the next higher level has been the problem. Think of a house that is built with bricks. You can possess all those basic building materials, but you still have to organize them properly to form a house. That's been a huge problem in origin-of-life research—organizing the basic building blocks by purely chemical and material mechanisms.

Here, however, I want to focus less on the particulars of the experiment as on the logic underlying it. The Miller/Urey experiment was intended to count as evidence for evolution (chemical evolution and, by implication, biological evolution). Why? Because scientists could reproduce this experiment. By running the experiment again one could, with high probability, get those same amino acids, those same basic building blocks of life. But what happens when you started trying to go to the next level? There, it seems, we keep running into roadblocks. Scientists have not able to get material forces, without intelligent assistance, to do the organizing work needed to take the chemistry of life to the next level.

So why was the success of the Miller/Urey experiment in generating amino acids used as evidence for evolutionary theory, but the subsequent failure of experimental research to form the next level of life's chemistry not used as evidence against evolutionary theory? There's clearly a double standard here. But wait, there's more. It's not just that we have problems with material forces when we try to go to the next level of biological complexity. It's also that we're finding things at that next level that exhibit the hallmarks of intelligent design.

There has been a revolution in biology in the last thirty years. When we look inside the cell, we find that our best metaphor for describing what is there is an automated city. You find tiny machines that are doing all sorts of nifty things: carrying loads down monorails; delivering packages using automated parcel addressing; storing, processing, and retrieving information. Everywhere you look you find high-tech, high-efficiency, nano-engineered machines.

Darwin, and even several generations after him, suspected nothing like this. Recall that Darwin did not write on the origin of *life* (except in a letter to Hooker); he wrote on the origin of the *species*. Why? Well, for him the origin of life was not a problem. When he looked at the cell, given microscopy as it was back then, he saw a blob of jelly enclosed by a membrane. His colleague Thomas Henry Huxley likewise thought that the origin of life was not a problem. He thought that spontaneous generation, in which life could arise from nonliving mud, worked just fine. It was getting all this great diversity and complexity of life after it had originated that was the problem, at least as they saw it.

But our contemporary knowledge of life has changed all that. Even the simplest life-form is amazingly complex. But is it just sheer complexity that renders spontaneous generation implausible? Lots of things grow in complexity. Take nearby Atlanta. Atlanta has grown tremendously in complexity over the last thirty or so years. Has there been any central planning? Not much, I suspect. Much of its complexity has arisen spontaneously. Complexity can arise in various ways. Some of it happens spontaneously, some of it requires intelligence. What about complexity in biology? Where did it come from? And how is it best explained?

To address these questions, I will continue to focus on the subcellular level—what is going on inside of the cell. I don't have my PowerPoint here, but if I did, I would at this point in my talk put up a slide—perhaps Michael will have the same one—of what has become the icon of intelligent design: the bacterial flagellum. The bacterial flagellum is a little, bidirectional, motor-driven propeller on the back of certain bacteria that can spin at up to a 100,000 RPM and change direction in a quarter turn. When you examine it with electron microscopy and other techniques, the first thing you notice is a long whiplike tail. But there's also a hook, which serves as the universal joint. There are O-rings, a drive shaft, discs that mount this apparatus to the cell membrane, and an acid-powered drive. And that doesn't describe the transduction circuitry that tells this mechanism when and how to operate.

So you have this machine of tremendous complexity and efficiency. Howard Berg at Harvard has, in his public lectures, called it "the most efficient machine in the universe." How does something like this originate? Are there good evolutionary explanations for it? Does evolution, conceived as a blind material process, one in which intelligence is not playing any substantive role, have an explanation for this molecular machine? I would put it to you that the scientific community does not have a good explanation for how this or other such systems arose.

Michael Behe, in his book *Darwin's Black Box*—which is a seminal text for the intelligent design movement—drew attention to this system ten years ago. It has remained the icon of intelligent design throughout that time. Nor has "the other side" mounted any serious challenge to its status as the icon of ID. Indeed, the other side has not even been able to imagine a putative evolutionary pathway, to say nothing of providing a detailed, step-by-step, fully articulated, testable evolutionary pathway to the flagellum. The only thing the other side has been able to come up with is a subsystem of the flagellum, a microsyringe known as a type III secretory system.

A flagellum consists of about forty protein parts, and this subsystem consists of about ten of those parts. It is, as it were, embedded in the flagellum. And so we have this subsystem that conceivably could have been subject to selection pressure and served as an evolutionary precursor to the flagellum. But note: what you have here is not a fully articulated path but an island (the type III secretory system) and a huge jump to the next island (namely, the flagellum). If evolution is going to try to explain how you can island-hop from Los Angeles to Tokyo, basically what the evolutionist has found is the Hawaiian islands—and nothing else. What the evolutionist has *not* found is the entire archipelago that will take you across. So that's the problem. The problem is unresolved.

Now is the problem I've identified here just an isolated instance? Are there numerous other systems, besides the flagellum, of comparable complexity that evolutionists have adequately explained? Have I just focused on this one renegade system? And if the evolutionist finds a solution to this one problem, will I simply retreat to some other unresolved problem? No, I'm not moving any goalposts. I spoke at the University of Texas at Austin a few years back, and one of the biologists during the Q&A remarked, "Just because you don't know how this system [the flagellum] could have come about by evolution, don't go telling me that it didn't." I responded, "Look, the problem isn't that I don't understand its evolution; the problem is that you don't understand it. And you're the biologist. You've got tenure and research funds. But it's not just that you don't understand it; none of your colleagues understand it, either."

I'm not exaggerating the seriousness of the problem and the abject failure of evolution's valiant defenders to resolve it. You will find some biologists who come clean about the extent of the problem—how pervasive and unyielding it is. These molecular machines inside the cell that I've been describing are absolutely indispensable for life to exist at all. So how do they come about? And why is standard evolutionary theory, which eschews design, so ineffective at dealing with this problem? Many biologists regard evolutionary theory as the greatest idea in all of science, providing unity for the whole of biology. This theory, which is supposed to account for how all the great complexity and diversity of life came about, did not anticipate this complexity within the cell, has repeatedly failed to explain it, and offers no prospect of explaining it.

Thus you have biologists who are not intelligent design proponents, such as Franklin Harold of Colorado State University, who writes in his book, *The Way of the Cell* (Oxford University Press, 2001), that we have to reject as a matter of principle intelligent design and stay with the dialectic, as he calls it, of chance and necessity. Notwithstanding, he then does an about-face and adds that there are no detailed Darwinian accounts for any of these systems, but "only a variety of wishful speculations."

Let that phrase "wishful speculations" sink in. When you are talking about wishful speculations, you are talking about "imagining an evolutionary path." You don't have the path; it's not experimentally supported. That very phrase, "wishful speculations," was also used by James Shapiro, a molecular biologist at the University of Chicago, in a review of Michael Behe's book. In that review, Shapiro likewise admitted that evolutionists offer no detailed testable evolutionary pathways to the systems Behe discusses, only a variety of wishful speculations. James Shapiro e-mailed me a few years back, saying, "I hear that you are citing me in your talks as supporting ID." I replied, "Yes, I cite you. But I always make it very clear that you are not an intelligent design proponent." Indeed, it helps to show that evolutionary theory is in disarray by citing people like Shapiro who have no truck with ID.

Here, then, you have people with no stake in intelligent design who are admitting the depth of the problem. But is it just a matter of ignorance? Am I simply offering an argument from personal incredulity, that we haven't figured out how material forces could account for such biological structures, therefore they must have been designed? Yet you can turn this around. Indeed, there's a comparable argument from personal incredulity on the other side: you haven't seen how such systems could have been designed, therefore they must have arisen by material forces. You can always flip these arguments around—they cut both ways.

The way out of this impasse is to realize that scientific explanations need to be causally adequate. Simply put, scientific explanations need to invoke causes that are adequate to account for the effects they are proposing to explain. This may seem so obvious as not to need stating. But consider, we don't have any good evidence for blind, undirected material processes producing feats of engineering. And such processes are all that the Darwinian mechanism and its extensions give us. Talk to the evolutionary biology community, and you will find that they are delighted that teleology (that is, design) has been removed from biology. Indeed, they're not trying to reintroduce it. And yet the only causally adequate account we have for these complex molecular machines inside the cell arises from engineering and, therefore, requires design.

The adamant refusal on the part of the evolutionary biology community to admit that evolutionary theory fails the causal adequacy test has created a stumbling block for how it makes sense of design in biology. It seems that we now have good evidence for the design of certain molecular machines inside the cell. We look at something like a bacterial motor, and it's not just that we don't have an adequate materialistic explanation—we don't—nor is it just that we are defaulting to design automatically. It's not because of what we *don't* know but because of what we *do* know that we infer design. Here we have a system that bears all the hallmarks of intelligence. It is a bidirectional, motor-driven propeller. Humans invented systems like this long before they even knew what a bacterial flagellum is or does; and then they found these motors in biological systems.

The only causal power we know that is able to produce systems like this is intelligence. So, what is the great leap in invoking intelligence here? I think the real problem centers on the implementation of design. How did the design get into those biological systems? (Note that evolution is a perfectly valid way of implementing design, though any evolutionary process that implements actual design would be thoroughly non-Darwinian.) Now, is it reasonable to argue that because we don't understand how the design of biological systems was implemented that it didn't happen by design at all? Or is it rather that we're in the position of somebody with very limited technology looking at a much higher-order technology, and we just don't understand how it could have been designed?

What would ancient humans (we don't even have to go to the Stone Age—someone like Aristotle, or any of the Ancient Greeks, will do) have thought of the latest computer technology? How would they have understood it? Could they have understood it? Thinking of life as an engineer, we find in living systems technological sophistication that dwarfs anything human designers have accomplished. Understanding design always presupposes certain background knowledge and certain technology with which we have facility. This observation points up the tension between mathematicians and engineers on the one hand and biologists on the other. I have found mathematicians and engineers to be much more favorably disposed toward intelligent design than biologists. Perhaps that shouldn't be surprising.

So far I've been careful to define evolution, but I have yet to define intelligent design. What, then, is intelligent design? The definition I would put to you is this: the study of patterns in nature that are best explained as the result of intelligence. Many special sciences already fall under this definition of intelligent design. Think of archaeology: "Is that an arrowhead or just a random chunk of rock?" "Is that just a naturally formed mound or a burial mound?" Or think of forensic science: "Did that person die of natural causes or was there foul play?" The very language of how we make sense of the world depends on this fundamental divide between these modes of explanation: Is the object under consideration the result of accidents, chance, randomness, or is it the result of purpose, intention, design?

This distinction applies not just to human artifacts, to instances of human intelligence. You can find it with animal learning and intelligence. You can find it in the search for extraterrestrial intelligence. Is that radio signal coming to us from outer space the result of an intelligence cause or is it the result of material forces? Notice that the arguments here are purely circumstantial. We don't have access to the intelligences. It's not like *E.T.*, where the little green guys come to earth and we can do medical experiments on them. All we have are these signals from outer space. Are they just random radio noise or are they the result of intelligence?

If you saw the movie *Contact*, fictitious radio astronomers in it observed a flamboyant signal sent to Planet Earth. Most of the real-life SETI research looks for narrow bandwidth transmissions because these are the types of transmissions that we typically get from human sources. But in the movie, there was a far more flamboyant signal; namely, a long sequence of prime numbers. Notice that it was a long sequence. Okay, what are prime numbers? (*audience laughter*) Prime numbers are numbers divisible only by themselves and 1. So it was 2, 3, 5, 7, 11, all the way up to 101. If you represent that sequence as a sequence of beats and pauses (that is, two beats then a pause, three beats then a pause, and so on), it would take over a thousand bits (0s and 1s) to represent it.

So you have this long sequence of prime numbers. It has to be long, because if it was a short sequence, say, just two beats and a pause, you couldn't contact the *New York Times* science editor and say, "We've found evidence of extraterrestrial intelligence, they've mastered the first prime number." You're not going to do that—it's possible that some alien intelligence was intending to bang out a long sequence of prime numbers but happened to have a heart attack just before he could move past the first prime number. But you could never know that, because if you are monitoring millions of radio channels from outer space (as actual SETI researchers do), you are bound to see a short sequence—any short sequence. But when you get into the long sequences, those are going to be hard to reproduce by chance.

But that's not enough. You're also going to need an independently given pattern, or what I call a *specification*. This is where much of my research has focused, on developing a method or criterion for design detection, which I call *specified complexity*. The signal in the movie *Contact* exhibits specified complexity—it is both complex (that is, hard to reproduce by chance) and specified (that is, satisfies an independently given pattern). As a consequence, this signal triggers a design inference. I have a whole book on specified complexity; it is titled *The Design Inference: Eliminating Chance through Small Probabilities*, which came out in 1998 with Cambridge University Press. I trust that we'll be talking about some of the details of that work here, both formally and informally. Wesley Elsberry, who is one of the respondents as well as one of my main critics, thinks that there are problems with this method of design detection. Let's talk about that.

In setting the stage for the discussion that follows, let me say a few final words regarding intelligent design and creationism. Many people mistakenly think that they are the same. I spoke at the University of Kansas just a week or two ago, where a professor named Leonard Krishtalka has gained some attention for calling intelligent design "creationism in a cheap tuxedo." I think he's since modified that classification because my colleagues in the ID community are now supposed to be getting all this fabulous funding; so now it's creationism in an expensive tuxedo—we've been upgraded! But if you're going to argue that way, then you would have to say something like, "Aristotle was a creationist in a cheap toga" or "Isaac Newton was a creationist in a cheap wig." Both were committed to intelligent design, yet neither would have embraced creationism as it is understood today.

If you are committed to collapsing the two, creationism and intelligent design, what are you going to do with someone like Antony Flew, who, until Richard Dawkins displaced him, had been the most prominent atheist in the

English-speaking world? Flew is no longer an atheist. Which is not to say he has become a Christian—he does not, for instance, believe in an afterlife. But he does think that the arguments for intelligent design, especially at the origin of life, have proven decisive. Flew throughout his career had argued for a presumption of atheism—atheism is the default position until good evidence for an intelligence behind the world is found. He claims now to have found such evidence.

How, then, do intelligent design and creationism differ? Creationism, at the very least, is always about a doctrine of creation. Where does everything come from? What is the source of being? A creator—an infinite, personal, transcendent creator god—is the source from which everything springs. But if you go with my definition of intelligent design, as the study of patterns in nature that are best explained by intelligence, you can't logically reason your way to such a creator. Where do those patterns reside? They reside in finite, material objects. You cannot, from patterns that are embedded in finite material objects, infer to or draw any conclusions about an infinite, personal, transcendent, creator god.

One way I like to illustrate this is to imagine that you have before you a pan balance. A one-pound weight can be seen on one of the pans, but a veil occludes the other. The one-pound weight is up, the other side is down. How much weight is on the other side? One and a half pounds? Two pounds? A million pounds? You know it's more than one pound. But you don't know how much more. That's the problem of moving from design to designer. A design inference can reliably tell us that there's an intelligence sufficient to account for some phenomenon. But it cannot tell us the ultimate extent or nature of that intelligence.

So, if you are a Christian, as I am, and you want to make sense of the designer behind biology, you will have to bring theological resources to bear. You are not going to be able to get to the Christian God from intelligent design. And yet, intelligent design does have apologetic value. It's not so much that ID argues positively for the truth of Christianity as that it argues negatively against what is perhaps the leading ideology that keeps people from seriously considering the Christian faith; namely, the scientific and Darwinian materialism that undergirds so many people's rejection of Christianity in Western culture. If intelligent design, as an intellectual and scientific movement, proves successful, it will sweep that ideology away and thereby render the faith that much more plausible.

Let me leave it there. We have a lot to discuss. Now I'll turn it over to Michael.

Opening Statement
Michael Ruse

Well, thank you very much for having me. My name is Michael Ruse, I'm an evolutionist. I am a philosopher too. To answer the question that I'm sure is going to be going through the back of the minds here, looking at someone who is sixty-five years old, who so clearly doesn't have much longer on this earth, and then who's going to take the long escalator down—I'm not a practicing Christian. In fact, I'm not a Christian, period. I was brought up as a Quaker in England. I went to a Quaker school. I didn't have a "road to Damascus" experience leading to my nonbelief. It was just one of those things like stamp collecting, and baked beans, those things that in my childhood were the most important things in my life. At the age of about twenty, suddenly I woke up and said, "I really don't care much for baked beans; I haven't looked at my stamp album for a long time; and I don't particularly want to go to Quaker meetings."

It was really a rather sad parting of the ways in a sense, although I really don't find myself drawn strongly to become a Christian again. I would not describe myself as an atheist. I suppose if you wanted a term, I'm an agnostic or a skeptic or something like that. But one thing I always do say, and this does separate me from people like Dan Dennett or Richard Dawkins, is that if you grow up as a Quaker, it's very hard to hate Christianity, even if you give it up. It's just not part of my nature. As you will hear, I think that people like Bill Dembski are deeply, deeply mistaken. I don't want to mince words about that. And I think the same of other people of the same ilk. So I suspect that most of you people here are deeply, deeply mistaken. But I would like to think that having said that, we can approach these issues in a sense of what I shall call *Christian friendship*—if that's not a presumptuous word to use.

If you asked me, "What does it mean to be made in the image of God?" I would say, part of it means to have an intellect and to have moral responsibility and to try to puzzle out this strange, mysterious, exciting, frightening world in which we live. So tonight I'm very happy to be here with you. As I say, I'm not going to, in any sense, conceal my deep disagreements, not only with Bill, but as I say, I suspect with many of you. But I'm glad to be here, and I want to share with you in, as I said, if it's not presumptuous, a Christian spirit, the reasons why I think Bill is deeply, profoundly wrong.

Now, although I am a philosopher, I normally talk to scientists. And my experience is that if I don't come with slides or a PowerPoint presentation before scientists, then their little faces drop. Whereas, if I turn up with them before philosophers, they're not quite sure what I'm doing. And so, consequently, you are going to have the fruits of my experiments with scientists, except, of course, being a philosopher, it means I really don't know how to work the technology. Here we go. (*Ruse shows a slide of the cover of his book,* The Evolution-Creation Struggle, *published by Harvard University Press in 2005.*)

I'm going to be talking about Bill Dembski, and I'm going to be mentioning his book, so I thought I might start off by mentioning my own. A lot of the ideas I am expressing are to be found in this book, and I hope you will see why I find this whole thing an absolutely fascinating debate, and why I don't just think it's important, but I think that it's also incredibly exciting and I feel that I'm awfully lucky to be in the midst of the whole thing.

Let me start by telling you a little about my own position and where I stand, and then I want to talk a little bit about ID and where Bill stands, and I want to show you that whereas I am standing on granite, Bill is standing on very shaky sand. The person that I obviously look to—I don't look to him as a saint, I don't think of him as a secular saint, but I do think of him as a very great scientist—is Charles Robert Darwin, who was born in 1809. In fact, he was born on February 12, 1809, the same day as Abraham Lincoln. He died in 1882. He was an Englishmen, a great scientist, and a naturalist. He was not the first evolutionist, but he is generally known as the Father of Evolution because it was he who made evolution, as it were, the dominant paradigm in the biological sciences.

Often people say, "I believe in evolution because of the fossils" or "I don't believe in evolution because of the fossils." In fact, for Darwin, I don't think that it was the fossil record that was the key thing that turned him into an evolutionist. It was biogeography. He went on board H.M.S. *Beagle* for some five years, going round the world. In 1835, they went to the Galápagos Archipelago, which is a group of islands in the Pacific. While he was there, Darwin was told that from island to island—and those islands are only about ten miles apart—the tortoises were significantly different. Then Darwin realized that the birds were too. At this point, I don't think Darwin was a Christian, but he was certainly a believer in a god—a god as an unmoved mover—what is known as a Deist. At this point, I think Darwin quite openly said: "It would not have made sense for God to put different birds and different tortoises on the different islands like that. It would make much more sense for the birds and tortoises to have come to the islands and then diversified when they got there." And so Darwin became an evolutionist.

Darwin knew, however, that it wasn't enough just to be an evolutionist. He also had to be somebody who looked to causes. Why did evolution occur? For Darwin, who had incidentally had a religious background, the big thing that had to be answered (apart from the sheer fact of evolution) was about the matter of functionality. Why do organisms seem to be well put together? Why do they seem to work? He found an answer in 1838. Then, for some reason for which we still don't have a full explanation, he sat on his answer for some twenty years. Finally, in 1859, Darwin published his ideas in his book, *On the Origin of Species by Means of Natural Selection*. What Darwin said was that more organisms are born than can survive and reproduce; only some will get through; and those that do get through will, on average, be different from those that don't. Moreover, the things that they have will be the sorts of characteristics that enable them to succeed in what was known as the "struggle for existence," although it's really a struggle for reproduction. It's no good being Tarzan if you've got the sexual desires of a philosopher, or something like that. Reproduction is what really counts, and so Darwin said that it's those characteristics, those adaptations, that really count.

Let me show you another slide. (*Slide of Darwin's finches from the Galápagos.*) These are birds that are now known as Darwin's finches. These were actually drawn or painted by the ship's painter or artist on H.M.S. *Beagle*, when Darwin visited the Galápagos. If you look at those birds, the most significant thing about them is that they have huge beaks. These beaks are there in order to eat cactus and nuts and those sorts of things. There are others of Darwin's finches with very fine beaks, they are insectivorous. There's even one species, or perhaps two species, that actually pick up twigs with their mouths and poke around in the bark and the insects come out. These finches actually use tools. All of these are examples of adaptation. These are all things that the natural theologians before Darwin had said obviously had to be designed, and clearly they were designed by the Great Designer in the Sky. What Darwin said was: "No, I think that these came about through unbroken law and there's no need to invoke a Designer to get them. Natural selection can do it."

Now, do notice what Darwin says. He does not say that evolution through natural selection makes a Designer impossible. What he says is that there's no need for one. Or, as Richard Dawkins says: "After Darwin, it's possible to be an intellectually-fulfilled atheist." Now Dawkins feels that he is an intellectually fulfilled atheist. Let's leave that one for next year, when we come again. The point I want to make is that I think Darwin made it *possible* to be a nonbeliever. I do not think Darwin made it *obligatory*. In fact, I think that, at the time Darwin himself discovered his theory (as I hinted above), he still thought that there was a god, a god who was a designer, but one who worked through unbroken law. In other words, one does not and should not look for interventions, as it were, as we go along. In other words, although Darwin had never heard the term, he is clearly putting himself in a position which is in stark opposition to ID.

And so as I say, this is the position to which I subscribe. Now, you might say: "Well, what about evolution? You've said that you're an evolutionist, or Darwin's the father of evolution. What right does one have to be an evolutionist?" Well, let me just simply say (or agree), in thinking about evolution, the idea that all organisms came, as it were, by a natural process from one or a few primitive forms, Darwin is dealing with something that we don't see. But Darwin's method of approach, or method of argumentation, is very much the method of argumentation one uses in the courts of law. When you don't see something happen, you don't say: "Ah ha! Well, I cannot convict!" Let us say, you walk in here, and your senior pastor is lying here in blood and gore, and you turn to the choirmaster and say: "I convict you." But nobody saw it, so the choirmaster says: "I'm okay, I wasn't seen." "No," you say, "look! There are clues! We know that you and the minister had been arguing about the hymns. He likes 'The Old Rugged Cross,' and you say, 'I'm never going to play that again.' We know there's been bad blood between you, and if I tried to stab him, I would be jab-jab-jab. But we know that you the choirmaster have been in the commandos and have learned to do it efficiently. It's done with an oriental knife, and we know that you the choirmaster's parents were missionaries in Korea." One adds up all the clues and they point to "you done it," and "you done it" explains all the clues. This is the kind of argumentation that Darwin uses in *Origin*. He says: "Give me evolution, evolution through natural selection, and then I can explain all of the wonderful things in biology. All of the sorts of things that Bill Dembski was talking about: the fossil record, biogeographical distribution, embryos being similar. All of these things! These are the clues that I can explain and conversely these clues justify my and your belief in natural selection."

I want to say that, after Darwin, masses of new evidence have come in. To give you just one example, Darwin said: "Yes, obviously, the fossil record is very incomplete because of incomplete fossilization." But he also said: "As we keep looking at the fossil record, we will find more and more evidence to suggest that there was indeed evolution." And in the 1860s, very shortly after *Origin* was written and published, one of the best clues that evolutionists have was discovered in Germany. This is Archaeopteryx. (*Slide showing Archaeopteryx.*) It is a bird, it's got feathers, but it also has all sorts of reptilian features like separate digits, teeth, and so on. And Darwin said: "Yes, that's exactly the sort of thing that I would have expected." So, as I say, I'm an evolutionist because of that kind of legal argument that Darwin puts forward. Give me a hypothesis, and I can explain the clues. The clues, in turn, justify the hypothesis.

I'm also a believer in natural selection, because, like Bill Dembski, I think that the world is very much "as if" designed. Bill thinks it was done by an intelligent designer. On one level, I don't even want to get into that (because I am not tonight arguing about the existence or nonexistence of God). But I do want to say the world is "as if" designed. However, I think that the proximate cause was natural selection. Whether or not there was an ultimate cause, whether or not there was a God behind the whole thing, is a separate issue.

Let's pick up now and address the other side, the ID side. Christians, of course, right from the beginning, were wrestling with the whole question of origins—"Where do we come from?"—as much as they were wrestling with questions of eschatology—"Where are we all going to go to?" One of the big issues that early Christians had, in fact, was how were they to treat the Jewish Bible. The Jews had rejected the Christians, so the Christians had to go it alone. Yet what about the Old Testament? Did this then mean that the Christians should reject the Old Testament? There were many Christians back then who said: "Yes!"

One of them was the young St. Augustine, about 400 C.E. He belonged to the so-called Manicheans, who rejected the Old Testament. One of the things that the Manicheans used to do was to go through the Old Testament and find all the problems—the two Genesis stories and the inconsistencies and these sorts of things. When Augustine converted, or reconverted, to Christianity, he said: "Of course, the Old Testament is true." There were good reasons for Christians taking on the Old Testament. Primarily because it made sense of the New Testament. Why did Jesus have to die on the cross for our sins? Because we are sinful. How do we know that we are sinful? Because of the Adam and Eve story.

When Augustine became a Christian, he insisted that the Old Testament was true. But, he cautioned, one doesn't necessarily have to take it as literally true. If science shows it is not literally true, then we must go with science. After all, science is something that comes through our reason, and this is very much part of being made in the image of God. So we're not turning from God by doing science—truth cannot be opposed to truth—we are trying to find some overall synthesis of it. Note that I am not saying that I think people at this time rejected Adam and Eve—of course they didn't, they had no reason to do so. Yet, it was always part of Christian tradition that this is an open possibility.

By the nineteenth century, in fact, more and more people were finding that the evidence of geology just simply did not go with the Old Testament taken absolutely literally. There was not, for instance, evidence of a universal flood. Actually, and more precisely, at the beginning of the nineteenth century, folk thought there was evidence of such a flood, but by about 1830, the evidence was coming in really strongly that hopes of any kind of universal flood were fading fast. This did not mean that people immediately rejected the notion of a local flood, but the literal universality was not on any longer. So by the early nineteenth century, Christians—Catholics and Protestants—were getting to the point where they were—I'm not saying they were rejecting the Bible, including the Old Testament—but they were increasingly reading it in a metaphorical or allegorical sense. Except in America! Particularly in the American South, for various reasons. (One major reason was that the Old Testament was considered as justifying slavery—the New Testament also.)

Moving forward to the time after the Civil War (and staying with America), one found that there was a very strong dichotomy between North and South. And nowhere more than over the interpretation of the Bible and the attitudes that Christians should take. Particularly in the South, and as the nation grew into the West, there developed an indigenous form of Protestant evangelicalism, one which was very heavily based on a literal reading of the Bible. This was not a traditional reading of a traditional Christianity, but it was a development of various parts of America in the nineteenth century.

This led eventually to the famous clash in 1925 in Tennessee, when a young teacher was put on trial and prosecuted by William Jennings Bryan, three times presidential candidate for the Democrats, and defended by Clarence Darrow, noted lawyer and agnostic. This was the Scopes Monkey Trial. As it happens, Scopes was found guilty and fined one hundred dollars, but it was overturned on appeal on a technicality. The main thing was that one had the ongoing clash between the North and South and their religious divides were still very significant.

Things remained uneasy right through the twentieth century. There were many so-called literalists or fundamentalists or creationists—often "young-earth" creationists—and they had some successes and some failures. And so we come to the end of the twentieth century, when this new movement, ID, developed. Bill has mentioned Michael Behe. I think Behe's book, *Darwin's Black Box*, is a seminal work. Bill is too modest to say this, but Bill himself has equally been important in the development of these ideas, thanks to his book, *The Design Inference*, and many others. And I think Bill would agree with me that the overall backbone, the great mentor of the movement, is Phillip Johnson, a former law professor at the University of California-Berkeley. Johnson is, as it were, the godfather, the Saint Paul of the movement, or at least something along those sorts of lines.

This, as you know, led eventually to the court case at the end of last year (2005) in Dover, Pennsylvania, where the school board tried to introduce ID. Even if it were not to be actually taught in the classrooms, then at least it had to be acknowledged in the classrooms. As it happened, it was not a good time for ID. The school board got kicked out and, in fact, the judge, at the beginning of December (2005), ruled very firmly against ID. The reason why I mention this—apart from saying "Ha ha, my side won!"—is to stress that it is not just my opinion that ID is not a scientific theory. Indeed, this is shown by its supporters. Who got right into the act immediately? None other than Pat Robertson, who seems to get into an awful lot of acts these days, when he's not slagging off Venezuela or the Israelis over the Gaza strip. He made it very clear what he thought of the new anti-ID school board in Dover, Pennsylvania. Specifically, Pat Robertson made it very clear that God is not pleased: "I'd like to say to the good citizens of Dover, if there is a disaster in your area, don't turn to God, you just rejected him from your city. God is tolerant and loving, but we can't keep sticking our finger in his eye forever. If they have future problems in Dover, I recommend they call on Charles Darwin; maybe he can help them."

So, I really think that to say that ID has nothing to do with religion is to miss the elephant in the room. It really is. Whether or not ID has any scientific merit, and I don't think it does, I have to say I see ID as part of the overall American, "indigenous Protestant evangelical," sort of position. It is true that I've mentioned Michael Behe, who is a Roman Catholic, but as everybody knows, American Catholics are much more like American Protestants than they are like European Catholics. The Vatican knows that, and it worries them to no end!

What is intelligent design theory that we are talking about? I can go quickly on this because Bill did give a full discussion of what it is. Behe's *Darwin's Black Box* is authoritative. If nothing else, I know that Michael Behe is an absolutely brilliant teacher. *Darwin's Black Box* has done well, and deservedly so. I would love to take a regular course in biochemistry from Michael Behe. His feeling for an analogy or an idea or a concept is simply brilliant. It must be a real privilege to take a class with him.

In explaining ID, Michael Behe focuses on the notion of irreducible complexity. He says some things are so complex that they could not have come about through blind, gradual law. He instances a mousetrap that has five parts. Take away one part, and the mousetrap does not work. It must have been put together in fell swoop. Likewise, says Michael Behe, we find many such examples in the organic world. He gives many instances, one of which is blood clotting. Blood clotting, Behe says, is a very complex system. It's not just one thing. It's a cascade. One thing happens, then another, and then yet another, in order for blood to clot. Michael Behe says in effect: "Take one thing out. The clotting cascade doesn't work. Hence, since it cannot have come about gradually, there must have been some kind of intervention, an intelligent designer."

I think this is the crux of the ID idea. It's simple, but that doesn't make it wrong. Great ideas are often very simple. Nevertheless, I do think it's wrong. The idea of irreducible complexity just doesn't work. Take the mousetrap example. You will not be surprised to learn that this claim that mousetraps have to have five parts has given us evolutionists ten years of happy work! We've been able to show that you can make mousetraps out of four parts, out of three parts, out of two parts, and you can even make a mousetrap out of one part. And I gather we're working on making a mousetrap out of no parts, and we hope to succeed very soon!

The mousetrap is not a very good example, and this casts big doubts upon the real examples, such as blood clotting. Perhaps you don't need all of the steps of the cascade. However, I have deeper worries about ID than the analogies. After all, analogies are analogies. You can use them one way, you can use them another way. My deeper worries are that first of all, Behe is simply wrong in his assumptions about the way that nature works. Look at a dry-stone bridge. Now if you started to build from the bottom up, and necessarily at some point began to move the top stones on either side toward the middle, you know what would happen before you got the stones to link up—the stones would fall down. And yet we've seen dry-stone bridges that don't fall down. What has happened? We know perfectly well that first you build a trestle or you build an embankment, then you lay the stones on it, and once they're in place, the stresses keep the bridge in place, and then you can remove the scaffolding or the embankment. Analogously in biology. It's not good enough to say simply:, "Ah ha! All these parts were in place, and therefore if one would be removed, then it breaks down. Therefore it couldn't come about by natural processes." Sure, if you look at it now things cannot be replaced. But historically often you'll have a process like dry-stone bridge building. Things will piggyback, they'll start to work, and natural selection will wipe away the scaffolding. I think that often that is the sort of thing that happens. I just don't think that that Behe's stand is something which is scientifically justified.

My second worry about Behe's position—an even greater worry—is theological. Take the great impressionist Henri de Toulouse-Lautrec. His legs would keep breaking. He was dwarfed. We're now pretty clear that this was a genetic disorder. As we now know, often genetic disorders involve just some very simple change in the genetic code. What I want to say is, If God has to get involved in order to produce the irreducibly complex, why couldn't God, or the Designer, have spent a few minutes clearing up the simple, but the simple that leads to absolutely awful effects? Often genetic diseases are a case of one or two molecules out of place, and what I want to know is, If you have an Intelligent Designer doing the complex, why couldn't the Intelligent Designer take a few minutes off and clear up the awful simple? So as I say, I've got major theological objections to ID, quite apart from the scientific ones. (Note that I am not saying that there is no designer or that the designer is necessarily bad. I am saying that if the designer gets involved in altering the creation then the designer has to take blame for the mistakes as much as credit for the successes.)

Now, finally, I do want to say I do not think that Bill Dembski is an old-fashioned creationist. I do not think that Bill Dembski believes in a young earth or anything like that. I know he does not. But is he in the tradition of American biblical literalism—American fundamentalism, American creationism, creation science—as these various movements have been called. Does this mean that ID is creationism lite? I want to argue: *Yes it is!* I want to say this because ID is not only a religious position, it is also very much bound with being a moral position. It is a social, cultural, and moral position—one that is properly identified with creationism. Bill himself recognizes this. Let me quote now from something Bill has said: "Despite my disagreements with Morris and young-earth creationism [Henry Morris was a leading creationist and the coauthor of *Genesis Flood*], I regard those disagreements as far less serious than my disagreements with the Darwinian materialists. If you will, young-earth creationism is at worst off by a few orders of magnitude in misestimating the age of the earth. On the other hand, Darwinism, in ascribing powers of intelligence to blind material forces, is off by infinite orders of magnitude."

This does not sound to me like a guy who's repudiating a tradition. I, of course, want to skewer Bill in front of all of you. I'm a professor, that's my job. But on another level, I want to say: "Bill, I think that you're absolutely right—because I do see you as part of something that is a continuing theme in American religious life." I see this very much also in the writings of Philip Johnson, whom (as I have said) I regard as the mentor, the godfather of the whole movement. If you read Johnson's writings, particularly the writings after *Darwin on Trial*, you will soon find that Johnson is not lying awake worrying about gaps in the fossil record. Neither, I think, is Bill Dembski. I don't think that's what worries them. I think it's the social and the moral issues. I think it's things like abortion—they think that we materialists are altogether too casual with the fetus and that sort of thing. I think it's things like gay marriage—we materialists, we Darwinians, are too readily inclined to say: "Well, you know, if it feels good, rub uglies. Do whatever you want to do, however you want to do, with whomever you want to do. It's all pleasure, rather than commitment, and these sorts of things."

I don't find it strange that people like Philip Johnson link their thinking about evolution to opposition to ways of thinking and behaving like this. We can add in other things like capital punishment. We can also bring in the president. He is an evangelical. He has doubts about evolution. He is against abortion, against gay marriage, strongly in favor of capital punishment. It is, as I say, a package deal. This is why I see ID as part of a tradition. I see ID as a sophisticated form of "indigenous American Protestantism," that has been developing since the nineteenth century. In a sense, it's the division we saw in the last election between America Red and America Blue. In a way, I see the evolution/ID debate not as a debate in its own right, but in some way as a litmus test for deeper divisions in the country. And, that is where I go out. Thank you.

Dialogue

RUSE: I'm not going first because I am better or worse. But somebody has to go first. My question to you, Bill, is the following: If intelligent design is indeed a truthful scientific paradigm or research program, what results in science are you actually getting? In other words, where is the bang for the buck? What are you ID people actually getting in the biological world that we evolutionists are not?

DEMBSKI: Good question. There are two ways to approach it. One is to ask: What is going on in the biological world already? Is it more naturally construed as falling under or supporting intelligent design or as supporting evolutionary theory? So I would say that there's a lot of ongoing research already that's relevant to answering this question. William Lawrence Bragg, a Nobel laureate, once remarked that the important thing in science is not to discover new facts, but new ways of thinking about facts. Thus, I don't think the burden on intelligent design is simply to come up with new experiments, new facts. The important thing is to find new ways to make sense out of them. I believe that we are making better sense out of them than the evolutionary biologists. The point of my joke about imagining an evolutionary pathway was that we have not been given any detailed evolutionary pathways. I think the more interesting question is, "Are there fundamental insights that intelligent design is giving or promises to give that could not be had within the Darwinian paradigm?" I think an affirmative answer to this question is being borne out.

My own research has been focused more on mathematical information theory. I'm working with some engineers, and I'm getting some interesting results there. They have to do with what is called the "no free lunch theorem," or what I'm calling displacement; that is, how information gets generated and tracked in biological systems. So this sort of research tends to be pretty theoretical. What about actual biological research supporting ID?

Here, the emphasis these days is on the evolvability of systems. From the evolutionary perspective, there is an unlimited plasticity to organisms; they can just evolve and change with very few constraints. That's now changing a bit even in more conventional evolutionary circles: there's a little bit of talk that there could be constraints (Simon Conway Morris's work on convergent evolution comes to mind).

But there's this deep sense in the biological community that you really can get from any point A to any point B—maybe not directly—but certainly from a common ancestor. But are there limits to evolvability? Can we figure out now just what the mechanisms in evolution are but also what their limitations are? Standard evolutionary theory says that you can get from point A to point B by using certain resources such as natural selection, random variation, and various other mechanisms (for instance, genetic drift and symbiogenesis). Are those mechanisms adequate?

We ask these sorts of questions in a lot of different contexts. If you are at the base of Mt. Everest and you need to get to the top, a Chevy Nova is not going to be an adequate resource for getting you there. What are the adequate resources for getting you up to the top of Mt. Improbable, as Richard Dawkins puts it? There's a new institute, the Biologic Institute in Seattle, which is run by Douglas Axe. The *New York Times* recently ran a story on it. I think Douglas Axe is really a key person to watch in this regard. He's looking at the evolvability of certain enzymes. He's focusing on this question because he's motivated by an intelligent design research program. So I think that there is work that is beginning, and there's a lot more that needs to be done. There is an emerging ID community; and there is work that is now getting out in the peer-reviewed literature.

My question, to Michael Ruse: I want to read a passage from your book, *Can a Darwinian Be a Christian?* And I'd like you to comment on it. "You are saying here . . ."

RUSE: You can see we've done this kind of thing before! (*Laughter*)

DEMBSKI: You are talking about the origin of life, and you remark, "At the moment, the hand of human design and intention hangs heavily over everything. The work is going forward rapidly to create conditions in which molecules can make the right and needed steps without constant outside help. When that happens, as one researcher puts it, 'The dreaming stops and the fun begins.'" Now what I want to explore is this: here we have origin-of-life research that's proceeding not as it would in nature; that is, driven by purely material or natural forces. Rather, it is proceeding by intelligent design or intelligent intervention. So, really, all the evidence at this point in these origin-of-life studies is pointing to intelligent design bringing about these systems. And yet you seem to have this overwhelming confidence that at some point you can just get rid of all this evidence for intelligent design and that these systems will be explained by material forces. It just seems to me to be a real disconnect; there's no induction from past experience going on here. The evidence right now is pointing toward intelligent design, and yet you are convinced that this will give way to a purely materialistic or naturalistic explanation. How do you come to that conclusion?

RUSE: Well, Bill, obviously, above all I believe in intelligent design. I think this computer was intelligently designed. I think it was designed by a squad of geeks out in California. That's where people live on avocados and that sort of thing. Clearly I believe in intelligent design. I agree also that scientific experiments are intelligently designed. Of course they are. But relevant to our discussion is the matter of trying to simulate situations that you think are natural. The point is, Bill, I'm not denying that the world is "as if designed." This is not our quarrel. I'm right with you all the way on that. The question is: Is the world—the living world particularly—intelligently designed by a human being, or some other being like a super-intelligent monkey or something like that? Or is it from my natural selection? Or is it done by something else?

So my point is that I am happy to accept the notion of intelligent design as such. It is something done by human beings here on earth. I'm excited about the work going on in origin-of-life studies. Obviously, these are intelligently designed at the moment. But I don't see that these concessions, if you will, in any sense threaten my overall position. What we're trying to do is set things up so we can see that, in the real world, these things happen—or did happen—without the need of intelligent design. They came about through the working of blind law, of natural selection in particular. My position is that if we argue for anything else, then our stance is so problematic that I don't know what we're saying. Are you seriously suggesting that some grad student on Andromeda is running an experiment for his Ph.D., and we're it? That this being is fiddling around with Planet Earth like that? Of course you're not! You're invoking God. And that's just not acceptable in science, and not necessary theologically since Darwin.

DEMBSKI: So the grad student on Andromeda is more acceptable than God?

RUSE: Well, I think the grad student on Andromeda is at least a plausible, naturalistic explanation. Of course I don't believe it, any more than I believe that the center of the moon is made of green cheese. But I would at least know what it would be like to say that a grad student was doing the work. Just like I know what it would be like if aliens landed and captured Elvis or brought him back. I don't believe that this is going to happen—except when I'm in the supermarket waiting at the checkout, and then having read the magazines on offer, I'm absolutely convinced! My point is this: I'm not against intelligent design, in the sense of thinking it a logically impossible notion, like a round square or something like that. Weapons for peace. I'm modest Michael—my demands are not absolute. I'm not against the notion of intelligent design in itself. But I don't think you can simply say: "Oh well, I don't have to answer that question. It's just intelligent design and not part of my query." I think that is cheating. If you invoke the idea of intelligent design, then you must go on to say something about the nature of that designer, and then you are caught with the ridiculous—the grad student on Andromeda—or the unacceptable in science—God.

Q&A with Panelists

William Lane Craig, Martinez Hewlett, Wesley Elsberry, and Francis Beckwith

WILLIAM LANE CRAIG: My question is for Michael Ruse. As a nonnaturalist, I'm honestly ready to follow the evidence wherever it leads, so I'd like to hear more about the evidence that the mechanisms that you have talked about can produce and actually have produced the biological complexity that we see in the world today. I think the evidence that you gave in your opening talk was rather thin. We heard about tortoises on Galápagos, Darwin's finches, the transition from reptiles to birds. These represent, of course, a very tiny portion of the animal kingdom. The extrapolation from that sort of evidence to a grand Darwinian theory of evolution represents enormous extrapolation from that evidence. Let's look at this PowerPoint slide, which I borrowed from Chris Peterson, of the various animal phyla that exist. All of the examples you gave come from the first phylum, the chordates, and even from a subclass within that, the vertebrates. which includes things like fish, mammals, and birds. Now even given vertebrate evolution, one can see that this is an utterly nimiscule part of the whole animal kingdom. The examples you cite are slmost trivialities in comparison with the whole. So what I want to know is, what would justify the extrapolation that all these phyla have evolved by these mechanisms from a common ancestor, as you envisioned? We know that in science these kinds of extrapolations often fail. For example, Einstein's attempt to extrapolate from a special theory of relativity to a general principle of relativity turned out to be a failure. What is the evidence that this extrapolation is warranted? Why should I, as an open-minded nonnaturalist, accept the grand Darwinian story?

RUSE: Let's back up a moment. I take it then, Bill, that you are not actually against the notion of natural selection or natural selection having fairly significant effects.

CRAIG: Right.

RUSE: Today we need a lot more penicillin now than we did in the Second World War. You're quite happy with putting that down to natural selection.

CRAIG: Sure.

RUSE: And I take it—I'm just trying to find out where our disagreements are—you are able to swallow Archaeopteryx without too much trouble. You accept the existence of intermediaries between the reptiles and the birds.

CRAIG: For the sake of argument. . . .

RUSE: Well, I don't want you being nice to me just because you're a Christian. No, I don't want any of that. (*audience laughter*) You see, the thing is, it seems to me, that to a certain extent, we've agreed that this stuff works. Now it's a question of how far we're allowed to take it.

CRAIG: Right, that's my question.

RUSE: You see, what I find very strange is your're quoting, I take it, from Sean Carroll. Am I right about that?

CRAIG: The source is, yes. . . .

RUSE: Yes. As you well know, a lot of this is material that we've only recently uncovered. A lot of this is new information. People like Sean Carroll, are in fact, discovering unbelievable things in evolutionary development. One of the most incredible things that they have found is the way that organisms are put together rather like on a Lego. You don't need to design everything from scratch. You take pieces that are shared in common and build very different organisms, just as in Lego you take the same pieces and build either the White House or a rocket ship. For instance, we now know that there are significant similarities between the development of fruit flies and humans.

The same genes are involved in both cases. This is something flatly denied forty years ago.

What I find really strange about your position is that we are galloping ahead. We know that natural selection works. We know that the overall evolutionary pattern is at least plausible. If you can accept Archaeopteryx, you really are on the plausible side of things. So we've gone that far, and we're now discovering all sorts of new things. For instance, about how organisms are put together by natural selection. We're discovering all of this. And yet you say: "Oh yes, but the problems are so great that I have to be a nonnaturalist." That seems to me to be silly, or indicative of the fact that you have a nonscientific agenda. The whole point about science—the whole point about good science—is not that we have all the solutions, but that we have a whole lot of interesting problems and they are giving way to a lot of naturalistic answers.

Sure, if you want a concession, I've always said that naturalism is an act of faith, if you want to use that sort of language. I would feel more comfortable saying that . . . (*audience claps*) All right, are you done? I would be more comfortable saying it's a metaphysical commitment of some kind. Of course it is. I don't think metaphysical commitments are stupid. What I'm saying to you is: Why would you be a nonnaturalist other than the fact that you've got burning other concerns? You're worried that if you're not a nonnaturalist you're going to get yourself on the wrong side with the fellow up there and, despite your youthful look, the clock is ticking. So I think that your position is one of covering your—well, you are covering—whatever it is one would say outside a Baptist church. You're not motivated by scientific concerns. You can't be. The science is going forward so rapidly.

I think you're motivated by factors that make you afraid to be a naturalist. The science is terrific. People like Sean Carroll are putting the science of life all together. They are showing how life works. They are showing how all of the parts fit together. They are showing that our whole picture is consistent. They are showing that the fossil record and the molecular genes and evo-devo all fit together in one glorious consilience. All I can say to you my friend is: "Join us! You won't be disappointed and God won't be cross with you. Take it from me!"

Martinez Hewlett: Both of you agree that there is design, we don't disagree about that. . . .

Ruse: Oh, I do. I say that the world is designlike. I didn't say that the world was designed. This—my computer—is designed. Your appearance is designed, in the sense that you got up this morning, asked yourself about what would make you look sexy and masculine in front of all these good Georgia Baptists. I certainly believe in design! But I don't think that asking about the design of organisms, in a literal sense, is a scientific question.

HEWLETT: Well, there's another word you both use that I haven't heard either of you really define, at least as far as I'm concerned. You're both using the word *cause* and you've used it in a variety of ways. Bill, you mentioned natural causes at one point in your book, and another point you also mention intelligent causes. Michael, you've mentioned proximate causes. I'd like for you both to explain what you mean when you use that word *cause*.

DEMBSKI: Michael and I are using *design* differently. For Michael, design or intelligence arises at the end of an evolutionary process. It's not something that's there at the start. The intriguing possibility that intelligent design is raising is whether intelligence is not simply an evolutionary offshoot, but whether there is an unevolved intelligence behind evolution. I think that's the crucial difference. Now what intelligent design is saying is that all definitions at some point end up being circular or end in some primitive notion. Intelligence, intentionality, what is it really? I think from an intelligent design perspective, intelligence ends up being a primitive notion. It is a cause that is not going to be reducible to what in my written work I've called natural causes, though that's probably not the best way to describe it.

What we've really been talking about are materialistic causes: material entities ruled by blind, unbroken, physical laws. Richard Feynman, the great physicist, once asked, "If all physical knowledge were destroyed but for one sentence, what sentence should we keep?" He then formulated a sentence stating the atomic hypothesis: that there are atoms and that they are governed by fixed laws of interaction. That, roughly, is what the materialist is committed to. Insofar as the materialist gives credence to intelligent design, it is intelligence that is ultimately reducible to this underlying materialist substrate. So, metaphysically speaking, intelligent design seems committed to treating intelligent causation as irreducible to materialist causes.

RUSE: I think that causes are what make things happen. Suppose Marty Hewlett—sitting next to me—started to turn bright green. I'd ask: "What was the cause of you turning bright green? Was it that you had too many peas at supper? Was it that you got some vile disease? Is it some sort of optical illusion?" Causes are what make things happen. I'm glad you asked this question, because I think that this is the crux of the issue, something that goes back to William Lane Craig's question. Can we explain the world in a natural fashion, or do we have to invoke nonnatural causes? I'm not denying the possibility of nonnatural causes. My question, rather, is whether in doing science it is necessary to invoke nonnatural causes? Or if we agree by definition that science cannot invoke nonnatural causes, whether it is necessary, therefore, to accept that there are questions about the world that science cannot answer because they demand nonnatural answers? My difference with Bill is that whereas I bar nonnatural causes, he would say it's necessary to invoke nonnatural causes sometimes.

DEMBSKI: It seems to me that intelligence can be a perfectly natural cause. The reason you're calling it nonnatural is because you have prejudiced the nature of nature. What is nature like? Already the metaphysics is feeding into how you answer this question. I think that this is precisely what we're talking about. Is intelligence something that is fundamental, that animates nature, and without which nature cannot be properly understood?

RUSE: I think you're making a huge theological leap, Bill, or you're just playing with words. Either you're prepared to bring God into the whole domain of science and say that the whole God issue is part and parcel of science or, at some level, you're not saying that. In which case, you're simply throwing the words around. Either God is a nonnatural phenomenon, or he/she/it is not. All I'm saying is . . .

DEMBSKI: But Michael, you're a philosopher. Was Aristotle a theistic believer who had a Judeo-Christian theistic conception of God? Of course not. For Aristotle, teleology was built into nature; there were final and formal causes built into nature. It was perfectly natural. Okay, that's why I don't bring up God and you do, because it's important . . .

RUSE: Oh yes, you do, William Dembski . . .

DEMBSKI: But in different contexts. In the discussion of the scientific status of intelligent design, I do not need to invoke God.

RUSE: Bill, back up for a moment. I want to say that this world of ours is an entirely natural phenomenon. Whether or not Bill Craig agrees with me, he knows what I mean by that. I mean that the living world was created by natural selection—aided, if you like—by mutation, random drift, and all of the other causes working according to the laws of nature. You say that there had to be an intelligent designer to get our world. Now my question to you is: "What about this intelligent designer?" You don't really think that the intelligent designer is a geek out in California.

DEMBSKI: Right.

RUSE: You don't really think that this intelligent designer is a grad student on Andromeda . . .

DEMBSKI: Okay, I know where you are going with this. . . . It's public knowledge that I'm a Christian and that I believe that God is ultimately behind everything. But designers can work through surrogate intelligences. We have thermostats; they regulate the temperature. We could have a little man or woman turn on the heat when it gets too cold or turn on the air conditioner when it gets too hot, but we automate it. God could work through organizing principles. Talk of organizing principles is everywhere in science these days. They could be teleological principles built into nature. This possibility is consistent with intelligent design.

   Or consider why the Oxford Center for Hindu Studies invited me to speak on intelligent design and warmly embraced what I'm talking about? Why am I in touch with people from all different religious and philosophical perspectives who are intrigued with intelligent design? Because with most of these perspectives, there is some sort of underlying purpose in the world. The one perspective that is not sympathetic to such an underlying purpose is the scientific materialism of which you are a proponent and which rules the academy and the Western intellectual world.

RUSE: I think we should bring this line of questioning to an end because I am winning so decisively! I hate to see a man down! But I have to say this. I believe that there are proximate causes that do the designing. Or, more precisely, that cause designlike effects. I call such causes natural selection.

DEMBSKI: What is the evidence for that? You're bluffing when you invoke the work of Sean Carroll to bolster your case. I mean, there's nowhere near the evidence that you're citing for the power of natural selection, and evolutionary developmental biology has deep problems of its own. (*RUSE says something under his breath . . . the audience laughs.*)

RUSE: Fellows, you refuse to give up! You chose to forgo your chance to surrender. This is getting nasty now. All these little old ladies in the audience who were hoping for blood, and they're getting it now. We are making happy all of those folk who watch wrestling on a Saturday afternoon on the telly. . . .

WESLEY ELSBERRY: Well, actually, I'm interested about the public-policy aspect of this whole thing. Now last month, I got on the weather-science database search and I looked up the term *cold fusion*, and it came up with nine hundred papers. Cold fusion is the poster-child for the "not ready-for-primetime-physics theory," something that is not ready for going into ninth-grade physics textbooks. We see the process of science in things like plate tectonics and the endosymbiosis theory and neutral theory and punctuated equilibrium. These are things that have earned a place in the textbooks because the people have put in the work, they have convinced the scientific community that they have points, and that's why they're in the textbooks. So what I'd like to hear from both of you: Is there a justification for giving intelligent design a pass on this process?

DEMBSKI: Who's first?

RUSE: No. (*Audience laughter*)

DEMBSKI: Well that was short; I think I could expand on that just a little bit . . . . (*Laughter all around*) A few years back, I wrote a paper that I delivered at a conference that you attended. It was titled "Becoming a Disciplined Science: Pitfalls, Problems, and Reality Check for Intelligent Design." In that paper, I addressed the concern that intelligent design would become an instrumental good used by various groups to further certain ends, but that the science would get short-shrifted. I also argued taht the science needs to be treated as an intrinsic good. And indeed, that's ultimately been my motivation for getting into this whole ID debate. I could make my peace with Darwinism if I had to. I'm theologically astute enough to do the fancy footwork, but it's the neo-Darwinism science itself that I think doesn't hold up. That is what motivates me to critique Darwinism and to develop intelligent design. As I argued in that paper, intelligent design has to be developed as a scientific program; otherwise, you can't get a pass on it. So I'm with you on that, Wesley. I was not a supporter of the Dover policy. Once it was enacted and the Thomas More Law Center was going ahead with it, I did agree to be an expert witness there. But I thought it was premature to mandate the teaching of ID.

FRANCIS BECKWITH: I'd like to ask the question actually about Dover and the recent opinion by Judge Jones, of whom both of you know and many in the audience know that in that particular case the school board of Dover passed a resolution or policy that requires teachers, ninth-grade biology teachers, had to read a five-paragraph disclaimer about evolution. Judge Jones argued in his 139-page opinion that the argument for intelligent design failed and that intelligent design is not science. But suppose the arguments for intelligent design did succeed, and this question is for both of you, do you think that this means that intelligent design could be taught in public schools and still not be science? Or do you think that it not being science would be sufficient to ban it even if it offers a successful argument?

RUSE: Well, I've thought a lot about this. I do not object to the topic of intelligent design coming up in schools. I'm a philosophy professor. I've been teaching about intelligent design in my classes for forty-one years. I do this because that's what we do in philosophy. I don't teach the argument from design as true. I try to point out the problems with it. But conversely, I don't teach the argument from design as false. I've always said to my students that I would be a bad teacher if, ultimately, I didn't say to you: "It's your choice." I always say to students that I never mark them on the last line of what they say. They never get a mark on their conclusion. I mark on how the student gets to the conclusion.

I would be very comfortable with intelligent design, along with other forms of Christianity, not to mention things like Islam and the beliefs of other religions, being taught in comparative religion or comparative philosophy classes in schools. I went to a Quaker school, and we had that sort of thing. I've always been glad that I had it. I truly want to see religion taught properly, straight up in a comparative, informational sort of way. I don't want it taught as has been proposed in California, where it's just a way of getting in religious indoctrination. And that is my worry. I think if religion is taught in a comparative, informational sense—no one is expected to believe the religion as true (or false)—then I am fine with that. And in such a case, if people like Bill Dembski or William Lane Craig are invited along to make their kind of case, I ain't got no problem with that at all.

DEMBSKI: Let me add something to the mix: string theory. There's currently no experimental evidence for it. The scale at which this theory operates and for which it would be confirmable are at levels of energy and means of instrumentation that no scientist can get an empirical handle on it. And yet string theory is taught in physics classes. There's a lot of nifty mathematics that comes along with it. So, what are you going to say—that's in science but that's not? I'm not sure you want to go that route. Can you understand Darwin's theory apart from intelligent design as its proper foil? Can you properly read Darwin's *Origin of the Species* without having some understanding of intelligent design? His notion of intelligent design, understood as special creation, comes up in that book about 120 times, explicitly referenced. My colleague Paul Nelson did a radio interview on NPR with Niall Shanks, a philosopher of science at Wichita State University. They went through book after book. Could Darwin's *Origin of the Species* be taught in high school biology? No, according to Shanks.

Could Stephen J. Gould's *Ever Since Darwin* be taught? No, because it raises the question of design. How far are you going to go with such exclusions before it undercuts the educational enterprise? It seems to me that, minimally, you can't understand the science of evolutionary biology historically apart from intelligent design. So, just in terms of good pedagogy, it has to be there.

ROBERT B. STEWART: Thank you.

2

The Evolution Wars

Who Is Fighting with Whom about What?

Martinez Hewlett

"Evolution Wars!" screamed the cover headline of *Time* on August 15, 2005, juxtaposing a chimpanzee in contemplation with Michelangelo's Creator God from the Sistine Chapel ceiling pointing his omnipotent finger earthward. The accompanying article dealt with the Dover, Pennsylvania, case, one of the central themes of the present volume, and covered in detail elsewhere in this book. My purpose here is to examine exactly what this warfare model is about. I will do this by asking and answering some questions, namely:

1. Just what is the task of science?
2. What is biological evolution and what is the evidence supporting it?
3. If this is a war, what are the supposed sides in the battle? What is atheistic materialism? What is scientific creationism? Most importantly, what is intelligent design?
4. Given all of this, is it really fair to say that this is a war between science and religion?
5. If this is a war, then what is the peaceful middle ground?

The Task of Science

Scientists, like everyone else, are human beings, and science is an all too human activity. It's a way of observing the world around us—it produces a view, sometimes called the scientific view. Is it privileged? Not really. It's a very powerful view, supported by a methodology that incorporates observation, hypothesis building, experimentation, and hypothesis revision. But this does not make it an exclusive view of the natural world. There is also the view of the artist, the writer, the philosopher, or the theologian to consider. Nonetheless, science has, in our modern world, come to be thought of as the "definitive" statement about the nature of reality.

Is this, in fact, the task of science? Niels Bohr, one of the founding fathers of the revolution in physics leading to quantum mechanics, said: "It is wrong to think that the task of physics is to find out how nature *is*. Physics concerns only what we can *say* about nature.[1]

If we substitute the word *science* for *physics* in Bohr's statement, we come to the understanding that the task at hand is to find a way to say something about the natural world, rather than to give an accurate description of that reality. What is this something science wants to say?

Science builds models of reality. Exactly what kind of model is this? Certainly, it is not a model in the way that we imagine in terms of toy trains and airplanes. Rather, scientific models are experimentally derived ways of making sense of observations. The models that scientists construct must have three features to be of any use:

1. The model must have explanatory value. This means that the model must allow the scientist to take data (observations) and come to explanations for them.
2. The model must have predictive value and be fertile. Scientific models are useful in that they generate new experimental approaches that yield new knowledge about the natural world.
3. Finally, the model must be falsifiable. It does no good if the model is not subject to experimental challenge. Science progresses as old models are challenged and revised or entirely new models take their place.

Scientific models, then, are ways of looking at, explaining, and probing the natural world using a method that allows experimental challenge and potential falsification. The model can also be called a theory.

It is popular with opponents of biological evolution to say, "but it's just a theory," as though this means there is no support for the idea. In science, the opposite is actually the case. Scientific theories are models for which there is abundant support in observations and experiments. Scientific theories meet the three criteria for models of reality that allow fertile new ground to be covered. When such theories no longer satisfy the criteria, they are replaced with more fruitful and explanatory versions. Such occurrences are termed "paradigm shifts," a phrase coined by Thomas Kuhn.[2]

Are such models reality? That is, can we say that scientific models and reality exactly coincide, and that the model is a complete and accurate description of the reality it describes? Let's take an example of a modern set of models. The gas hydrogen is the simplest form of matter (used in the modern, not the classical, sense of matter here) in the universe. It is a colorless, odorless, flammable gas. Science uses three conceptual models to describe hydrogen: the periodic table of the elements, the planetary model, and the quantum model. Each is a model that fits all three criteria, and yet none of these is meant to be the gas itself.

The periodic table of Mendeleev models the relationship of all of the elements, including hydrogen, to all other elements. In this description, hydrogen occupies the upper-left beginning position of the table, with the symbol and atomic properties described as ^{1}H. This table has explanatory value and its predictive value was so fruitful that all of the elements, as they were discovered, could fit into this same scheme. But it is not the gas; it is only a useful model.

The nature of the atom itself was first described by Niels Bohr as a small planetary system. In this model, hydrogen is drawn with a central spherical nucleus (the proton) around which orbits the small, spherical electron. This is a model with such important explanatory value that it still appears in elementary textbooks as a way to depict how two atoms join together to form a chemical bond. And yet no physicist would think that this is what hydrogen actually looks like. To a physicist, hydrogen, or at least the ground state of the electron in the first orbit, would look like this (see fig. 2.1):

$$\Psi_{1s} = \pi^{-0.5}\left[z/a_0\right]^{1.5}e^{-\sigma}$$

Figure 2.1

Is this wave equation, then, the reality of the gas? Not exactly, but it is a very useful model, both explanatory and fruitful. The computer upon which I write this text is possible in our world as a consequence of the quantum revolution in physics, of which this equation is one result.

Does this mean that scientific models have no relationship to reality? Certainly we use them precisely because we understand them to be, in some sense, indicative of some properties of reality. It's just that we need to keep in mind that they are powerful, useful, and ultimately revisable models.

Biological evolution is a theory in this sense. At present, it is the best explanatory and predictive model that we have to account for the diversity of life on our planet. It is so well supported by evidence that we can see no reason to revise or discard it in the near future. It is a model that serves us richly. Let's see exactly what this scientific theory maintains.

Biological Evolution: A Brief History and Description

In December 1831, a young naturalist, son of a wealthy British family and until recently a student at Cambridge, set sail on H.M.S. *Beagle* from Plymouth harbor on what would be a nearly five-year voyage around the globe. Charles Darwin left that day not knowing, I'm sure, the true destination that would be the result of his decision to join the ship's company.

Darwin's observations during his journey returned home with him in the form of books full of his notes and drawings. He did not come back to England convinced of his revolutionary model. Rather, he came back to years of labor as he worked to make sense of his observations. From 1836 until the publication of *The Origin of Species by Means of Natural Selection* in November 1859, Darwin carefully formulated his explanatory theory.

From his data, Darwin argued that all living things on the planet descended from a common ancestor with modifications that lead to the variety of species we now see. He stated that this took place because of the force of natural selection operating over geological time periods.

His use of the term *natural selection* was conscious. He was comparing the force he proposed in nature to the action of agriculturists who, for centuries, practiced selective breeding of plants and animals to encourage the propagation of desirable traits. In a similar way, he argued, the reproductive success of organisms was dependent upon the forces at work in nature, and such selection then influenced the traits of subsequent generations.

He was aware of the idea of geological or "deep" time. His grandfather, Erasmus Darwin, was one of the first to propose that the earth was much older than originally suspected. In addition, Darwin was a close associate of Charles Lyell, the great geologist of Victorian England.

It is possible to state the Darwinian model as a series of propositions. This version is taken from the work of the late evolutionary biologist, John Maynard Smith.[3]

1. Imagine a population of organisms (units of evolution) exists with three properties:

a. multiplication (one can give rise to two),

b. variation (not all entities are alike), and

c. heredity (like usually begets like during multiplication).

2. Differences between organisms will influence their likelihood of surviving and reproducing. That is, the differences will influence their fitness.

3. The population will change over time (evolve) in the presence of selective forces.

4. The organisms will come to possess traits that increase their fitness.

These four propositions are often summarized as "descent with modification."

Darwin's theory was not fully credible to other biologists at the time of its publication, mainly because he had no real idea how natural selection worked. As a scientist of his time, Darwin was working with little understanding of the mechanisms of heredity. True, in 1868, the Augustinian priest and scientist Gregor Mendel published what was to become another influential explanatory theory. However, it took almost fifty years for this quantitative law describing the behavior of genes to be accepted.

It was not until the 1940s that everything came together in what Julian Huxley then called "the modern synthesis."[4] This brought together the powerful explanatory theory of Darwin with the mechanism of heredity of Mendel, joined with an understanding of the nature of genetic variation as mutation and ultimately as changes in the sequence of DNA. Natural selection then becomes a force that, over gradual geological time, acts to promote the reproductive success of organisms whose genetic information contains favorable variations. This is now called the neo-Darwinian synthesis, and represents the current paradigm of biology.

How good is this model? Remember, in judging the model we need to keep in mind the three criteria of explanatory value, fruitfulness, and falsifiability.

The model is supported by and explains observational data from a wide variety of fields. Darwin saw it reflected in the fossil record, and paleontologists still mine this vast data set today. Biological evolution also explains the relationship of form that is seen throughout the living world. This relationship suggests descent from a common ancestor, and is seen whether one is examining the structure of organisms, organs, cells, or biological molecules. All of life shares common mechanisms and functional parts. Darwin's model predicts that this occurred over the long geological history of the planet, under the selective pressure of reproductive success.

Is the model fruitful? In December 2005, *Science*, the research publication of the American Association for the Advancement of Science, chose evolution as its "breakthrough of the year."[5] This was not done because evolution was a new discovery, but rather because it was a theory of such immense fruitfulness that several new areas of knowledge had opened up during that year as a direct result of the application of the Darwinian model.

Is the model falsifiable? The operation of science is such that every experimental investigation has the potential to falsify a theory. In fact, Karl Popper pointed out that science does not proceed by proving theories, but rather by falsifying them.[6] At this point, experimental evidence has not been observed that in any way challenges the basic model, although details of the model have been revised.[7]

The science is solid, supported by observations, and still leads in new and important directions that are important not only for our fund of knowledge, but also for our well being as a community of living beings. So, why the warfare issue? No similar outrages arise as a result of the law of gravitation or models of chemical reactivity. What is it about the science of biological evolution that continues to provoke such strong reactions?

Covering over the Science: Ideological Shrink Wrapping

It turns out that it's not the science that's the problem. Darwin's book was published on November 22, 1859. On November 23, a letter arrived for him from Thomas Huxley, one of the most influential thinkers of the nineteenth century. In this letter, Huxley says: "My dear Darwin—I finished your book yesterday, a lucky examination having furnished me with a few hours of continuous leisure."[8]

Huxley was one of the first proponents of Darwin's theory. He saw in it the intellectual justification for his coining of the word *agnosticism*. Out of this also grew his conviction that, as his grandson Julian Huxley would later say, he could discern the "lineaments of a new religion."[9] Within twenty-four hours of its publication, *Origin of Species* had become the centerpiece of what would eventually be an atheistic materialism and the core of the "religion" of evolutionary humanism.[10] Indeed, the modern proponents of this stance, such as Richard Dawkins, trace their philosophical and atheistic roots back to Thomas Huxley's overnight take on Darwin's scientific work:

> An atheist before Darwin could have said, following Hume: "I have no explanation for complex biological design. All I know is that God isn't a good explanation, so we must wait and hope that somebody comes up with a better one." I can't help feeling that such a position, though

logically sound, would have left one feeling pretty unsatisfied, and that although atheism might have been *logically* tenable before Darwin, Darwin made it possible to be an intellectually fulfilled atheist.[11]

In my opinion, that last sentence should really read, "Thomas Huxley, using Darwin, made it possible." That would be truer to what actually happened.

It was not only Huxley who championed Darwin's model beyond the science. Herbert Spencer, another intellectual star of the late nineteenth century, had already written extensively on biological issues and had, in fact, come up with his own theory of evolution.[12] His model did not have the force of natural selection as a mechanism and did not include the extensive observations that Darwin had made. And so it was that Spencer was inclined to agree with Darwin completely. In fact, the phrase "survival of the fittest" was coined by Spencer and added to the sixth edition of *Origin of Species* by Darwin himself, who wrote:

> I have called this principle, by which each slight variation, if useful, is preserved, by the term natural selection, in order to mark its relation to man's power of selection. But the expression often used by Mr. Herbert Spencer, of the Survival of the Fittest, is more accurate, and is sometimes equally convenient.[13]

Spencer, however, took the model beyond the limits of the data and scientific explanations for the natural world. He reasoned that, if organisms were subject to natural selection, so would be societies and economic systems. This layer of shrink wrapping is called Social Darwinism. In effect, Spencer argued for the survival of the fittest systems, economic or political. His idea was that those unfit systems, and the people that they affected, would simply die off.

Another great figure of Western Europe in the nineteenth century added yet a third layer over the science. This was closer to home for Darwin, because it was his cousin, Francis Galton, perhaps even more influential in his time than his now more famous relative. The argument he made was that if humans, like all other creatures of the living world, were subject to natural selection, then it made sense to influence the course of our evolution by guiding our own reproduction as a species. Galton invented the term *eugenics* to describe this process, meaning "good breeding." The best and brightest should be encouraged to have offspring (positive eugenics), while those "unfit" members of the community should be discouraged, or even prevented from reproduction (negative eugenics). Galton put forth these ideas in a book called *Hereditary Genius*.[14]

You can well imagine how these three layers of ideology would go over with people of religious convictions. If, as some of them believe, accepting Darwin's model as an explanatory and predictive tool also means accepting atheism, materialism, social Darwinism, and eugenics, then they would want no part of any of it, including the science. But is that the case? Are these ideologies inseparable from the science?

Some would have you believe so. Richard Dawkins argues for this in his most recent book, *The God Delusion*.[15] On the other hand, I am also a scientist. When I go into my laboratory to work on the molecular biology of viruses, I do not have to don atheist garb in order to make sense of my observations. There is no step in the scientific method where it says: "at this point, abandon belief in God." And yet, the neo-Darwinian synthesis, the paradigm of my science, is necessary for me to think about how viruses in our world, such as influenza, mutate and evolve.

Those who tell you that the science of Darwin leads inevitably to all of the ideology, including atheism, are selling you a bill of goods. What they are not being honest about is that their conclusions are philosophical, not scientific. These are prior commitments that many of them have to the ideology, and they are using the science in an attempt to justify it. The sad thing is that many of them hide these facts behind the cloak of science itself, pretending to be doing the task of modeling the natural world when they are, in fact, trying to convert you to their belief system (or lack of one).

The Somewhat Predictable Religious Reaction

In spite of what I just argued it seems that the ideologists have done their work all too well. Almost immediately, and continuing to this day, there were those in the religious community who saw biological evolution as a challenge to spiritual values, if not the very essence of evil itself. It must be stated that the extreme reaction was, and remains today, confined to the Christian communities of the West, for the most part those of the evangelical Protestant persuasion.

One of the most fervent antievolution movements to rise up has been scientific creationism. It is fair to say that, while those at the forefront of this position are religiously conservative and evangelical, they are also scientists and not theologians. Their respect for science leads to their conclusion that the problem of evolution is, at its heart, a misuse of science itself.

Notice that I have not called the scientific creationists "fundamentalists." This has been confusing in the popular mind. Ted Peters and I, in our two books on the evolution issue, have taken great pains to point out that American fundamentalism had, at its very beginning, no problem with

Darwinian evolution.[16] In fact, some of those responsible for composing the Five Fundamentals, such as B. B. Warfield, within the Presbyterian Church in the United States were themselves evolutionists.

The Supreme Court of the United States ruled in 1982, in the case of *McLean v. Arkansas Board of Education*, that scientific creationism is a form of religious ideology and cannot be taught in public schools.[17] Given that this court decision ended the attempts to insert this position into the biology curriculum, I will not deal with it further, but leave the reader to investigate the case.

Intelligent Design: A Science or an Alternative Ideology?

The subject of this volume, however, is intelligent design. What exactly is meant by this? From where does this position derive? What, if anything, is wrong with it as a science?

Intelligent design may be defined as follows: An object or process in the natural world is so complex that its existence cannot possibly be explained by standard, naturalistic models (that is, neo-Darwinian evolution). Therefore, the object or process must have had an intelligent designer.

Living systems simply beg for explanations that include design. When we observe the functional workings of organisms, organ systems, or cells, we are overwhelmed with the evident complexity of it all. This impressed Reverend William Paley who, in 1802, published *Natural Theology, Or Evidences of the Existence and Attributes of the Deity*.[18] Paley's book was required reading at Cambridge, and young Charles Darwin admitted that he had virtually memorized it. However, Paley's work is not the origin of this issue.

The great Greek biologist Aristotle had much to do with this. Did I say biologist? Yes, I did, for Aristotle actually published more treatises on living systems than he did on philosophy. It was his philosophical approach to descriptions of the natural world, however, that ultimately influenced Saint Thomas Aquinas.

Aristotle described the natural world in terms of four causes: the material cause (what a thing is made of), the formal cause (the form the matter takes for a particular thing), the efficient cause (the agent bringing about the change of matter into a particular form of a thing), and the final cause (the end result or purpose of the thing). With these four causes he could discuss any feature of the world he observed.

His body of work was lost for a time to the Western world, but was ultimately preserved and studied in the Muslim world. Great philosophers such as Ibn Rush'd (Averroes) and Ibn Sina (Avicenna) had written commentaries on Aristotle, and it was through these scholars that his philosophical system returned to medieval Europe. This is the pathway through which Thomas Aquinas encountered the Philosopher, as he called him.

Thomas wrote his own interpretation of Aristotelian thought, expanding on and critiquing the work done by his Muslim colleagues. In addition, he used this methodology to comment on theological issues. Among these commentaries are two treatises: *Summa Contra Gentiles* and his masterwork, *Summa Theologica*.

In composing these theological works, Thomas used Aristotelian philosophy as his method of choice, it being the cutting-edge academic discipline of his day. In the *Summa Theologica*, he begins by telling us that we cannot, in principle, know anything about God using our reasoning alone. As a result, God must reveal Godself to us through faith. On the other hand, we can demonstrate to ourselves that God does, indeed, exist, using analogous reasoning, in the Aristotelian style. This resulted in the *quinque viae*, or five ways of knowing.

In this series of analogies, Thomas reasons from effect to cause. Basically he argues that something we know from experience, such as the movement of objects in the natural world, tells us that there must be a cause for the effect, in this case the motion. The fifth of these ways deals with reasoning from the effect of an object's or event's end result to the cause of it. This uses the fourth and, for Thomas, the most important of the Aristotelian causes, the final cause.

The fifth way is not an "argument from design" as some have erroneously concluded, most recently Richard Dawkins in his, I'm afraid rather poorly constructed, criticism of Thomas.[19] Instead, Thomas argues from the governance of the world: *"Quinta via sumitur ex gubernatione rerum* (The fifth way is taken from the governance of the world)."[20] I will have more to say about the fifth way and the design arguments in a moment. For now, let's explore, for a moment, what Thomas means by analogous reasoning.

If Thomas is correct that we cannot have knowledge of God solely from our own reason, then anything we conclude about God from argument can, at best, be said to be an analogy. Thus, when we say the experience of a cause of something implies a prior cause, we are operating out of our understanding of natural processes in our world. If this reasoning leads us to conclude that there must be some ultimate cause, some "uncaused cause," that can be said to be a result of our logical induction. Now to say, as Thomas does, that this first efficient cause, or "uncaused cause" is what we call God is not, in fact, defining God, but rather arguing that God is something like and "uncaused cause." It is an analogy.

For Thomas, this aspect of God as the first efficient cause can also be called the primary cause. Again, using an analogy, we can say that God's action in the world is like a primary cause, and that everything else we see in the world is secondary to that, or what we would call secondary causes. In fact, it is the secondary causes of the world; that is, the behavior of natural objects and systems, that are the aim of science to investigate with its models. By definition, science cannot investigate primary cause since, as Thomas says, this is only an analogy and God is unknowable by reason to begin with.

We come now to the proposals of the intelligent design movement. This includes the nineteenth-century theologian Reverend Paley, but also the modern proponents, Michael Behe[21] and William Dembski.[22] For Behe and Dembski, the existence of complexity in living systems that they claim cannot be explained by naturalistic models argues for the direct action of an intelligent designer. They further argue that this is a realm for the investigative activities of science. In other words, if only science would look, it could find evidence of this designer's work, using the tools of science itself.

As reasonable as this appears at first glance, the proposal begins to fall apart on closer inspection. First, let's remember our criteria for good science. In order to build a useful model, we must have explanatory power, fruitfulness, and falsifiability. Intelligent design certainly is explanatory. For Paley, the human eye exists because God designed it directly. For Behe and Dembski complex structures such as the bacterial flagellum exist because an intelligent designer made them so.

These are explanations. However, are they fruitful? Do they lead to other kinds of experimental approaches, or are they dead-end arguments? For example, if the human eye is designed and not the end result of a selective process that includes an entire lineage of light-sensing organs in nature, then there is no reason to investigate, by comparative genomics, the mechanisms that underlie vision. After all, the eye of the fruit fly would have nothing to do with ours.

Are they falsifiable? If an intelligent designer did work to create these complex structures, is there a trace of this work? Apparently not, except in the final product. How does one falsify a hypothesis when evidence for or against can't be found?

One issue here is the nature of the intelligent designer. Robert John Russell, founder and head of the Center for Theology and the Natural Sciences at the Graduate Theological Union in Berkeley, has argued that there are two possibilities: either the designer is a natural agent or a supernatural agent.[23]

If, he writes, the designer is a natural agent, then there are two problems. First, the designer left no trace of his/her/its work, and therefore this cannot be subjected to the methods of science; there are no observations to make.

Second, if the designer is a natural agent, then who designed the designer? On the other hand, if the designer is a supernatural agent, then the subject is not one that belongs in a science class, but rather in a philosophy or theology class.

Finally, the intelligent-design proposal completely misses the point that Thomas made about primary and secondary cause. The complete statement of the fifth way from the *Summa Theologica* is as follows:

> The fifth way is taken from the governance of the world. We see that things which lack intelligence, such as natural bodies, act for an end, and this is evident from their acting always, or nearly always, in the same way, so as to obtain the best result. Hence it is plain that not fortuitously, but designedly, do they achieve their end. Now whatever lacks intelligence cannot move towards an end, unless it be directed by some being endowed with knowledge and intelligence; as the arrow is shot to its mark by the archer. Therefore some intelligent being exists by whom all natural things are directed to their end; and this being we call God.[24]

Let's draw out, if we can, Thomas's archer analogy. Imagine an archer, an arrow in flight, and a target. For Thomas, the arrow is the set of secondary causes at work in nature. This is the area that science investigates. Science can build models or theories related to the arrow. The archer, for Thomas, is the first efficient cause or primary cause, something like what God must be. The target is God's purpose. Neither of these can be investigated by science. By the way, this is not my restriction. This is the self-described role for science in viewing the natural world.

Proponents of intelligent design seek to force science into an improper role to accomplish an impossible task. Dembski wants to argue for two kinds of causes: natural causes and so-called intelligent causes.[25] What are these latter causes? Are they another class of secondary cause? If so, let's design experiments to test their validity. Are they really subsumed under primary cause? If so, let's not ask science to attempt the investigation, since this is an analogous description of something that is in the realm of philosophy and theology.

In summary, it would seem that intelligent design, for all of its pretenses to science, is really an ideology. It is a well-meaning but ill-conceived attempt to counter the ideological overlays that have plagued the Darwinian account since its first publication. By focusing on the rich scientific legacy of the model *per se*, however, we can perhaps avoid the philosophical pitfalls of both the atheistic materialists and the intelligent-design advocates. Let's see how this might work.

Theistic Evolution: Moving the Discussion onto Peaceful Ground

I contend that it is possible to be both a scientist and a person of faith, without any conflict, whether scientific, philosophical, or theological. How is this accomplished? We (Ted Peters and I, along with others in this field) call this position theistic evolution. It is the position taken by a surprisingly large number of scientists—surprising, at least, from the press that science receives with respect to faith. It is also the position of most mainline Christian denominations.

Admittedly, the spectrum of theistic evolution is quite broad, ranging from somewhat reluctant acceptance of the Darwinian theory (B. B. Warfield held this position) to full-fledged incorporation of the science into a complete cosmological and spiritual model (as, for instance, in the writings of Pierre Teilhard de Chardin). Most of us who fall into this category are between these two extremes.

Ted Peters and I have offered a list of features that characterize the theistic evolution position.[26] I will briefly discuss each of these in turn to conclude this chapter.

1. Theistic evolution accepts the fruitful science of evolution without the ideological shrink wrapping. We want the best science, both for the enrichment of our understanding of the natural world as well as for the continued benefit of our health and well-being. We hold that there is no requirement in or imperative from the science of evolution for atheistic materialism or any of the other ideological positions people on both sides of the war want to associate with it.

2. We wish to recover Thomas's concept of primary cause versus secondary causes. We recognize that science operates entirely in the realm of secondary causes. We also understand that primary cause was meant by Thomas as an analogous way of reasoning to God's action in the world and is not accessible to the scientific method.

3. A corollary of this statement is that science does not attempt to discern purpose *within* nature. Rather, we hold, as persons of faith, that God has a purpose *for* nature, which will only be revealed in the eschatological future. Of course science deals with purposeful behavior at all levels, especially in the living world. But this kind of purpose is not the same as the intentionality of Thomas's archer in his fifth-way analogy.

4. We want to use the theology of the incarnation, the cross, and the resurrection as ways in which we, as Christians, can attempt to rescue the brokenness of creation that is evidenced in the apparent

wastefulness of the evolutionary model. For Christians, it is important that God chose to partake in God's own creation in the person of Jesus. Such christological reflection does not answer the objections of those who see natural evil as a part of the evolutionary process, but it does allow the believer to reflect on the journey of "all creation groaning," as Paul writes.

5. Finally, we want to see science as a vocation to which our best and brightest might aspire. In this way, we want to go beyond the distaste that the faithful may have for the unnecessary ideologies and move toward the celebration of creation that is inherent in the scientific enterprise.

Theistic evolution has a wide number of proponents, not the least of whom was the late Pope John Paul II. The Pope was an outspoken supporter of biological evolution as the best explanation for the presence of the species we observe in the living world, including our own physical structure. He also embraced a dialogue between science and religion. In a letter to George Coyne, the head of the Vatican Observatory, Pope John Paul II wrote: "Science can purify religion from error and superstition; religion can purify science from idolatry and false absolutes. Each can draw the other into a wider world, a world in which both can flourish."[27]

3

Naturalism and Intelligent Design

William Lane Craig

Critics of the reigning evolutionary paradigm in biology frequently allege that the theory of evolution presupposes naturalism. Since naturalism is the expression of a philosophical, not a scientific, judgment, this allegation, if true, is an important one, for it implies that the theory's success is attributable, not so much to any scientific merits it might possess, but to presuppositions that are nonscientific and controversial.

Now at first blush, it seems that this allegation holds that the theory of evolution is true only if naturalism is true; that is to say, evolutionary theory implies naturalism. Accordingly, if naturalism is false, it follows logically that evolutionary theory is false. This conviction probably underlies much of the popular opposition to evolutionary theory. Since the vast majority of people are not naturalists but theists, they—particularly Christian theists—feel bound by their nonnaturalistic worldview to reject evolution.

The converse claim—that naturalism implies evolution—is, I think, relatively uncontroversial. Of course, there are naturalistic alternatives to evolutionary theory. Aristotle, for example, believed that natural kinds of organisms have always existed and that the kinds we observe are the remnants of those that existed in the past. Still, given the evidence of the historical sciences like cosmology, geology, and paleontology, such alternatives are not scientifically credible. In the absence of any creative intelligence, the only scientifically credible explanation of biological complexity is that such complexity must be the outcome of a long process of evolutionary development from quite simple primitive conditions. As Alvin Plantinga has famously remarked, if naturalism is true, then evolution is the only game in town.

The modern naturalist, then, must be an evolutionist. But must an evolutionist be a naturalist? Can one embrace both evolutionary theory and nonnaturalism?

Does Evolutionary Theory Imply Naturalism?

In order to get at this question, we need to define our terms. Naturalism is frequently defined as the view that there are no nonnatural entities, where a natural entity is one that is reducible to the entities required by our best theories of physics. These will include not only material objects but also any abstract objects like classes or mathematical objects such as are required by the truth of our scientific theories. Since abstract objects are causally effete, they can in this context be safely ignored, so that naturalism effectively reduces the domain of existents to the material contents of space-time, along with space-time itself. Naturalism in this sense implies atheism.

William Dembski, however, understands naturalism by a weaker claim. He takes naturalism to be the view that "the physical world is a self-contained system that works by blind, unbroken natural laws."[1] By a "self-contained system," Dembski appears to mean "causally isolated." There is no causal input into such a system from anything outside the system. By "unbroken" natural laws, Dembski appears to mean that there are no miracles in the system, no events that are different than what was predicted by the natural laws describing the system. To say that the natural laws are "blind" is to say that they are undirected; there is no teleology characterizing the laws. On such a definition, naturalism implies not atheism, but what we might call theistic indifferentism. According to Dembski, "Naturalism doesn't come right out and say there's nothing beyond nature. Rather it says that nothing beyond nature could have any conceivable relevance to what happens in nature. Naturalism's answer to theism is not atheism but benign neglect. People are welcome to believe in God, though not a God who makes a difference in the natural order."[2] If God exists, he may have created the system initially and may act *on* the system to conserve it in being, but God does not act *in* the system, nor are the system's laws created with any internal telos in view.

Now does evolutionary theory imply naturalism in either of these senses? The very fact that Dembski can describe a weaker form of naturalism that is compatible with evolutionary theory suffices to show that evolutionary theory does not imply naturalism in the strong sense. Otherwise, establishing the truth of weak naturalism would suffice to refute evolutionary theory, which it clearly does not. It is mistaken, then, to think that evolutionary theory commits us to atheism or the nonexistence of nonnatural beings.

So must the evolutionist be a naturalist in Dembski's sense? In order to get at this question, let us look more closely at Dembski's characterization of naturalism. In a later, more nuanced discussion, Dembski distinguishes four brands of naturalism: (1) antiteleological naturalism, (2) methodological naturalism, (3) antisupernaturalist naturalism, and (4) pragmatic naturalism.

Antiteleological Naturalism

The first of these, antiteleological naturalism, is, says Dembski, "the predominant form of naturalism—it's what usually is meant by the term *naturalism*."[3] According to Dembski, "Antiteleological naturalism is at the heart of most varieties of naturalism, including philosophical naturalism, metaphysical naturalism, epistemological naturalism, reductive naturalism, scientific naturalism, scientific materialism, materialism and physicalism. . . . If one speaks of naturalism simpliciter. . . , one typically means antiteleological naturalism."[4]

Unfortunately, Dembski's characterization of this form of naturalism is not consistent with his earlier characterization. According to Dembski's earlier characterization, it will be recalled, naturalism does not "come right out and say there's nothing beyond nature"; it may even allow that some sort of Deism is true. But now Dembski says that "Antiteleological naturalism takes nature to be all there is and views nature . . . as operating purely by blind natural causes."[5] Here Dembski describes the sort of strong naturalism we mentioned a moment ago. We've seen that the evolutionist need not be committed to so strong a claim. So let us retain Dembski's earlier characterization of naturalism as taking nature or the physical world to be a closed system rather than "all there is."

The hallmark of antiteleological naturalism is that "it leaves no room for any fundamental teleological principles operating in nature."[6] The denial of teleology in nature has two implications. First, the only causes operative in nature will produce their effects solely by chance and necessity. Although Dembski writes frequently of chance and necessity, it is not always easy to tease apart what he means by these terms. Typically, when we say that an event happens by chance, we do not mean that it is causally undetermined. Only in the case of events resulting from indeterminate quantum processes would we say that the event is not necessitated by its causes. Rather, in saying that some event occurred by chance, what we mean is that the event is a result of the intersection of two independent causal chains. Given its causal antecedents, the event could not have failed to occur; but because there was no interaction between the causal lines producing it, we say that it happened by chance. By contrast, to say that something happens by necessity typically means that in any world governed by the same natural laws as ours in which the same initial conditions are given, the event occurs. Thus, apart from quantum indeterminacy, chance is not really a causal factor in nature. Chance is merely a word we use to describe an event resulting from the intersection of two independent causal chains, in contrast to an event that constitutes a link in a single causal chain. Both events occur necessarily, given the relevant initial conditions and the laws of nature. If we do factor in quantum indeterminacy, then we shall say that antiteleological naturalism implies that everything that happens in the universe is the result of the conspiration of quantum randomness and deterministic causes operating on initial conditions. The problem with this understanding, however, is that antiteleological naturalism basically reduces to determinism, and determinism does not seem to be incompatible with design. If one is a compatibilist with respect to human choices, then the effects of human choices are determined and yet often deliberately designed as well. But then naturalism would not exclude intelligent design.

Dembski, however, does not use the terms *chance* and *necessity* in this way. He says, "I approach chance and necessity as a probabilist for whom necessity is a special case of chance in which probabilities collapse to zero and one."[7] On this perspective, the antiteleological naturalist holds that everything happens by chance, but that given the laws of nature and initial conditions, the chance of a particular event's occurring is one. The probability theorist must presuppose that he is dealing with processes that are not directed by intelligence, lest his probability calculations be subverted. Once you learn that there is a card shark at the table, all bets are off! So on this understanding, the antiteleological naturalist treats all events in nature as the product of chance, that is, causes that do not prevision certain ends and aim to bring about those ends. Such a philosophy would preclude intelligent design.

The second implication of antiteleological naturalism is that the laws of nature were not themselves designed with any end in view. A deist who agrees that all causes operative in nature are nonteleological could nonetheless maintain that the whole arrangement of natural laws and initial conditions was set up by a designer with the end in view of the production of biological complexity or intelligent life. Indeed, some ID theorists like Michael Denton seem to hold just this view. Such a deistic perspective seems to be quite popular among participants in the contemporary dialogue between religion and science who have a distaste for miraculous interventions by God in the natural order but who think that the set-up of natural laws and initial conditions seemingly aimed at the production of intelligent life bespeaks the existence of a divine designer. If antiteleological naturalism is to be incompatible with intelligent design, then it must exclude not only intelligent causes acting within the universe but also intelligent causes acting on the universe with certain ends in mind.

Now, at this point, someone might object that antiteleological naturalism, so defined, is obviously false, since not all causes operative in nature are nontelic in character. For human beings, at least, clearly are causes that produce their effects with certain ends in mind. So there are obviously causes directed by intelligence in nature, contrary to antiteleological naturalism. But this objection ignores a crucial word in Dembski's characterization of this brand of naturalism. Antiteleological naturalism denies that there are "any *fundamental* teleological principles" operative in nature. What Dembski has in mind here is *irreducible* teleological principles. Naturalists, he says, are quite willing to admit causal explanations adverting to intelligent agents who are themselves explicable in terms of undirected causes. "Any such design or teleology must evolve as a result of more basic laws controlled ultimately by chance and necessity. . . . Only designers reducible to non-designers are acceptable within . . . naturalism."[8] So, the antiteleological naturalist is prepared to admit directed causal activities within nature, so long as the agents of such activities are not themselves irreducible to nontelic processes.

With this characterization of antiteleological naturalism clearly understood, we now ask ourselves, Must an evolutionist be a naturalist? What emerges from our discussion is that the evolutionist need not embrace full-blown antiteleological naturalism. For antiteleological naturalism involves two implications or theses, and it is open to the evolutionist to affirm the first while denying the second. That is to say, he may agree that there are in nature no fundamental telic causes, while maintaining that nature itself is constructed with the end in view of the evolution and existence of intelligent life. The view commonly known as theistic evolution would be a religious version of this perspective. It represents the classic deist view of God's relation to the world. God has overall ends in mind for the world and for humankind, but God does not act in the series of secondary causes in the world, acting instead only as a primary cause in creating and conserving the world in being.

It might be objected that this sort of design hypothesis is untenable in light of quantum indeterminacy. Given indeterminacy, even on the subatomic level, it becomes impossible to arrange, in advance, boundary conditions that will with any acceptable probability lead to the evolution of intelligent life. Although quantum effects are immediately miniscule, they can be amplified in various ways to impact events on the macroscopic level. For example, the spatial range permitted by Heisenberg's Indeterminacy Principle for the position of a photon emitted from the star Betelguese is, for us on earth, about ten feet! Accordingly, the designer must get involved in the series of secondary causes so as to direct them toward the production of intelligent life. Thus this attempt to combine evolutionary theory with design is untenable.

But there are two difficulties with this objection. First, there is no reason at all to think that quantum indeterminacy is ontic rather than merely epistemic. A good many physicists are quite disenchanted with what one theorist has called the "mumbo jumbo" of the Copenhagen Interpretation and are therefore pursuing deterministic interpretations such as David Bohm's. If indeterminacy is merely a reflection of our ignorance rather than characteristic of objective reality, then there is no reason that the designer of the universe who established such laws should not know the deterministic outcome of quantum processes so as to factor them into the production of intelligent life via undirected evolution from initial conditions in accordance with natural laws. Second, even if quantum indeterminacy is ontic, design of an undirected evolutionary process leading to intelligent life is feasible if the intelligent designer possesses what theologians call "middle knowledge," that is to say, knowledge of certain subjunctive conditional propositions concerning contingent events.

Jesuit theologians of the Counter-Reformation attributed to God just such knowledge of human free acts, so that logically, prior to creation of the world, God knew what any free creature would freely do in any set of circumstances in which God might place him. Contemporary philosophers call such propositions "counterfactuals of creaturely freedom." Now by the same token, there will be counterfactuals of quantum indeterminacy as well, concerning how any quantum mechanical system would behave given any initial description of that system. A designer with knowledge of such counterfactuals could choose to arrange the appropriate boundary conditions and constellation of natural laws that God knew would lead, via a blind evolutionary process, to intelligent life. For these reasons we cannot treat dismissively the theistic evolutionary perspective.

So it is clear that an evolutionist need not be committed to antiteleological naturalism. Indeed, Dembski is emphatic that the ID theorist need not envision the designer's intervening in the series of secondary causes in the world. Exactly when or how the designer injected design into the cosmos is an open question for proponents of intelligent design. Dembski is quite willing to entertain the hypothesis that design was, as he puts it, "front-loaded" into the Big Bang at the beginning of the universe.[9] Such a hypothesis envisions the designer's setting up the initial conditions and selecting the laws that would eventually lead to intelligent life. Thus, far from being an antiteleological naturalist, the evolutionist might actually be a proponent of intelligent design.

At this point one might think that the evolutionist must be committed to at least the first thesis of antiteleological naturalism, holding that the only causes operative in nature are undirected causes. Indeed, there have been statements issued by the National Association of Biology Teachers affirming specifically that according to evolutionary theory, the processes leading to biological complexity are "unsupervised," a statement that led to protests from Alvin Plantinga and Huston Smith and, finally, to a retraction. With good reason! As Dembski emphasizes, an intelligent designer can mimic a random process so as to "hide his tracks," so to speak.[10] To all appearances, the end product would appear to be undesigned, the unprevisioned product of chance, when in reality it was purposefully designed and created.

With regard to the origin of biological complexity, it is open to the evolutionist to maintain that the designer actually intervened in the series of secondary causes, miraculously causing the specific genetic mutations that would be preserved by natural selection in preparation for the next step. As Dembski emphasizes, in such a case, complex organisms would be the result of intelligent design, even though it would be impossible for us to detect it. That is why Dembski holds that while it is possible to prove that a product is designed, it is impossible to prove that a product is not designed.[11] It follows that the design hypothesis is not falsifiable; it is, Dembski maintains, refutable; that is to say, one can show that the hypothesis has no warrant and is therefore scientifically irrelevant; but one cannot prove it false.[12] It follows, then, that the evolutionist need not be committed even to quasi-antiteleological naturalism.

Methodological Naturalism

The second form of naturalism that Dembski discusses is methodological naturalism. According to this perspective, science must be carried out "as though antiteleological naturalism is true."[13] That implies, says Dembski, that "scientists must invoke only 'natural processes'," that is, "processes operating entirely according to unbroken natural laws and characterized by chance and necessity."[14] In fact, it implies more than that; Dembski should have added that it also excludes invoking intelligence as an explanation for the whole set-up of nature's laws and initial conditions. Methodological naturalism, as the assumption of antiteleological naturalism for the project of doing science, precludes, for example, cosmologists' invoking an ultra-mundane intelligence in order to explain the origin of the universe or the fine-tuning of its initial conditions for life.

Again, there seems to be no reason to think that the evolutionist need be committed to methodological naturalism. The theory of evolution is a theory about the origin of biological complexity, not a philosophy of science prescribing a methodology. The theory just has nothing prescriptive to say about how to do science. The evolutionist has the freedom to adopt whichever philosophy he prefers. Given that an evolutionist can be even a theist, as we have seen, he may be quite open to theistic science, willing to invoke God as a cause in order to explain certain phenomena. As a theistic evolutionist, he may be convinced that God's causal activity is in fact the best explanation of the otherwise extraordinarily improbable course of evolutionary development. He may be an ID proponent. So it is evident that evolutionary theory has no implication of methodological naturalism.

Antisupernaturalist Naturalism

The third form of naturalism considered by Dembski is what he calls antisupernaturalist naturalism.[15] This is really something of a misnomer. As Dembski characterizes it, it is really a sort of religious naturalism, postulating a God who works only within the bounds of nature. Specifically, the God of this view cannot bring about events that are beyond the productive capacity of nature. Miracles are *streng verboten* on this view. It is obvious that an evolutionist need not be a religious naturalist. An evolutionist could be an atheist or an antiteleological naturalist. The theory does not obligate him to adopt a religious view of reality.

Pragmatic Naturalism

Finally, the fourth form of naturalism mentioned by Dembski is what he calls "pragmatic naturalism."[16] He has reference here to the so-called naturalized epistemology of W. V. O. Quine. Quine's naturalism amounted to a methodological disposition to accept only the deliverances of the physical sciences as evidence. He eschewed what he called "first philosophy," which is logically prior to science and seeks to justify its deliverances. For Quine, science is simply where we begin in our effort to understand the world, and that project needs no justification. Now it is evident that there is nothing about the biological theory of evolution that commits us to Quine's naturalized epistemology. One might accept an evolutionary account of origins and yet be open to sources of knowledge other than the physical sciences, such as rational intuition or even divine revelation. Evolutionary theory does not prescribe an epistemology.

   In sum, I do not see why an evolutionist need be committed to any form of naturalism. Antiteleological and methodological naturalism may commit us to evolutionary theory, but the reverse is not the case.

Naturalism's Connection to Evolutionary Theory

So are those who claim that evolutionary theory presupposes naturalism simply mistaken? I don't think so. Let me explain how I think their claim is best to be understood.

According to the model of inductive reasoning employed in scientific explanation, which is called "inference to the best explanation," the scientist begins with a body of data to be explained. In the present case, these data comprise facts about living organisms discovered by biologists, geneticists, paleontologists, geographers, and so on. In order to explain these data, the scientist assembles a pool of competing hypotheses offering various explanations of the data. Since the number of possible hypothesis is potentially infinite, the scientist cannot survey them all and so will limit his pool of hypotheses to live options, excluding the crazies as not worthy of examination. For example, no one would for a second take seriously the hypothesis that the world replete with its multifarious organisms sprang into being *de novo* five minutes ago with built-in appearances of age.

Having assembled a pool of live options, the scientist then subjects his competing hypotheses to various tests to determine how well they meet certain criteria for being a good explanation, such as explanatory power, explanatory scope, degree of *ad hoc*-ness, and so forth. The hypothesis that outstrips significantly its rivals in meeting these criteria will be deemed the best explanation of the data. The scientist will accept the best explanation as the explanation of the data.

Now the claim on the part of many critics of evolutionary theory that evolution presupposes naturalism is to be properly understood, I think, as the claim that evolutionary theory's status as the best explanation of biological complexity depends crucially on excluding from the pool of live explanatory options nonnaturalistic hypotheses. Philip Johnson has often said that he would have no objection to evolutionary theorists' claiming that evolution is the best naturalistic hypothesis available for explaining biological complexity. What he protests is the claim that evolutionary theory is the best explanation *simpliciter.* Were we to admit into the pool of live explanatory options nonnaturalistic hypotheses, then it would no longer be evident that evolutionary theory is the best explanation of the data. It is in that sense that the theory presupposes naturalism. The theory itself does not imply naturalism; rather it is the theory's current exalted position as the best explanation that depends crucially on excluding from consideration nonnaturalist alternatives.

When detractors of intelligent design denounce ID as religion, not science, or seek to bar it from science classes and to relegate it to religion classes, when scientists or philosophers of science insist that science can only consider natural causes operating according to natural laws, when intelligent design is classified as pseudo-science, philosophy, or, worse, theology masquerading as science, then these observations only serve to confirm the accuracy of the above analysis. All these objections represent attempts not even to permit the hypothesis of intelligent design into the pool of live explanatory options. The design hypothesis is to be classed among the crazies that do not merit consideration and so do not even make it into the pool. Far from demonstrating the inadequacy of the design hypothesis, such attempts to exclude intelligent design from the pool of live options actually preclude its being assessed as inadequate, since it never even gets to the stage of theory assessment. Such refusal even to consider it a live option only reinforces the suspicion that evolutionary theory's triumph as the best explanation represents a cheap victory, won only because certain competitors were barred from the field.

This refusal to admit nonnaturalistic hypotheses into the pool of live explanatory options is an expression of methodological naturalism. The claim that evolutionary theory presupposes naturalism should then be understood as the claim that evolutionary theory's current status as the best explanation of biological complexity is propped up by methodological naturalism. What is striking about methodological naturalism is that it is a philosophical, not a scientific, viewpoint. It is not an issue to which scientific evidence is relevant; it is about the philosophy of science. As such, it is notoriously difficult to justify.

As Dembski has said, "If methodological naturalism were merely a working hypothesis [or better, guideline], maintained because it supposedly has served science well in the past, that would be one thing. As a working hypothesis it would be optional, and scientists who found the hypothesis no longer helpful would be free to discard it."[17] But when treated as dogma, methodological naturalism "is a straitjacket that actively impedes the progress of science."[18] Perversely, it would prevent us from inferring design even if we were to discover that every atom carried the label "Made by God." More seriously, suppose that life and biological complexity really were the result of creative, miraculous interventions at various points in the past; suppose that we actually live in a world like that. It would be a tragedy, would it not, both scientifically and personally, if we were debarred from discovering the truth about reality simply because of a methodological constraint? Methodology is supposed to aid us in the discovery of the truth about reality, not hinder us in it.

Why can't the scientist postulate a Godlike being as a theoretical entity in order to explain certain observable data, just as high-level physicists postulate strings, hyperspaces, parallel universes, and sundry unobservable theoretical entities in order to explain observable data? This need not represent a blending of religion and science, since the postulated deity would serve merely an explanatory function, not a cultic one. In Aristotle's physics his Unmoved Mover, which he called God, was not an object of religious devotion but served merely as the engine that turned the crank to set in motion the system of the spheres.

It might be objected that such a God, while not religious, is nonetheless supernatural, and so inadmissible in scientific theorizing. But supernaturalism is not really the boogeyman in this debate. Methodological naturalists would have no more truck with a naturalistic God such as is envisioned by a religious naturalist like Paul Davies. Davies's God is subject to the laws of nature and so is not supernatural, yet methodological naturalists would have no more sympathy for the theoretical postulation of such a cause than of a supernatural deity.

Dembski is therefore on target, I think, when he diagnoses the sticking point not as the prohibition of the supernatural in science, but rather as the prohibition in science of fundamental teleological principles in nature. The methodological naturalist is not content merely to bar religion or God, whether conceived supernaturally or naturally, from science. It is the exclusion from science of teleology in nature that is the root issue here. It was Charles Thaxton who, to my knowledge, first made this diagnosis years ago. The naturalist's bugaboo is not really God or the supernatural, but final causes; that is to say, causes that operate with a view to some previsioned end.

Such a proscription of final causes from science would force us to regard archaeology as not a science, in which case we might want to know how the archaeologist's methods differ from, say, the geologist's. Are archaeologists less scientific than geologists in their study of the detritus of the past, simply because they study human history rather than earth history? The methodological naturalist could avoid the awkward implication that archaeology is not a science by placing on final causality Dembski's condition of *being fundamental*: methodological naturalism proscribes from science only final causes which are not reducible to undirected causes. But I suspect that Dembski is being charitable to methodological naturalists in assuming that they exclude only fundamental final causes from science. I doubt that they have thought the matter through so carefully; I suspect that the vast majority simply rest content with arbitrarily permitting the introduction of final causes in some fields of science while banning it in others.

Indeed, I must say that the physics community is not nearly so enamored with methodological naturalism as are the biologists. Historically, God has played a significant role in physics. I have already mentioned Aristotle's physics, but one thinks also of Newton's physics, in which divine eternity and omnipresence lay the ontological foundations for absolute time and space.[19] Newton's famous words at the end of General Scholium to his great *Principia Mathematica* come to mind: "And thus much concerning God, to discourse of whom from the appearances of things does certainly belong to Natural Philosophy." In the transition to relativistic physics, God appears in the role of Henri Poincaré's *intelligence infini* (infinite intelligence), H. A. Lorentz's *Weltgeist* (world spirit), and Sir Arthur Eddington's "being co-extensive with the world."[20]

On the contemporary scene, one finds not infrequent references to God in discussions over cosmogony, fine tuning, and the Anthropic Principle. Some of these references, to be sure, may be merely metaphorical, such as Stephen Hawking's "mind of God." But others are more literally intended. I am amused when I hear detractors of intelligent design state that such hypotheses are not discussed in scientific journals. I wonder what such spokesmen would say of an article I read recently by Lin Dyson, Matthew Kleban, and Leonard Susskind titled "Disturbing Implications of a Cosmological Constant," in which these three physicists struggle to explain the presently observed state of thermodynamic disequilibrium in the universe. Restricting their attention to our causally connected patch of the universe and taking as their point of departure Henri Poincaré's argument that in a closed box of randomly moving particles every configuration of particles, no matter how improbable, will eventually recur, given enough time, Dyson, Kleban, and Susskind argue for the inevitability of cosmological Poincaré recurrences, allowing the process of cosmogony to begin anew within our causal patch. They then state: "The question then is whether the universe can be a naturally occurring fluctuation, or must it be due to an external agent which starts the system out in a specific low entropy state?"[21] They recognize that the central weakness of the fluctuation hypothesis is that there are "far more probable ways of creating liveable ('anthropically acceptable') environments" than those that begin in a low entropy condition. Therefore, the fluctuation hypothesis is unacceptably improbable.

They then turn to the hypothesis of an external agent, commenting, "Another possibility is that an unknown agent intervened in the evolution and for reasons of its own restarted the universe in the state of low entropy characterizing inflation."[22] Now, what is interesting is that they do not treat this hypothesis dismissively by brushing it aside as religion, not science, or as having no place in science. Rather, they treat it seriously and try to refute it. They write, "However, even this does not rid the theory of the pesky recurrences. Only the first occurrence would evolve in a way that would be consistent with usual expectations."[23] But in so saying, they have misconstrued the hypothesis. The hypothesis was not of an external agent who "restarted" the universe but of "an external agent which *starts the system out* in a specific low entropy state." On such a hypothesis, "some unknown agent initially started the inflation high up on its potential, and the rest is history."[24] On this hypothesis the recurrence problems do even not arise.

By contrast, Dyson, Kleban, and Susskind, by rejecting the hypothesis of an external agent as well as the fluctuation hypothesis, are finally driven to suggest that "Perhaps the only reasonable conclusion is that we do not live in a world with a true cosmological constant,"[25] a desperate hypothesis that flies in the face of powerful evidence that there is a positive cosmological constant. Whether their refutation of the hypothesis of the external agent is successful or not, however, the main point remains that, contrary to the allegations of the detractors of intelligent design, they do treat the hypothesis as a scientifically legitimate alternative that is subjected to the normal criteria of theory assessment.

Why couldn't this also be done in the biological sciences? I note with interest that the man who has been called "Darwin's rotweiler," Richard Dawkins, despite his strong antipathy to religious belief, implicitly rejects methodological naturalism and treats intelligent design as a scientific hypothesis which should be assessed like any other scientific hypothesis. Dawkins repeatedly insists that what he calls "the God hypothesis" is "a scientific hypothesis" offered to explain the appearance of design in the natural world and should be treated as such.[26] Interestingly, Dawkins does not reject the inference to a cosmic designer *tout court*: he recognizes that we might be products of some super-human designer, and he offers no in principle objection to inferring such an intelligent designer of the universe.[27] What Dawkins objects to is identifying this super-human designer with God. He argues that since the *explanans* (God) is as complex and, hence, improbable as the *explanandum* (the complex order in the world) yet admits of no further explanation, being eternal and uncaused, no explanatory advance is made by positing a divine designer. Hence, he insists, if we do infer to intelligent design, the designer must be a non-divine being which is itself the product of some prior evolutionary process.

Ironically, it is I.D. theorists themselves who have repeatedly insisted that the design inference is *not* an inference to theism but merely to some sort of intelligent agency. Thus, whatever the merit of Dawkins' objection,[28] design theorists will be unfazed by it, since it is strictly irrelevant to a design inference on the basis of biological complexity. Dawkins, then, finds himself in agreement with the most fundamental tenets of intelligent design theory: (i) that intelligent design is a scientific hypothesis which should be assessed as such, (ii) that it is illegitimate to exclude *a priori* from the pool of explanatory options hypotheses which appeal to final causes or even super-natural beings, and (iii) that the design inference is not to be equated with an inference to theism. What follows is that intelligent design is not religious creationism masquerading as science and that it should not be excluded from the science classroom on the grounds that it is religion, not science. It is remarkable that someone who is so dogmatically committed to Darwinism and so derisive with respect to religious belief should nonetheless find himself so supportive of some of the central tenets of Intelligent Design.

Conclusion

The question we need to face squarely, then, is, What happens to evolutionary theory if we do not assume, metaphysically or methodologically, antiteleological naturalism? If we permit design hypotheses to compete on a level playing field with the evolutionary hypothesis, which emerges as a better explanation? I honestly do not know the answer to that question. But Dembski has repeatedly charged that evolutionary theory has failed to provide detailed, testable accounts of how complex, specified biological systems could have emerged on earth apart from intelligent direction. Such an allegation would surely be taken with deadly seriousness were it not for the confidence inspired by the assumption of antiteleological naturalism that there *must* be such accounts. It is time to find out whether such confidence is not misplaced.

4

The Collapse of Intelligent Design

Wesley R. Elsberry and Nicholas Matzke

The Defeat of Intelligent Design

In 2005, the intelligent design (ID) movement had its day in court, in the form of *Tammy Kitzmiller, et al. versus Dover Area School District, et al.* (usually shortened to *Kitzmiller v. Dover* or just *Kitzmiller*). The case began after a school board in Dover, Pennsylvania, passed a policy mandating that ID be introduced into the biology curriculum and that an ID textbook, *Of Pandas and People: The Central Question of Biological Origins*,[1] be made available to students. Eleven parents from Dover filed a constitutional challenge, represented pro bono by the American Civil Liberties Union (ACLU) of Pennsylvania, Americans United for Separation of Church and State, and attorneys from Pepper-Hamilton, a private Philadelphia law firm. The plaintiffs also received assistance from the National Center for Science Education, which contributed pro bono advice on science, creationism, and science education (both of us worked extensively on the case throughout 2005).

The Dover Area School District was defended by the Thomas More Law Center, a nonprofit law firm describing itself as "the sword and shield for people of faith."[2] The Law Center had been seeking a test case on ID for years,[3] and in 2004 it found in Dover a school board willing to adopt an

ID policy and textbook (*Of Pandas and People*). This was sure to bring a constitutional challenge and a media circus rarely seen since the 1925 Scopes Monkey Trial in Dayton, Tennessee. Indeed, Richard Thompson, director of Thomas More Law Center, explicitly stated his hope that the *Kitzmiller* case would put his group on the map, much as the Scopes Trial had done for the ACLU in 1925.

The *Kitzmiller* case, filed on December 14, 2004, was litigated for just over a year. On December 20, 2005, after months of pretrial discovery, depositions, and hearings, a six-week trial, hundreds of exhibits and briefs, and unprecedented media coverage of ID and its claims, Judge John E. Jones III issued a 139-page ruling that struck down a policy promoting ID in the Dover public schools.[4]

The surprising feature of the decision was not that ID lost the case; this had been widely predicted, based on the behavior of the school board (although the Thomas More Law Center said repeatedly it hoped to appeal the case to the Supreme Court). What surprised many[5] (but not us[6]) was the crushing nature of the defeat. Not only did the judge rule that the Dover Area School District's ID policy violated the Constitution's prohibition against government establishment of religion, the judge also found that the ID movement's claim that ID was science failed on multiple grounds, that ID was intrinsically a specific religious view and, even more damaging, that ID was just creationism given a new, more secular label after the court defeats of "creation science" in the 1980s.

The ruling therefore knocked down each of the main pillars on which ID proponents had based their fifteen-year campaign for respectability in academia and constitutionality in public-school science classrooms. The *Kitzmiller* decision was not appealed (the pro-ID school board was voted out in November 2005), and therefore it did not establish a binding precedent as would a Supreme Court case. The ruling was widely seen as setting a persuasive precedent, however, in part because the judge's detailed and unequivocal ruling was based on a massive evidentiary record, including hundreds of exhibits and six weeks of sworn testimony, much of it from the leading proponents and opponents of ID. Future courts would therefore likely pay close attention to the *Kitzmiller* ruling, much as a similar 1982 district court decision against creation science, *McLean v. Arkansas,*[7] influenced the 1987 Supreme Court decision *Edwards v. Aguillard.*[8] Another reason *Kitzmiller* set a persuasive precedent is that the ruling came not from a left-wing liberal judge, but a churchgoing Republican who had been recommended for the federal bench by Pennsylvania Senator Rick Santorum and appointed by George W. Bush—two politicians strongly supported by religious conservatives, and who had both supported teaching ID in the public schools. If ID lost big even before a conservative appointee, school boards had little reason to suspect ID policies would fare better in future court cases.

The persuasive value of the *Kitzmiller* decision became evident following the decision. The 2006 calendar year contained a string of reversals for the ID movement. Santorum, who in 2001 attempted to add pro-ID language authored by Phillip Johnson to the federal No Child Left Behind Act, resigned from the board of the Thomas More Law Center immediately after the ruling. Despite this and other attempts to increase his appeal to political moderates, he lost his reelection bid in November 2006. School boards in California and New Mexico dropped antievolution policies, as did the Ohio Board of Education. A common argument made against antievolution policies was that while they might appeal to religious conservative voters, they set up a "Dover trap" for the governmental body—referring to the fact that the Dover school district, after losing the *Kitzmiller* case, had to pay $1,000,011 to the plaintiffs—$1 to each plaintiff in symbolic damages, and $1 million to partially cover over $2 million in fees accumulated by the plaintiffs' legal team. The Kansas Board of Education, which had a 6-4 creationist majority and passed extensive pro-ID changes to the science standards in 2005 (while vociferously claiming it was not requiring ID),[9] never got the chance to see its strategy tested in court, because two creationists were defeated by proscience candidates in the August 2006 Republican primary.[10] Several other pro-ID candidates around the country lost in the November 2006 elections. Finally, in December 2006, almost exactly one year after the *Kitzmiller* decision, the four-year-old case of *Selman v. Cobb County School District*, a case concerning the constitutionality of "warning label" stickers placed in the front of biology textbooks in Cobb County, Georgia, was resolved when the school district threw in the towel rather than face a retrial where the plaintiffs' case was strengthened by the *Kitzmiller* decision and lawyers and experts who had worked on the *Kitzmiller* case.[11]

During all this, the Discovery Institute's Center for Science and Culture[12]—the Seattle-based think tank that since 1996 has served as the main institution supporting ID—vehemently disclaimed any support for Dover's policy. This occurred despite the fact that, early in the case, five of the Discovery Institute's fellows had signed up as expert witnesses for the Defense (three of whom—Angus Campbell, William Dembski, and CSC Director Stephen C. Meyer—dropped out midway through the case for reasons that remain obscure[13]), Dover's textbook *Of Pandas and People* was heavily promoted on the Discovery Institute Web site, and a Discovery Institute video, *Icons of Evolution*, helped to radicalize the creationist leaders on the Dover school board. Even more incredibly, the Discovery Institute also claimed it had always opposed any official policies promoting ID in the public schools, apparently forgetting that just a few years earlier its own 1998 strategic plan, titled "The Wedge," had explicitly declared that one of their "Five Year Objectives" was to have "ten states begin to rectify ideological imbalance in science curricula & include design theory" and then "pursue possible legal assistance in response to resistance to the integration of design theory into public school science curricula."[14] In a public confrontation at an American Enterprise Institute event that took place in Washington, D.C., while the *Kitzmiller* trial was ongoing, Richard Thompson accused the Discovery Institute of changing its tune. Thompson quoted a 1999 "legal guidebook" coauthored by David DeWolf (law professor and Discovery Institute fellow) and Stephen Meyer (the director of the Discovery Institute Center for Science and Culture) that stated, "school boards have the authority to permit, and even encourage, teaching about design theory as an alternative to Darwinian evolution—and this includes the use of textbooks such as *Of Pandas and People* that present evidence for the theory of intelligent design."[15] Thompson concluded, "you had Discovery Institute people actually encouraging the teaching of intelligent design in public school systems. Now, whether they wanted the school boards to teach intelligent design or mention it, certainly when you start putting it in writing, that writing does have consequences."[16]

In summary, in spite of recent denials, the ID movement and the Discovery Institute cannot avoid responsibility for creating the situation—the claim that intelligent design is science, the handy public-school biology textbook, *Of Pandas and People*, and the legal strategy and encouragement—that would sooner or later result in a courtroom showdown. Even if *Kitzmiller v. Dover* had never occurred, some similar case would have come about sooner or later.

Both the ID movement's recent defeats, and the Discovery Institute's shameless denial of its own history, make it apparent that the 2005 *Kitzmiller* decision has dealt the ID movement a defeat at least as damaging as the defeat that the 1982 McLean decision inflicted on the then-popular creation science movement. While traditional creation science is still popular with many fundamentalists, it is no longer taken seriously as a legal strategy with any chance of success in American courts. ID was the new hope of creationists, but now it too is probably dead as a legal strategy. However, we are not so foolish as to think that intelligent design and its proponents will disappear from view; after all, creation-science groups like Answers in Genesis are still the biggest antievolution groups, and still the most influential within the evangelical/fundamentalist public, if not the media and politicians. We suspect, at least in the arena of public schools, that history will repeat itself: creationists will again move to new strategies, as they have in the face of previous court defeats.

The Constitutionality of ID: Pre-*Kitzmiller* Claims

Before the *Kitzmiller* case, the ID movement produced a substantial body of legal commentary confidently asserting that ID should and would pass constitutional muster, where previous creationist policies had not.[17] These works doubtlessly provided encouragement and guidance to the Thomas More Law Center during its decisions to construct and litigate the *Kitzmiller* case. After the ID legal strategy crashed and burned in *Kitzmiller*, ID proponents seem to have retreated somewhat from their initial strong promotion of ID in the public schools, and are switching to a pure "evolution-bashing" strategy, as represented in a new Discovery Institute supplemental biology textbook, titled *Explore Evolution*.[18] This is somewhat difficult to accept at face value, given the brash confidence ID proponents expressed just few years before. And despite recent backpedaling, a new post-Kitzmiller law review article showed that ID proponents still promote the central pillars on which the ID movement rests, to wit: (1) ID is not creationism in disguise, (2) ID is instead a scientific theory that is a responsible scientific alternative to modern evolutionary theory, and (3) therefore ID is constitutional to teach in public-school science classrooms, just like any other scientific theory.[19]

Although these claims are the central issues in virtually every work promoting or critiquing ID, and although we believe they were definitively debunked during the Kitzmiller trial and the judge's ruling, we feel it would be worthwhile to examine them again, specifically in the light of the ID movement's pre-Kitzmiller legal claims and the subsequent *Kitzmiller* decision. Court cases like *Kitzmiller* are where the rubber meets the road for legal scholarship. By conducting a postmortem, and examining what went wrong, larger lessons can be learned.

Background: Legal History of Creationism in the Public Schools

To explore these questions, we must briefly review the legal history of anti-evolutionism in the United States. The four most important cases are *Scopes v. Tennessee* (1925–1927), *Epperson v. Arkansas* (1968), *McLean v. Arkansas* (1981–1982), and *Edwards v. Aguillard* (1981–1987). We will pick up the story with the aftermath of *Epperson* and the rise of creation science. For further details of the legal history, including other important cases, readers are referred to Ed Larson's excellent book *Trial and Error*.[20] For more background on the historical origins of ID from creationism, readers are referred to recent articles.[21]

The Second Creationist Strategy: Equal Time for Creation Science.
In 1968, the first creationist strategy—namely, banning evolution from the
public schools outright, as fundamentalists had successfully and scandalously
done from the 1920s to the 1960s—was ruled unconstitutional in the U.S.
Supreme Court's *Epperson v. Arkansas* decision.[22] But creationism did not go
away: it evolved into a second antievolution strategy. According to Ronald
Numbers's definitive history of scientific creationism, *The Creationists: The
Evolution of Scientific Creationism*, creation science was born in 1969.[23] The
basic idea was that if creationism was portrayed as science instead of a particular theological interpretation of the Bible, then it would be constitutional
in the public schools. Henry Morris, the leader of the creationist resurgence,
said, "Creationism is on the way back, this time not primarily as a religious
belief, but as an alternative scientific explanation of the world in which we
live."[24] ID proponents more or less admit, although usually only implicitly,
that creation science wasn't really science and was instead just a scientific
veneer over a particular literalist reading of Genesis, so we will not argue the
point further here.

Creation science grew in popularity throughout the 1970s. The movement peaked in 1981 when Arkansas and then Louisiana passed laws mandating "equal time" for creation science (similar bills were proposed in
dozens of other states, but were not passed). The ACLU challenged the
Arkansas law first on behalf of a diverse set of plaintiffs, including teachers
and ministers. Both sides called in their top experts for the trial. A two-week
trial was held in Little Rock in December 1981. A battle of the experts took
place, with leading scientists such as Stephen Jay Gould, Brent Dalrymple,
and Francisco Ayala lining up on the plaintiffs' side, and leading creation-
science witnesses lining up to support the state of Arkansas' defense of the
law. These included Norman Geisler (then a theology professor at the Dallas
Theological Seminary), a number of witnesses from the Adventist Geosci-
ence Research Center, and most significantly, Dean Kenyon, a young-earth
creationist who actually held a tenured faculty position in a biology department at a major public university, San Francisco State.

To make a long story short, the creationists were trounced. Most of the
defense witnesses had joined creationist organizations that had membership
statements committing them absolutely to a strict literalist reading of Genesis
and, furthermore, had failed to get their claims published in peer-reviewed
scientific journals. Geisler, an old-earth creationist but a leading advocate of
biblical inerrancy, attempted to argue in court that supernatural creation was
not necessarily a religious doctrine, but got tripped up when, "under cross-
examination, Geisler tarnished his credibility somewhat by declaring that
UFOs were agents of Satan."[25] As for the creationists' best weapon, Dean

Kenyon (a follower of Henry Morris[26]), he flew to Little Rock to be deposed before his testimony, but he "fled town after watching the demolition of four of the state's science witnesses on day 1 of the second week."[27] It later emerged that Kenyon withdrew from the case on the advice of Wendell Bird, the young-earth creationist and ally of the Institute for Creation Research who in 1978–79 had published the legal rationale for the constitutionality of creation science in prestigious law-review journals.[28] Arkansas attorney general Steve Clark threatened Bird with legal action for interfering.[29] Bird was to head the defense of Louisiana's Balanced Treatment Act, and apparently wanted to save Kenyon's credibility for the Louisiana case.

After the courtroom debacles, even the creationists did not have much hope for a positive result in the McLean case. On January 5, 1982, Judge Overton issued a long and detailed opinion ruling Arkansas' balanced-treatment law unconstitutional. Overton found that creation science failed to be science on numerous grounds, and more importantly, that the content of creation science was through-and-through a religious view.[30] It was a crushing and embarrassing defeat for the always brash creation scientists. Moody Monthly, a fundamentalist magazine highly sympathetic to creation science, declared in a May 1982 cover story that Arkansas was "Where Creationism Lost Its Shirt."[31]

The Second (and a Half) Strategy: Redefine Creation Science in *Edwards v. Aguillard.*

The definition of creation science in Louisiana's Equal Time law was changed the day after the ACLU filed suit against the Arkansas law.[32] The Louisiana legislature removed explicit references to a young earth, a global flood, and special creation of humans and the Genesis "kinds." This was part of a legal strategy to make creation science less vulnerable to the charge that it was religion in disguise.

The litigation of the Louisiana case was complex because in 1981, Wendell Bird got a jump on the ACLU and filed a preemptive suit in state court the day before the ACLU filed in federal court. Resolving the resulting tangle took until 1984, at which point the case was headed for a federal district court trial with the ACLU as plaintiffs and Wendell Bird heading the creationist defense for the state. Both sides named and deposed expert witnesses in preparation for trial. Many of the witnesses for both sides had been used in McLean, but this time Bird had Dean Kenyon and Walter Bradley—two future leaders of the ID movement—on his list.[33] For the summary judgment litigation, Kenyon wrote an expert-witness affidavit presenting the case that "creation-science is as scientific as evolution." Contrary to the claims of the ID proponents, who say that creation science is always strictly defined as

Genesis literalism and therefore ID is different, Kenyon claimed "Creation-science does not include as essential parts the concepts of catastrophism, a world-wide flood, a recent inception of the earth or life, from nothingness (ex nihilo), the concept of kinds, or any concepts form Genesis." Instead, said Kenyon, "Creation-science means origin through abrupt appearance in complex form."[34]

Unfortunately for the creationists, before a trial was held in Louisiana, the ACLU filed a summary judgment motion and won. A summary judgment motion argues that a trial is unnecessary because the agreed-upon facts (which included the legislative history of Louisiana's equal-time bill), even construed in favor of the party opposing summary judgment, are sufficient for the judge to reach a decision. The ACLU was able to cite clear evidence of creationist and apologetic claims from the 1981 legislative history, which included the testimony of various creation scientists. Doubtless the McLean trial, which had already dealt with a very similar law, helped the ACLU's argument.

When Judge Duplantier ruled summarily for the plaintiffs, some thought that the creationists were at the end of their rope. But Wendell Bird was just beginning to fight. He appealed the summary judgment decision to the circuit court. Losing before a three-judge panel, he appealed to the full circuit court en banc, and again lost, but this time only by an 8-7 vote. Finally, Bird appealed to the Supreme Court, and in December 1986, oral arguments took place. Bird referred repeatedly to the affidavits of Kenyon and several other experts, and did the same in a written brief. But it was all for naught; on June 19, 1987, the Supreme Court decided 7-2 against overturning the summary judgment against the Louisiana law, ruling "The Act impermissibly endorses religion by advancing the religious belief that a supernatural being created humankind."[35] Regarding Bird's argument that expert testimony in a full trial might change the outcome, the Court ruled, "The District Court, in its discretion, properly concluded that the postenactment testimony of these experts concerning the possible technical meanings of the Act's terms would not illuminate the contemporaneous purpose of the state legislature when it passed the Act. None of the persons making the affidavits produced by appellants participated in or contributed to the enactment of the law."[36] The only place Kenyon's affidavit was cited was in the dissent, written by Justice Scalia, who cited Kenyon no less than fourteen times.

Ignoring the substantive holding that supernatural creation was a religious view and therefore unconstitutional for the state to advocate in science classes, creationists took heart from this passage in the Court's ruling:

> We do not imply that a legislature could never require that scientific critiques of prevailing scientific theories be taught. Indeed, the Court

acknowledged in Stone that its decision forbidding the posting of the Ten Commandments did not mean that no use could ever be made of the Ten Commandments, or that the Ten Commandments played an exclusively religious role in the history of Western Civilization. In a similar way, teaching a variety of scientific theories about the origins of humankind to schoolchildren might be validly done with the clear secular intent of enhancing the effectiveness of science instruction. But because the primary purpose of the Creationism Act is to endorse a particular religious doctrine, the Act furthers religion in violation of the Establishment Clause.[37]

Creationists, including those of the ID variety, have henceforth cited the first and third sentences in this passage (but not the fourth) almost robotically in every single discussion of the constitutional issues surrounding their views.

Although young-earth creation science is probably still the most popular view amongst evangelicals, it gradually faded from the national scene after Edwards. In several cases, rather than requiring that creationism be taught, creationists attempted strategies such as disclaimers or teachers teaching creationism on their own initiative. However, these have all failed in district and appeals courts.[38]

Intelligent Design, *Kitzmiller*, and Science

We now turn to intelligent design. ID appeared on the creation/evolution scene in 1989 with the publication of the supplemental biology textbook *Of Pandas and People*, produced by the Foundation for Thought and Ethics (FTE).[39] As Jon Buell, the head of FTE, wrote in a 2004 preface for the third edition of *Pandas*, "this book was the first intelligent design textbook. In fact, it was the first place where the phrase 'intelligent design' appeared in its present use."[40] The movement grew in popularity with works like Phillip Johnson's 1991 *Darwin on Trial*, Michael Behe's 1996 *Darwin's Black Box*, and a variety of works by William Dembski, Jonathan Wells, Paul Nelson, Stephen Meyer, and others. Since 1996, Meyer was the head of the ID program at the Discovery Institute.

The standard line put out by the ID movement, in arguing for the constitutionality of ID, is that ID is scientifically credible and that it is definitely not creationism. All of the major law-review articles arguing for the constitutionality of ID rely on these background premises. In addition, the standard line is available in almost every book, article, and Web site promoting ID. These exact arguments were employed by the Thomas More Law Center in defending the Dover Area School District in the 2004–2005 *Kitzmiller* case. In its formal answer to the plaintiffs' complaint (each of these documents is a written brief submitted to the court at the beginning of the case), the defense argued:

> Intelligent Design is a scientific theory based on interpretation of scientific data by scientists; it is endorsed by a growing number of scientists who assert that intelligent causes are necessary to explain the complex, information-rich structures observed by biologists. It does not presuppose any supernatural being. It is not Creationism, which in its basic form holds that the biblical account of creation recorded in the Book of Genesis is scientifically accurate.[41]

In a brief supporting summary judgment in favor of the defendants, the defense argued:

> Plaintiffs also want this court to ignore the reality that the Board is ultimately responsible for the educational policy of the school district and that they believed that intelligent design was a scientific theory advanced by at least some credentialed scientists—and they were correct. Moreover, *Pandas*, as this Court can readily judge for itself, is a book about science. It does not contain citations to Sacred Scripture nor does it discuss the Biblical account of creation as found in the Book of Genesis.[42]

And finally, after the trial, the defense submitted to the court a 950-point *Proposed Findings of Fact and Conclusions of Law*. From point 939:

> a. Although Plaintiffs allege that IDT [intelligent design theory, the Defense's preferred term] is a non-scientific argument that is inherently religious, the evidence shows that IDT is a scientific argument, advanced by scientist [sic] relying on evidence and technical knowledge proper to their specialties.
>
> b. Although the Plaintiffs claim that IDT is Creationism, the evidence shows that IDT is not Creationism.[43]

And from point 950, the very last paragraph of the Defense's 232-page submission:

> 950. In sum, the Court [should find] that Edwards, supra, actually supports the Defendants policy in this case precisely because the Supreme Court took pains to point out that "teaching a variety of scientific theories about the origins of humankind to school children, might be validly

done with the clear secular intent of enhancing the effectiveness of science instruction."[44]

We feel it necessary to belabor this point, for the following reasons. After the trial, the Discovery Institute and other critics of the *Kitzmiller* decision not only argued that the judge was wrong in his ruling that ID was not science and was creationism—an argument that of course they are entitled and expected to make—but they furthermore argued, indignantly and vociferously, that the judge had no business whatsoever ruling on these questions. In light of the defense's explicit and prominent arguments on exactly this question—the core of their entire defense strategy—and the fact that the defense was simply making use of the arguments that the ID movement's legal minds had been boldly promoting for years in books and law-review journals, this objection to the *Kitzmiller* ruling is unbelievable and mendacious. If the ID movement didn't want a court to rule on whether or not ID was scientific, then ID advocates should not have put forward the "ID is science" argument in the first place. As has long been observed, you reap what you sow.[45]

The Claim That ID Is Science

Due to space limitations, we can only briefly rebut the claim that ID is science. ID is strong on bold rhetoric and confident boasting, but extremely deficient in serious self-criticism, careful qualification of its claims, or anything approaching the scientific behavior usually exhibited by dissidents attempting to overthrow established scientific opinion. Blustering about science may work well in newspapers, law-review articles, and conferences designed to promote ID—but when scientists who know better see it, all it does is convince them that ID is just another one of the hundreds of crank science movements out there.

As it turns out, blustering also doesn't work well in court—or at least it didn't work in the *Kitzmiller* case, where six weeks of trial time were available for careful examination and cross-examination of each of claims made. Time after time in the *Kitzmiller* case, common ID talking points—the very talking points that are confidently put forward in law-review articles on ID—were confidently put forward, but then collapsed on examination by plaintiff experts and the court.

For example, the Discovery Institute attempts to show that it has serious scholarship behind it by displaying a list of "peer-reviewed and peer-edited" articles supporting ID. The Discovery Institute even submitted this list to the judge in *Kitzmiller* via an amicus brief,[46] a venue that avoids cross-examination in open court.

Unfortunately, like virtually every ID argument in science, philosophy, or law, the claim to have peer-reviewed backing was a house of cards, built mostly on wishful thinking. In fact, when the peer-review issue came to a head in the *Kitzmiller* trial, the defense and its witnesses did not even try to use most of the Discovery Institute's literature list. When it came to the key issue, the real measure of science—original empirical research published in peer-reviewed science journals—the entire ID movement came up empty. "The evidence presented in this case demonstrates that ID is not supported by any peer-reviewed research, data or publications. Both Drs. Padian and Forrest testified that recent literature reviews of scientific and medical-electronic databases disclosed no studies supporting a biological concept of ID."[47] Furthermore, the judge was even able to quote Michael Behe, the ID movement's leading expert, to this effect:

> On cross-examination, Professor Behe admitted that: "There are no peer reviewed articles by anyone advocating for intelligent design supported by pertinent experiments or calculations which provide detailed rigorous accounts of how intelligent design of any biological system occurred."[48]

When the ID movement's own star science expert gives testimony like this—under oath, when it really counts—it destroys ID proponents' attempts to obfuscate this issue elsewhere. Just to be thorough, however, we feel it is important to note that even if the ID movement did somehow produce a few research articles in peer-reviewed journals that claimed to support ID, the movement would have just taken the first tiny baby step toward scientific credibility. Cold fusion, homeopathy, and Bigfoot have all been published in the scientific literature to a greater extent than ID, and yet none of these areas is considered credible science worthy of inclusion in public-school science classrooms.

As *Kitzmiller* lawyer Eric Rothschild noted, one of the plaintiffs' experts, paleontologist Kevin Padian, by himself has written more than a hundred peer-reviewed scientific articles. When leading publications such as *Science* or *Nature* publish a research study claiming to support intelligent design, then ID will be something worth discussing seriously as science in the biological community. Only if ID becomes well-accepted within the biological community will ID have earned a place in the textbooks. This hard route is the one taken by all other modern scientific theories—plate tectonics, the big bang, and so forth. Did the proponents of the big bang skip doing the hard work, and instead lobby school boards and legislatures in order to force their views into public-school science classrooms? The very thought is ridiculous. The proponents of the big bang did the experiments, made their case in the science journals, won over the physics community, and won their Nobel Prizes, and eventually their place in textbooks. This route is the only respectable one in science, and it is the ID movement's only chance of ever being taken seriously as science.

What about the Arguments?

Perhaps we have been unfair in not addressing the scientific details of the claims made by the ID movement. We cannot do everything in one short essay, but to sum up our view, the vast majority of the writing put out by the ID movement, even when it is not precisely republished material, is redundant. About 75 percent of the ID movement's biology-related argumentation could be summed up in one essay by Meyer on the origin of genetic information, an essay by Dembski on specified complexity, and an essay by Behe on irreducible complexity. The rest is unsystematic assertion about fossils and the like, adopted practically unmodified from the creation scientists.

For the most detailed scholarly critiques of the ID movement's scientific claims—critiques that will have to be acknowledged and met in detail for ID to ever become accepted by scientists—we refer readers to the key references listed in a recent review.[49] Many of the basics of the problems with ID arguments were covered in the expert testimony at the *Kitzmiller* trial, which is freely available online, and summarized in the judge's opinion.[50]

The Claim That ID Is Not Creationism

If the ID movement's claims to scientific status break down, then what is the real identity of ID? In the *Kitzmiller* case, the plaintiffs had to make the case against ID being science, but this was only a secondary argument (though obviously important) made in rebuttal to the likely defense argument. The plaintiffs' main argument had to establish that ID was a religious view, because the Constitution prohibits governmental entities from establishing religion through policies that have the primary purpose and/or effect of promoting a particular religious view.

On the one hand, this turned out to be easy—the Dover school board members who passed Dover's ID policy had made it clear that they were trying to promote their religious views in the public schools. The fact that in the summer of 2004, Dover school board president Bill Buckingham stood up in front of his church and took a collection to gather money to purchase the copies of *Of Pandas and People* that were later "anonymously" donated the Dover classrooms, also didn't help the defense case. This was especially true when Buckingham lied to hide this fact in the sworn depositions, later exposed during a dramatic courtroom cross-examination.[51]

Critics of the *Kitzmiller* decision have regularly suggested that the case should have been decided merely on the basis of the actions and statements of the Dover Area School Board. The plaintiffs did not know going into the case, however, that the school board members were going to lie in their depositions or that this would be provable by documents brought to light during the discovery period of the case. Furthermore, the tests used in religious establishment cases specify that secondary religious purposes or effects do not override a policy if the primary purpose and effect are secular. Thus the defense might argue that even if some of the school board members happened to have the personal motive of promoting their religious views, intelligent design was not a religious view, and therefore the primary governmental purpose and effect of teaching ID was to enhance science instruction—a secular goal, endorsed by the Supreme Court in *Edwards*. Predictably, the defense ended up relying heavily on this argument, as we saw above.

The Establishment Clause and Religious Purpose

This sort of argument has become popular in general among ID proponents, who would like to have a way to argue that ID or other antievolution policies are constitutional despite the fact that these policies are inevitably passed by fundamentalist politicians who are typically not shy (until coached by lawyers) about declaring their goal of promoting their creationist religious views via the public schools. It should be noted that ID proponents are often confused about what the words *religious purpose* mean in a constitutional context. In establishment-clause court cases, a policy is declared unconstitutional if a court finds it was enacted for a religious purpose; that is, in violation of the well-known "purpose prong" of the Supreme Court's Lemon test. ID proponents object, asserting that the religious purpose test means there is a general ban on governmental actors using their religious beliefs in making decisions, voting on legislation, and so forth, and that therefore the Lemon test itself is an unconstitutional form of religious discrimination. If ID proponents' understanding of the term *religious purpose* were correct, they might have a point. However, it is not. In the legal context of judicial review of governmental policies, the phrase "this policy has a religious purpose" does not mean "this policy was enacted for religious reasons" but instead means "this policy was enacted for the purpose of having the government establish a religious view."

In other words, the Constitution bars the government from promoting any particular religious view. Government establishment of religion is the key concern for courts, not the personal motives of legislators. The latter may be relevant in a particular legal situation, but not always. For example, a law that required public-school science classes to teach Mormon views on North American archaeology (which include many beliefs, such as the idea that ancient Israelites traveled to the Americas, that are not supported by modern archaeology) would be an unconstitutional establishment of a particular religious view whether or not the legislators who passed that policy personally believed that those views were based on religion or science. A court well-informed by relevant experts would easily conclude that (1) the Mormon archaeological view is not actually derived from scientific evidence but instead is derived from the book of Mormon and (2) the governmental policy clearly has the purpose of pushing that religious view. Thus the policy has a religious purpose in the legal sense. Even if the legislators sincerely believed with all their hearts that Mormon archaeology was scientifically supported, it would still be unconstitutional.

We acknowledge that the shorthand phrase *religious purpose* lends itself to the kind of confusion we are warning against. But a careful understanding of what religious purpose means avoids the quandaries that are raised by foes of the purpose prong. Passing a bill to help the poor because legislators believe that the Bible commands them to help the poor is perfectly constitutional—the governmental action that results is helping the poor, not governmental promotion of a particular religious view. Passing a bill that required public schools to put a sign in every classroom saying "help the poor because the Bible says so" would be entirely different matter.

Intelligent Design Is a Religious View: The Evidence

With the above context in place, we can see why it was important for the plaintiffs to argue positively that ID was intrinsically a religious view, separately from the question of what the Dover Area School Board said while passing the policy. During the discovery period of the *Kitzmiller* case, some evidence on this point came to light that was truly "astonishing" (this was the word the judge used in his opinion).

Readers will recall that the Dover school board adopted the ID movement's biology textbook, *Of Pandas and People*, and in an official policy recommended it to students who were "interested in gaining an understanding of what Intelligent Design actually involves."[52] *Pandas* was the book that systematically use the intelligent design terminology, and was also the first book to put "intelligent design" in a glossary. Here is a definition from *Pandas* commonly cited at the *Kitzmiller* trial: "Intelligent design means that various forms of life began abruptly, through an intelligent agency, with their distinctive features already intact—fish with fins and scales, birds with feathers, beaks, and wings, etc."[53] Even at face value, this definition is rather obviously a description of the traditional creation-science doctrine of special creation, where various groups of organisms are created fully formed by God, as described in Genesis. ID proponents claim that ID does not rely on the Bible, but in fact careful readers of *Pandas* will find evidence of exactly this reliance, only slightly disguised. For example:

> An additional issue concerns the matter of the earth's age. While design proponents are in agreement on these significant observations about the fossil record, they are divided on the issue of the earth's age. Some take the view that the earth's history can be compressed into a framework of thousands of years, while others adhere to the standard old earth chronology.[54]

These are clearly references to young-earth and old-earth creationism—yet the views are being called "intelligent design" instead! Even ID advocates admit that young-earth views are based on a particular reading of the Bible, so they have already lost the argument that intelligent design is something different. Here is another example: "design proponents point to the role of intelligence in shaping clay into living form."[55] This seems like a bizarre statement until it is realized that it is a reference to the verse in Genesis where it is said that God created organisms from "dust of the ground." Based on this and other evidence, reviewers of *Pandas* were sure that intelligent design was creationism in disguise. In fact, this was clearly stated in print starting in 1989 and continuing throughout the 1990s.[56] And this was before any details were known about the history of intelligent design.

In the spring of 2005, we discovered some evidence indicating that *Pandas* not only made use of recycled creationist arguments, but that it also had actually used creationist terminology in early drafts. For example, consider a small announcement published in a 1981 creationist newspaper. The front-page headline of the newspaper read, "Lawsuit prospects dim in Arkansas, bright in Louisiana." Beneath the main article, a short announcement stated, "A high school biology textbook is in the planning stages that will be sensitively written to 'present both evolution and creation while limiting discussion to scientific data.'"[57] This is an early reference to the *Pandas* project, eight full years before the book was published. Notably, the book is supposed to be a two-model work—exactly the approach the creation scientists were using at the time! Furthermore, the two models are not evolution and intelligent design, but creation and evolution.

A second document that turned up in research was a 1987 prospectus for a textbook called *Biology and Origins*. At the time, a manuscript textbook (also by Kenyon and Davis, and thus the same book as the *Pandas* project) was being shopped around to potential publishers by the Foundation for Thought and Ethics. Even in 1987, the textbook topic was described as creation and evolution, not intelligent design. These and other clues led to the suggestion in April 2005 that the *Kitzmiller* plaintiffs should attempt to recover the drafts of the *Pandas* book via subpoena. After several months of battling over the subpoena, the drafts were turned over. To our amazement, not one, but five different prepublication drafts of the *Pandas* textbook were recovered. They were eventually introduced into evidence in the *Kitzmiller* case with the following titles and exhibit numbers: *Creation Biology* (1983, P-563), *Biology and Creation* (1986, P-560), *Biology and Origins* (1987, P-561), *Of Pandas and People* (1987a, P-562), and *Of Pandas and People* (1987b, P-652).

If the progression of titles wasn't clear enough, examination of the text was even more revealing. Consider the earlier-cited quote from *Pandas*, "Intelligent design means that various forms of life began abruptly. . . ." In the drafts, the quote appears, but in somewhat modified form: "Creation means that various forms of life began abruptly through the agency of an intelligent Creator with their distinctive features already intact—fish with fins and scales, birds with features, beaks and wings, etc."[58]

Was this the only time this delightful change of words occurred? No. Similar switches, between the word *creation* and its cognates (*creationist* and the like) and variations on *design* (*intelligent design*, *design proponents*, and so forth) occurred over one hundred times throughout the book. The rebranding took place between the two 1987 drafts titled *Of Pandas and People*.[59] Both drafts cite the then-recent *Edwards* decision, which the Supreme Court issued on June 19, 1987. Evidently, what happened was that the creationists working on the *Pandas* book—including Kenyon, an expert who was advocating the creation-science position in *Edwards* at the same time that he was writing *Pandas*—decided that creation science was legally dead, and if they wished their book to have a chance in public schools, they had better find a new term.[60]

Here we have the glorious origin of ID. Not in a conference, definitely not in a peer-reviewed scientific journal, but in a shoddy attempt to avoid the Supreme Court's *Edwards* decision. Although the Pandas drafts were utterly unknown before the *Kitzmiller* case, this is exactly what the critics of ID had always claimed. ID is literally creationism relabeled.

Conclusion

Naturally, the legal implications of this evidence in the *Kitzmiller* case were devastating for the argument that ID is constitutional. The *Pandas* relabeling evidence almost makes a district court judge's decision for him. A judge's job is to follow the Supreme Court's precedents. The Supreme Court had already ruled against creation science, in the 1987 *Edwards* decision, and ID emerged in a trivial relabeling attempt that was then systematically hidden as a dark secret for fifteen years. Thus the Supreme Court has in effect already made the decision, and what is left for the district court judge to do is apply the precedent.

We do not review all of this in order to gloat over the defeat of ID. There is a moral here, even for people who are sympathetic to the ID movement. The moral is that wishful thinking does not get you very far. Sunny claims, such as the notion that ID has substantial scientific support, or even that it is an up-and-coming challenger to evolution with peer-reviewed scientific backing, might work with sympathetic and uncritical audiences such as those found at apologetics conferences (the major venue at which ID is promoted). But they won't work in situations where informed critics can reply, such as court cases or academia, and they won't even work in media/political debates beyond the short term. Eventually the inconvenient facts come out, and even groups that are naturally sympathetic to ID, such as conservative evangelical Christians, end up with a bad taste in their mouths. We are convinced that in the long run, Christian believers will not condone the use of euphemisms like "ID" to disguise views to get around Supreme Court decisions.

Unfortunately, it appears that the Discovery Institute is a long way from learning this lesson. Instead of doing the only intellectual responsible thing— following the path of everything else in science and making its case to the scientific community before pushing its fringe view in public schools—the Discovery Institute is instead going to have yet another try at the *Of Pandas and People* strategy. The Discovery Institute's new public-school biology text-book, *Explore Evolution,*[61] is essentially *Pandas* with "intelligent design" deleted. The content of the book (which we have reviewed) shows that behind various denials and obfuscations, the book is promoting the same old religious doc-trine of special creation. The Discovery Institute is thus ensuring that legal battles and the culture war over evolution will continue for the foreseeable future.

5

Intelligent Design, Religious Motives, and the Constitution's Religion Clauses

Francis J. Beckwith

The topic the editor invited me to address—intelligent design, public schools, and the First Amendment—is one that can be tackled in a number of different ways. However, given the 2005 opinion of Judge John E. Jones in *Kitzmiller v. Dover*,[1] I thought it would be helpful to offer not only my own understanding of the First Amendment and intelligent design but also to assess an aspect of Judge Jones's opinion that I believe is the most inconsistent with our tradition of religious liberty as well as the U. S. Supreme Court's free-exercise jurisprudence.

Intelligent Design and Constitutional Law

Any exploration of this issue must begin with the checkered jurisprudential history of the disputes that are often placed under the heading, "The Creation/Evolution Debate." After reviewing that history and the constitutional principles that may be reasonably extracted from the Supreme Court's most recent holding on the matter, I will explain what I understand ID to be and why I do not think it can be constitutionally prohibited from the public-school classroom.

The Creation/Evolution Debate

Because Darwinism appeared to conflict with the dominant reading of the Bible in late-nineteenth- and early-twentieth-century America, some states passed laws that prohibited the teaching of evolution in public-school classes. One of those states, Tennessee, featured the first real legal battle over such a law, the Scopes Trial. The trial took place in 1925 in the small town of Dayton. The case involved John Scopes, a local teacher who used a textbook that included sections explaining and defending Darwinism. Scopes's arrest was orchestrated with his consent by a group of prominent Dayton officials and businessmen who wanted to increase the visibility of their small town. Drawing the attention of a worldwide audience, the Scopes Trial featured the legendary civil-liberties attorney Clarence Darrow, who represented Scopes, and the three-time Democratic presidential candidate William Jennings Bryan, who was part of the prosecution's legal team. Although Scopes was convicted, it is widely believed that the Scopes Trial was a cultural victory for Darwinism.[2]

It was not until 1968 that the U.S. Supreme Court dealt with an anti-evolution statute. In *Epperson v. Arkansas* (1968),[3] the Court struck down an Arkansas law that was similar to the statute upheld in Scopes. The Court held that the statute "must be stricken because of its conflict with the constitutional prohibition of state laws respecting an establishment of religion or prohibiting the free exercise thereof."[4] The Court concluded that the statute proscribed evolution solely because it is inconsistent with the creation story in the biblical book of Genesis. Thus the statute had no secular purpose.

In the face of *Epperson*, opponents of evolution developed a "balanced treatment" approach, a strategy that resulted in the crafting of statutes that required a balanced treatment in public schools between evolution and "creation science," a unique religious doctrine transparently derived from a literal reading of the first chapters of Genesis though portrayed by its proponents as a scientific alternative to Darwinian evolution.

Balanced-treatment acts in Arkansas and Louisiana were struck down as unconstitutional by a federal district court in *McLean v. Arkansas* (1982, Arkansas)[5] and by the U.S. Supreme Court in *Edwards v. Aguillard* (1987, Louisiana).[6] Although the statutes were not identical, they were similar and the reasoning that the courts applied to each was similar as well. The courts held that the real purpose of the acts was to advance a particular religious viewpoint, creation science, and thus held that the acts violated the establishment clause. Four issues dominated the analysis in both cases:

1. The statute's historical continuity with *Scopes* as well as the creation/evolution battles throughout the twentieth century;
2. How closely the curricular content required by the statute parallels the creation story in Genesis, and/or whether the curricular content prohibited or regulated by the statute is treated as such because it is inconsistent with the creation story in Genesis;
3. The motives of those who supported the statute in either the legislature or the public square;
4. Whether the statute was a legitimate means to achieve appropriate state ends.

The courts in *Epperson*, *McLean*, and *Edwards* were convinced that the statutes had no secular purpose and that they became law for only one reason: to protect or advance a particular religious belief derived from special revelation, the creation story in Genesis. The courts concluded that in a nation whose constitution prohibits government establishment of religion, and which contains a citizenry with diverse religious points of view, a public-school curriculum may not include one of these religious points of view unless it provides public, nonsectarian reasons for its inclusion. The courts found no such reasons in either the statutes' texts or legislative histories. To employ the language of ID-critic Robert Pennock, the courts rejected the employment of private epistemologies as a justification for shaping public-school curricula.[7]

However, the U.S. Supreme Court, unlike Pennock, seems to understand state impartiality as permitting alternatives to evolution even if those alternatives may be inconsistent with the epistemology and metaphysics, the philosophical, not scientific, presuppositions of the "knowledge class."[8] In *Edwards*, the Court maintained that its holding does "not imply that a legislature could never require that scientific critiques of prevailing scientific theories be taught."[9] The Court affirmed that "teaching a variety of scientific theories about the origins of humankind to schoolchildren might be validly done with the clear secular intent of enhancing the effectiveness of science instruction."[10] Justice Powell writes in his concurring opinion that "a decision respecting the subject matter to be taught in public schools does not violate the Establishment Clause simply because the material to be taught 'happens to coincide or harmonize with the tenets of some or all religions'."[11]

In addition, the Court pointed out, with apparent approval, that the unconstitutional Balanced-Treatment Act was unnecessary because the state of Louisiana already did not prohibit teachers from introducing students to alternative points of view.[12] So the teaching of a nonnaturalist view of origins may be consistent with state impartiality as long as it is justified by public or secular reasons.

Intelligent Design and the Law

Because Professors Dembski and Craig have already offered their definitions and cases for ID, my comments on what I understand ID to be will be brief, with an emphasis on the constitutional implications of that understanding. Intelligent design is not one theory. It is a shorthand name for a cluster of arguments that offer a variety of cases that attempt to show, by reasoning unaccompanied by religious authority or sacred scripture, that intelligent agency rather than unguided matter better accounts for apparently natural phenomena and/or the universe as a whole. Some of these arguments challenge aspects of neo-Darwinism. Others make a case for a universe designed at its outset, and thus do not challenge any theory of biological evolution. Nevertheless, they all have in common the notion that the human intellect has the capacity to acquire knowledge of, or at least have rational warrant to believe in, an inference that mind, rather than nonmind, best accounts from some apparently natural phenomena or the universe as a whole.

But even ID advocates who criticize neo-Darwinism are technically not offering an alternative to evolution, if one means by evolution any account of biological change over time that claims that this change results from a species' power to accommodate itself to varying environments by adapting, surviving, and passing on these changes to its descendents. This is not inconsistent with a universe that has earmarks and evidence of intelligent design that rational minds may detect.

A good way to understand what I mean by ID is to contrast it with its polar opposite, the view that extranatural agency is unnecessary in order to account for the order and nature of things. A succinct and instructive version of this narrative is published on the Web site of the Wright Center for Science Education at Tufts University:

> At the beginning of a whole new millennium, modern science is now helping us construct a truly big picture. We are coming to appreciate how all objects—from quark to quasar, from microbe to mind—are interrelated. We are attempting to decipher the scenario of *cosmic evolution:* a grand synthesis of all the many varied changes in the assembly and composition of *radiation, matter,* and *life* throughout the history of the Universe . . . . These are the changes, operating across almost incomprehensible domains of space and nearly inconceivable durations of time, that have given rise to our galaxy, our star, our planet, and ourselves. . . . Now emerging is a unified worldview of the cosmos, including ourselves as sentient beings, based upon the time-honored concept of change. *Change*—to make different the form, nature, and content of

something—has been the hallmark in the origin, evolution, and fate of all things, animate or inanimate. From galaxies to snowflakes, from stars and planets to life itself, we are beginning to identify an underlying pattern penetrating the fabric of all the natural sciences—a sweepingly encompassing view of the formation, structure, and function of all objects in our multitudinous Universe.[13]

This is why it is incorrect to think of ID as "stealth creationism," as some, including Judge Jones,[14] have labeled it. For, as we have seen, this word *creationism* is a term of art in constitutional law that refers to a belief that a literal interpretation of Genesis's first thirteen chapters is true. Because that belief served as the primary reason for some states to ban evolution or teach creationism, the Supreme Court struck down those laws as violations of the establishment clause.[15]

Because ID arguments do not contain Genesis and its tenets as propositions, and because ID advocates build their cases from inferences that rely on empirical facts and conceptual notions, ID does not run afoul of the U.S. Constitution. Of course, the cases for ID may indeed fail as arguments, but that is not a violation of the establishment clause.

As a matter of policy, I believe there are good reasons why a public school should *not require* the teaching of ID. Nevertheless, there are no good constitutional reasons to prohibit a teacher from teaching it or a school board from permitting or requiring it.

Kitzmiller v. Dover (2005)

In November 2004, the board of the Dover Area School District of Pennsylvania formulated and promulgated a policy that required Dover High School ninth-grade biology teachers to read in class a series of brief paragraphs:

> The Pennsylvania Academic Standards require students to learn about Darwin's Theory of Evolution and eventually to take a standardized test of which evolution is a part.

> Because Darwin's Theory is a theory, it continues to be tested as new evidence is discovered. The Theory is not a fact. Gaps in the Theory exist for which there is no evidence. A theory is defined as a well-tested explanation that unifies a broad range of observations.

> Intelligent Design is an explanation of the origin of life that differs from Darwin's view. The reference book, *Of Pandas and People*, is available for

students who might be interested in gaining an understanding of what Intelligent Design actually involves.

With respect to any theory, students are encouraged to keep an open mind. The school leaves the discussion of the Origins of Life to individual students and their families. As a Standards-driven district, class instruction focuses upon preparing students to achieve proficiency on Standards-based assessments.[16]

Several parents of Dover schoolchildren, assisted by counsel from the American Civil Liberties Union of Pennsylvania, soon brought suit against the school district, and thus prevented the policy to take effect. These citizens argued that the policy violated the establishment clause of the Constitution's First Amendment. Judge Jones agreed, and ruled in their favor.

Even if one is convinced that Judge Jones ruled in favor of the wrong party, one should not embrace the policy of the Dover school board. There are at least two problems with the policy's disclaimer. First, implying that Darwinism is a theory about the origin of life may be misleading if one is talking about biological evolution, which concerns how living things that already exist change over time. Second, the claim that evolution is "not a fact" is inconsistent with the school board's call for it students to "keep an open mind." The board cannot say that evolution is not a fact and at the same time suggest to students that they should have an open mind on the subject, since having an open mind requires that they critically consider the possibility that evolution is a fact.

Religious Motive Analysis

Although Judge Jones offers several reasons for his opinion, he relies heavily on what I call the "religious motive analysis" to dismiss the policy in Dover as a violation of the establishment clause.[17] According to this test, a policy or law is unconstitutional if the legislators and/or citizens who support the policy or law have exclusively religious motives. Although this sort of analysis found its way into *McLean*[18] and *Edwards*[19]—two cases cited by Judge Jones—and some uncharitable descriptions of the intelligent design movement,[20] it is both logically fallacious and constitutionally suspect.

Concerning the former, labeling a point of view, or the motives of its proponents, "religious" or "nonreligious" contributes nothing to one's assessment of the quality of the arguments for that point of view. Either the arguments work or they don't work or, more modestly, they are either reasonable or unreasonable, plausible or implausible. To suggest, as Judge Jones did, that an argument is religious because of the apparent or perceived cultural pedigree or motivational beliefs of its proponents is to commit the genetic fallacy. And as far as I know, the genetic fallacy is still a logical fallacy, even if it is offered as a principle of jurisprudence by a federal judge in rural Pennsylvania.

In terms of constitutional law, I want to argue that because this test targets motives, a type of belief, for the purpose of segregating citizens from the public square on the matters on which these beliefs touch, this test is in violation of our nation's long tradition of absolutely prohibiting government inspection of its citizens' beliefs. I will first explain the difference between motive and purpose and then I will explain why a motive is a type of belief and that beliefs are protected absolutely under the U.S. Constitution.[21]

Distinguishing Motive from Purpose

Consider a modest example derived from a familiar case. Imagine that it is 1802 and you are a leader in the Danbury Baptist Church of Connecticut and you are not pleased that your state has levied a tax to support its established church, Congregationalism. Although Connecticut does allow Baptists and other citizens to request that the state redirect their tax money to their own churches, the process requires that "they first . . . obtain, fill out, and properly file an exemption certificate."[22] And because "Baptists [are] a harassed minority, some communities [make] it difficult for them to receive these exemptions,"[23] which is why you and your fellow Baptists share your complaint with President Thomas Jefferson. The president replies in what has become a famous letter. In that reply, Jefferson writes that he agrees "with you that religion is a matter which lies solely between Man & his God, that he owes account to none other for his faith or his worship, that the legitimate powers of government reach actions only, & not opinions." Jefferson goes on to announce his reverence for the American people's embracing of that portion of the First Amendment that declares that Congress "should 'make no law respecting an establishment of religion, or prohibiting the free exercise thereof,' thus building a wall of *separation between Church & State.*"[24]

Suppose that you agree with the president's sentiments and wish that your state, Connecticut, would include religion clauses in its constitution similar to those found in the federal constitution and extolled by the president in his reply. So, in principle, you support religious free exercise for all faiths, including your own. You see, correctly, that *the purpose* of such a constitutional amendment would be to increase religious liberty for all by forbidding the state to establish a religion and support it financially by taxing those of contrary faiths. However, your *motive* for advancing this constitutional amendment is so that the state may relieve your religion of a financial burden that is inhibiting evangelism. That is to say, your motive for supporting this constitutional amendment is religious: you believe that it is a good thing for people to convert to the Baptist faith and the current legal arrangement in your state makes such conversions more difficult. But that is not a complete account of your motive. It also has a state-restricting aspect to it. For you have no intention in establishing the Baptist faith as the state's official religion, even if you had the opportunity and power to do so, because you sincerely hold to the theological belief that faith resulting from coercion, however minimal, is not authentic faith. So, your motive for supporting a state constitutional amendment that protects religious liberty and forbids religious establishment is unequivocally to advance a particular understanding of religious truth. Nevertheless, the purpose of the proposed amendment is consistent with a liberal view of religious freedom and antiestablishment, which, by any account, is secular. So, we have a case in which a particular law's purpose is secular while the motive of its supporter is purely religious. And yet, it seems odd to say that this law, because of the motive of its supporter, would violate religious establishment. After all, the law, motivated by religious beliefs, *forbids* religious establishment.

Now imagine that you are a resident of Virginia, and you, with the help of the president, convince your fellow citizens that the state should place in its constitution an amendment that consists of religious liberty and antiestablishment clauses that is identical to the amendment proposed in Connecticut. Suppose, however, that your motive for proposing this amendment is not religious at all. Rather, your beliefs in religious liberty and antiestablishment are motivated by the belief that a good community is one that ought to rid itself of any vestiges of a bygone era in which citizens persecuted each other for political power so that the state may endorse, establish, and support a particular ecclesiastical body. Although the purpose and wording of the amendment offered in Virginia is identical to the one the Baptists are suggesting for Connecticut, the first is motivated by what most people would consider nonreligious beliefs while the second is religiously motivated. Yet, the motive of the supporters of each adds nothing to the content and purpose of the amendment. In conclusion, a law's purpose and a legislator's (or citizen's) motive are conceptually distinct.

Why Motives Are Types of Beliefs

A motive is a type of belief that is causally effective in contributing to the bringing about of an action by an agent (that is, a citizen). A motive, of course, is not a sufficient condition to bring about an action by an agent, since an agent may have a number of beliefs that, though potentially causally effective, never contribute to bringing about an action for a variety of reasons, including the absence of other conditions, such as the agent's failure to exercise the power to act. But the motive is not the act or policy itself, and neither is the motive the reason that justifies the particular policy or act. For two people can have the exact same motive for two contrary policies or acts—for instance, Bob opposes, and Fred supports, welfare reform because each is motivated by a desire to help the poor. Moreover, one policy or act may be supported by citizens with contrary motives—for example, Bob opposes welfare reform because he is motivated to help the poor; Tom opposes welfare reform because he is motivated to get reelected and most of his constituents oppose welfare reform. In addition, one policy or act may be supported by two citizens with the same motive but each may justify the policy or act for different reasons—for instance, Bob and Sid both oppose welfare reform because each is motivated to help the poor, but Bob justifies the policy by showing that a similar policy in California failed whereas Sid justifies the policy by appealing to what he thinks are sound principles of social justice. A motive in many ways is a belief properly basic to one's personal constitution, character, and inner life and cannot be "unbelieved" by an act of will in the way that one may willingly and without much difficulty offer different reasons or purposes for the same policies and acts one may advance throughout one's life.

For constitutional law, these distinctions are important. For the Supreme Court holds that "the Free Exercise Clause categorically prohibits government from regulating, prohibiting, or rewarding religious beliefs as such. . . ."[25] This is because the Court makes a distinction between belief and practice: "Laws are made for the government of actions, and while they cannot interfere with mere religious belief and opinions, they may with practices."[26] To be sure, government (including the courts) may assess its own actions and those of its citizens, as well as the reasons for those actions.

In the case of *Torcaso v. Watkins* (1961),[27] the Supreme Court declared as unconstitutional a Maryland law that required a declaration of belief in God's existence as a condition for holding public office. Justice Hugo Black wrote in the Court's unanimous opinion, "We repeat and again reaffirm that neither a State nor the Federal Government can constitutionally force a person to 'profess a belief or disbelief in any religion.'. . . This Maryland religious test for public office unconstitutionally invades the appellant's freedom of belief and religion and therefore cannot be enforced against him."[28] Although he leaves out the citation, Justice Black, in this passage, seems to be relying on an interpretation of the First Amendment he first offered over a decade earlier in *Everson v. Board of Education* (1947),[29] in which he states: "No person can be punished for entertaining or professing religious beliefs or disbeliefs. . . ."[30] Four years earlier, Justice Robert Jackson, seeming to rely on the same sort of reasoning, writes in *West Virginia Board of Education v. Barnette* (1943):[31] "If there is any fixed star in our constitutional constellation, it is that no official, high or petty, can prescribe what shall be orthodox in politics, nationalism, religion, or other matters of opinion or force citizens to confess by word or act their faith therein."[32] The principle that seems to ground this reasoning has its origin in what was once called "freedom of conscience":[33] *no citizen's religious beliefs may be employed by the government to disqualify that citizen from either public office in particular or political participation in general.*

Therefore, the beliefs that propel the citizen or legislator—that is, his or her motives—to embrace particular policies and engage in particular actions may not be used by government to limit a citizen's or legislator's legitimate liberties or powers.

Although it is probably the case that most critics of philosophical naturalism (and neo-Darwinism in particular) are religious believers who see nonnaturalistic accounts of origins as lending support to their worldview, it is difficult to believe that anyone would suggest in a liberal democracy that this motivation would be a good reason to declare as unconstitutional a policy that permits a modest, fair, and nonsectarian introduction to nonnaturalist views in the public-school science classroom. For this would impose a special burden on the political activity of religious citizens that has no logical relation to the content of, or public reasons for, the policy they are suggesting. It would result in political exclusion based on belief, something the Supreme Court has held is *de facto*, not just *prima facie*, unconstitutional.[34]

Aside from the constitutional problems already mentioned, the religious motive analysis provides sustenance to a political culture in which citizens are taught that any public disclosure of their beliefs that serve to motivate a legislative proposal may result in the judiciary's rejection of that proposal regardless of its content or the reasons offered for the proposal. Consequently, this test is an instrument of subtle coercion of, and thus provides an incentive to, religiously motivated citizens to pretend publicly as if they do not have the motives they in fact have. This presents a catch-22 that makes it nearly impossible for religious citizens to remedy public policies that they believe are uniquely hostile to their beliefs. For who but the citizens, whose views are marginalized, would be the most vocal critics of such policies and the most visible proponents of ways to mitigate them? This is a sort of burden not placed on secular political participation. And for this reason, it cannot be just.

In conclusion, the religious motive analysis employed by Judge Jones is tantamount to a religious test for civic participation. It literally penalizes citizens who fail to excise their own religious motives from their own minds, even in cases where these same citizens have fulfilled all their liberal obligations in providing public or secular reasons and have done so through the proper channels and institutions of government. I am not saying that the Dover school members offered such reasons in such a circumspect fashion. In fact, I believe that the Dover policy was unwise, poorly crafted, and ineptly defended by its school board apologists. Nevertheless, however relevant this may be to Pennsylvania politics or to other constitutional concerns raised by Judge Jones, his inspection of the religious motives of the Dover school board members violates their religious liberty, as understood by our founders as well as other federal courts in free exercise cases.

6

Dawkins, God, and the Scientific Enterprise

Reflections on the Appeal to Darwinism in Fundamentalist Atheism

Alister E. McGrath

In the last few years, Richard Dawkins has arguably become the world's most high-profile atheist. His 2006 book, *The God Delusion,* is now widely regarded as the manifesto of a new, hard-nosed, highly dogmatic atheism, which has led many cultural commentators to speak of the rise of "atheist fundamentalism."[1] Fundamentalism, once regarded as an essentially religious development, is increasingly expressing itself in antireligious embodiments, characterized primarily by their dogmatism, refusal to take alternative perspectives with any intellectual seriousness, and their hectoring, aggressive rhetoric.[2]

The growing militancy and stridency of recent atheist writers has been noted with interest by cultural commentators, and with concern by those who believe that the movement's new aggressiveness is losing it public sympathy, and that its overstatements and serious misrepresentations of religion are compromising its intellectual credibility.[3] This development is widely interpreted to point to the increasing defensiveness of the movement, especially in the face of the growing public influence and credibility of religion in many parts of the world, particularly the United States.

This development is of interest and importance in its own right. Yet in this essay, I wish to address one issue, and one only, that I believe to be of especial importance in the light of the themes of this volume: What role is played by Darwin in this new atheist fundamentalism? To what extent is *The Origin of Species* the new sacred text of this antireligious movement, which is, perplexingly, increasingly expressing itself in religious ways?

Dawkins is widely recognized as the High Priest of this movement.[4] As he was initially noted for his popularization of the neo-Darwinian synthesis, before gaining a somewhat more dubious reputation as an aggressive antireligious propagandist, it seemed entirely proper to explore how Darwinism is (mis)represented in contemporary atheist polemics, focusing on Dawkins as a luminous and important case study.[5] Yet it is important to note that he is not alone. Daniel Dennett's *Breaking the Spell* also advocates an antireligious agenda, based on an essentially Darwinian analysis of the origins of religion.[6] Yet such is Dawkins's influence over the movement that it is appropriate to single him out for special comment.

So who is Richard Dawkins? Clinton Richard Dawkins was born in Kenya on March 26, 1941, the son of Clinton John and Jean Mary Vyvyan Dawkins. He was educated at Oundle School, located near the cathedral city of Peterborough. In 1959, he went up to Balliol College, Oxford, to read zoology, gaining second class honors in 1962. Dawkins was placed high in his class, as he was allowed to go on to undertake research in Oxford University's department of zoology under the supervision of Professor Niko Tinbergen (1907–1988), joint winner of the Nobel Prize in Medicine and Physiology for 1973. Dawkins's doctoral thesis, titled "Selective Pecking in the Domestic Chick," set out to explore the mechanisms that account for the way in which a chick pecks at the stimuli around it. He married Marian E. Stamp, a fellow zoologist, on August 19, 1967. From Oxford, Dawkins went on to become assistant professor of zoology at the University of California at Berkeley in 1967, returning to Oxford as lecturer in zoology and fellow of New College in 1970. It was during this time that his most influential and creative works were published, including *The Selfish Gene* and *The Blind Watchmaker*. Following his divorce from Marian Stamp Dawkins in 1984, Dawkins married Eve Barham in 1984. The couple had one child—a daughter, Juliet Emma. After the collapse of this marriage, Dawkins married Lady Sarah (Lalla) Ward in 1992.

In 1995, he was appointed to a new academic position at Oxford University, made possible by the generosity of Charles Simonyi, then one of the Microsoft Corporation's foremost software architects, who went on to cofound the Intentional Software Corporation in August 2002. Dawkins was appointed "Charles Simonyi Reader in the Public Understanding of

Science." A further advance in his career took place in 1996, when Oxford University conferred on Dawkins the additional title of Professor of the Public Understanding of Science, thus saddling Dawkins with the distinguished, yet somewhat cumbersome, distinction of being both Charles Simonyi Reader in the Public Understanding of Science and Professor of the Public Understanding of Science. Oxford University recommends that he be styled as "Simonyi Reader, and Professor of the Public Understanding of Science."[7] He was made a Fellow of the Royal Society—the supreme acolade for a British scientist—in May 2001.

From an early stage, Dawkins took the view that the "most imaginative way of looking at evolution, and the most inspiring way of teaching it" was to see the entire process from the perspective of the gene.[8] The genes, for their own good, are manipulating and directing the bodies that contain them and carry them about. Throughout his writings, Dawkins has developed the rhetoric of a "gene's eye view of things"—not simply of the individual organism, but of the entire living world. Organisms can be reduced to genes, and genes to digital information.[9] On this view of things, as Dawkins famously observed, the universe has "no design, no purpose, no evil and no good, nothing but blind pitiless indifference."[10]

Yet this vigorously atheist public understanding of science that Dawkins has advocated with such ferocious intensity carries surprisingly little weight within the scientific community itself. Dawkins himself advocates the view found in the writings of the Chicago geneticist Jerry Coyne, which insists that "the *real* war is between rationalism and superstition. Science is but one form of rationalism, while religion is the most common form of superstition."[11] It is a form of absolute dichotomist thinking that is typical of fundamentalisms, whether religious or antireligious. Where some divide the world into the saved and the damned, Dawkins divides it into those who follow the ways of rationalism and superstition. It is either black or white; there are no shades of grey. It is, of course, a totally unsustainable distinction, marred by a failure to deal with recent critiques of rationalism and some of the more elementary aspects of the history and philosophy of science.[12] Yet it has a certain rhetorical force, not without its advantages in engaging a readership that is not well-informed at the philosophical and historical levels.

Within this way of looking at things, the figure of Charles Darwin looms large. For Dawkins, the advent of Darwin has changed everything. Before Darwin, scientists (such as Newton) believed in God; afterward, they do not—or at least ought not to. Darwin, Dawkins insists, has shown belief in God to be little more than "cosmic sentimentality," endowing life with a "saccharine false purpose," a naïve and dangerous belief that natural science has a moral mission to purge and debunk. Such naïve beliefs, he argues, might have been understandable before Darwin came along. But not now. Darwin has changed everything. Newton, Dawkins argues, would be an atheist if he had been born after Darwin. Before Darwin, atheism was just one among many religious possibilities; now, it is the only serious option for a thinking, honest, and scientifically informed person. To believe in God nowadays is to be "hoodwink'd with faery fancy."[13]

Once upon a time such religious beliefs would have been understandable, perhaps even forgivable. But not now. Humanity was once an infant. Now it has grown up and discarded infantile explanations. And Darwin is the one who marks that decisive point of transition. Intellectual history is thus divided into two epochs: before Darwin, and after Darwin. As James Watson, the Nobel Prize winner and codiscoverer of the structure of DNA, put it, "Charles Darwin will eventually be seen as a far more influential figure in the history of human thought than either Jesus Christ or Mohammed."

According to Dawkins, Darwin impels us to atheism. It is not merely that evolution erodes the explanatory potency of God; it eliminates God altogether. In an important essay of 1996, Dawkins argues that there are at present only three possible ways of seeing the world: Darwinism, Lamarckism, or God. The last two fail to explain the world; the only option is therefore Darwinism. "I'm a Darwinist because I believe the only alternatives are Lamarckism or God, neither of which does the job as an explanatory principle. Life in the universe is either Darwinian or something else not yet thought of."[14]

Now the rhetoric of his argument demands that Darwinism, Lamarckism, and belief in God are three mutually exclusive views, so that commitment to one necessarily entails rejection of the others. Yet it is well known that many Darwinians believe that there is a convergence between Darwinism and theism. The extent of that overlap is most certainly open to discussion, and it is far from being a settled issue. Yet Dawkins's conclusion depends upon proposing an absolute dichotomy—either Darwinism or God—when the theories themselves do not require such absolutist ways of thinking (though they certainly permit it).

So how does Dawkins appeal to Darwin in his apologetic for a scientific atheism? Dawkins appeals to Darwin at two significantly different levels. First, as a specific example of the general warfare between science and religion, which can only result in the triumph of science over its irrational, superstitious rivals. Second, Darwinism, considered as a universal worldview, offers a totalizing view of reality that totally eliminates God. In what follows, we shall consider these individually.

Atheism, Darwinism, and the Scientific Method

Dawkins's insistence that science in general, as well as Darwinism in particular, destroys faith in God is widely regarded as totally unsustainable. There is widespread agreement that the concept of nature is conceptually malleable, and is a patient of atheist, theist, deist, pantheist, and panentheist readings.[15] Three points should be noted here, whose justification is not dependent on religious presuppositions. The issue concerns how science is interpreted.

First, at the most general level, the scientific method is incapable of adjudicating the God-hypothesis, either positively or negatively. Those who believe that it proves or disproves the existence of God press that method beyond its legitimate limits, and run the risk of abusing or discrediting it. Some distinguished biologists (such as Francis S. Collins, director of the Human Genome Project) argue that the natural sciences create a positive presumption of faith;[16] others (such as the evolutionary biologist Stephen Jay Gould) that they have negative implications for theistic belief. But they prove nothing, either way. If the God question is to be settled, it must be settled on other grounds.

Second, Dawkins's arguments lead to the conclusion that God need not be invoked as an explanatory agent within the evolutionary process. This is consistent with various atheistic, agnostic, and Christian understandings of the world, but necessitates none of them. While it is clear that Christians have disagreed, and continue to disagree, over the implications of their faith for their attitudes toward evolutionary biology, it is evident that, as a matter of historical fact, many Christians have been able to accommodate evolution within their worldview without undue difficulty.[17]

A critical point to appreciate here is that the created order thus demonstrates causal relationships that can be investigated by the natural sciences. Those causal relationships can be investigated and correlated—for example, in the form of the laws of nature—without in any way implying, still less necessitating, an atheistic worldview. To put this as simply as possible: God creates a world with its own ordering and processes.

Third, the concept of God as watchmaker, which Dawkins spends so much time demolishing in his important work *The Blind Watchmaker*, emerged as significant in the eighteenth century, and is not typical of the Christian tradition. Its origins can be traced back to Robert Boyle (1627–1691), who compared the universe to the Great Clock of Strasbourg. The image was initially used to the highlight the ordering and apparent design of physical aspects of the world, such as the regularity of planetary motions. Yet the analogy was transferred to the biological sphere in the late eighteenth and early nineteenth centuries, especially in the writings of William Paley. Dawkins demonstrates the vulnerability of a historically contingent approach to the doctrine of creation, linked with the specific historical circumstances of eighteenth-century England. It was rejected as inadequate, possibly even unorthodox, before the advent of Darwin's theories, by many leading English theologians of the time, such as John Henry Newman. Yet, it was also dismissed as inadequate—again, before the advent of Darwin—by many scientists, who regarded it as failing to do justice to the aesthetic aspects of nature. The Scottish geologist Hugh Miller (1802–1856), for example, found Paley's comparison between nature and a piece of machinery distasteful. Machines can be ugly. How could the beauty of the natural world be adequately accommodated and expressed through such a flawed analogy?[18]

Dawkins's constant emphasis on the absence of any purpose within the natural realm occasionally results in serious inconsistencies within his thought. The most striking example of this is found in his *God Delusion*, in which he sets out to argue that religion is an accidental by-product of evolution. Dawkins there argued that essentially natural tendencies may have become misdirected, ending up as something fundamentally religious. Religion is thus an "accidental by-product" or a "misfiring of something useful."[19] Yet this is clearly inconsistent with his own universal Darwinism, which eschews any notion of purpose. How can Dawkins speak of religion as something accidental, when his understanding of the evolutionary process precludes any theoretical framework that allows him to suggest that some outcomes are intentional and others accidental?

Dawkins's appeal to Darwinism in defense of his atheism is a bold yet philosophically deeply problematic approach. One of the most important difficulties lies in Dawkins's characteristic tendency to smuggle in philosophical, metaphysical, and occasionally even religious ideas under the guise of scientific statements. To explore this question, let's consider a statement made by Dawkins in his first work, *The Selfish Gene*: "[Genes] swarm in huge colonies, safe inside gigantic lumbering robots, sealed off from the outside world, communicating with it by tortuous indirect routes, manipulating it by remote control. They are in you and me; they created us, body and mind; and their preservation is the ultimate rationale for our existence."[20] We see here a powerful and influential interpretation of a basic scientific concept. But are these strongly interpretative statements themselves actually scientific?

To appreciate the issue, consider the recent rewriting of this paragraph by the celebrated Oxford physiologist and systems biologist Denis Noble. What is proven empirical fact is retained; what is interpretative has been changed, this time offering a radically different was of looking at things. "[Genes] are trapped in huge colonies, locked inside highly intelligent beings, moulded by the outside world, communicating with it by complex processes, through which, blindly, as if by magic, function emerges. They are in you and me; we are the system that allows their code to be read; and their preservation is totally dependent on the joy that we experience in reproducing ourselves. We are the ultimate rationale for their existence."[21]

Dawkins and Noble see things in completely different ways. (I recommend reading both statements slowly and carefully to appreciate the difference.) They simply cannot both be right. Both smuggle in a series of quite different value judgments and metaphysical statements. Yet their statements are empirically equivalent. In other words, they both have equally good grounding in observation and experimental evidence. So which is right? Which is more scientific? How could we decide which is to be preferred on scientific grounds? As Noble observes—and Dawkins concurs—"no-one seems to be able to think of an experiment that would detect an empirical difference between them."[22]

So what about Darwin himself? What was his own understanding of the religious implications of his views? It would suit Dawkins's purposes admirably if Darwin could be shown to have abandoned any faith in God as a consequence of his theory of evolution. Yet Dawkins's discussion of the complex and fascinating interaction of Darwin's scientific and religious views is most disappointing, and fails to deal satisfactorily with the issues involved.[23] If everything was altered after Darwin, it is clearly important to determine what Darwin himself believed to have changed as a result of his new ideas.

The view that Darwin was indeed an atheist on account of his evolutionary doctrine was vigorously advocated in Edward Aveling's pamphlet *The Religious Views of Charles Darwin* (1883).[24] The evidence brought forward in this short work is far from persuasive, and it is unclear what weight should be attached to it. Darwin had earlier declined Aveling's request to dedicate his *Student's Darwin* to him. Aveson was one of Karl Marx's most dedicated English followers, and regarded Darwin's evolutionary views as reinforcing the basic ideas of Marxian materialism. Darwin did not wish to endorse such an association.

There are indeed several important passages in Darwin's writings that can be interpreted to mean that Darwin ceased to believe in an orthodox Christian conception of God on account of his views on evolution. The problem is that there are other passages which variously point to Darwin maintaining a religious belief, or to his losing his faith for reasons quite other than evolutionary concerns. A note of caution must be injected, however: on the basis of the published evidence at our disposal, it is clear that Darwin himself was far from consistent in the matter of his religious views. It would therefore be extremely unwise to draw any confident conclusions on these issues.[25]

There can be no doubt that Darwin abandoned what we might call conventional Christian beliefs at some point in the 1840s, although more precise dating of this must remain elusive. Yet there is a substantial theoretical gap between abandoning orthodox Christian faith and becoming an atheist. Christianity involves a highly specific conception of God; it is perfectly possible to believe in a god other than that of Christianity, or to believe in God and reject certain other aspects of the Christian faith. Indeed, the Victorian crisis of faith—within which Darwin was both spectator and participant—can be understood as a shift away from the specifics of Christianity toward a more generic concept of God, largely determined by the ethical values of the day.

In 1879, while working on his autobiography, Darwin commented on his personal religious confusion: "My judgement *often fluctuates*. . . . In my most extreme fluctuations I have never been an Atheist in the sense of denying God. I think that generally (and more and more as I grow older), *but not always*, that an Agnostic would be the more correct description of my state of mind." That seems entirely consistent with his stated views on the matter, and is generally considered to be the safest interpretation of his position.

Universal Darwinism and Atheism

Dawkins, of course, is noted particularly for his insistence that a Darwinian theory of evolution is fatally corrosive to belief in God, for reasons that have been explored elsewhere in this volume. As this aspect of Darwin's thought is examined in great detail elsewhere in this collection of essays, I do not propose to discuss it in greater detail here. Instead, I intend to consider the way in which Dawkins attempts to convert Darwinism from a provisional, revisable, scientific theory to a universal worldview.

Dawkins is adamant that "Darwinism is too big a theory to be confined to the narrow context of the gene." Instead, he attempts to convert Darwinism from a mere scientific theory to a worldview, a metanarrative, and an overarching view of reality. Darwinism could be transformed into a universal method, reaching beyond the specific domain of biological evolution to include the world of culture.[26] Yet this bold attempt to develop a universal Darwinism that would make Marxism seem parochial in comparison has failed to persuade.[27] The Darwinian paradigm is firmly and properly anchored to the sphere of biological existence, and has little relevance in other domains.

In a significant publication titled *The Limits of Science*, Sir Peter Medawar, an Oxford immunologist who won the Nobel Prize for medicine for the discovery of acquired immunological tolerance, explored the question of how the scope of science is limited by the nature of reality. Emphasising that "science is incomparably the most successful enterprise human beings have ever engaged upon," he distinguishes between what he calls transcendent questions, which are better left to religion and metaphysics, and questions about the organization and structure of the material universe. With regard to the latter, he argues, there are no limits to the possibilities of scientific achievement. He thus agrees with Dawkins's universalism—but only by defining and limiting the domain within which the sciences possess such competency.

So what of other questions, such as the existence of God or the meaning of life? As if preempting Dawkins's brash and simplistic take on the sciences, Medawar suggests that scientists need to be cautious about their pronouncements on these matters, lest they lose the trust of the public by confident and dogmatic overstatements. Though a self-confessed rationalist, Medawar is clear that there is indeed a limit upon science, which is evident from "the existence of questions that science cannot answer, and that no conceivable advance of science would empower it to answer." Medawar has in mind such questions as "What are we all here for?" or "What is the point of living?" He then makes an interesting comment: "Doctrinaire positivism—now something of a period piece—dismissed all such questions as nonquestions or pseudoquestions such as only simpletons ask and only charlatans profess to be able to answer."[28] Perhaps Dawkins's writings, especially *The God Delusion*, might have taken Sir Peter by surprise, on account of its late flowering of precisely that "doctrinaire positivism" that he had, happily yet apparently prematurely, believed to be dead.

Yet there is a further issue here: the provisionality of scientific theorizing. All scientific theories are supported, at least to some extent, by evidence. Some go on to achieve dominance, being widely regarded as the best explanation of the existing evidence. Yet this is a temporary resting place, not a permanent judgment. There is a sense in which every theory is actually underdetermined by the evidence, making it vulnerable to displacement and replacement. As the history of science makes clear, the process of radical theory change means that today's best explanation can easily become tomorrow's equivalent of phlogiston or caloric—ideas that were once regarded as stable and successful, but have since been superseded by superior alternatives, either through theoretical advance or the acquisition of additional evidence.[29]

As Michael Polanyi (1891–1976), a chemist and noted philosopher of science, pointed out in *Personal Knowledge*, natural scientists often find themselves being put in the position of having to believe some things that they know will later be shown to be wrong—but not being sure which of their present beliefs would turn out to be erroneous.[30] So how can Dawkins be so sure that his current beliefs are true, when history shows a persistent pattern of the abandonment of scientific theories as and when better approaches emerge? What historian of science can fail to note that what was once regarded as secure knowledge is often eroded through the passage of time?

Scientific theorizing is thus provisional. In other words, it offers what is believed to be the best account of the experimental observations currently available. Radical theory change takes place either when it is believed that there is a better explanation of what is currently known, or when new information comes to light that forces us to see what is presently known in a new light. Unless we know the future, it is impossible to take an absolute position on the question of whether any given theory is right.

The fundamental difficulty that this process of change raises for Dawkins is this: Darwinism may be regarded as the best option today by many. But is this a stable judgment? Is it not open to historical erosion? At one point, Dawkins concedes the force of this point: "We must acknowledge the possibility that new facts may come to light which will force our successors of the twenty-first century to abandon Darwinism or modify it beyond recognition."[31] So how can Dawkins present atheism as the certain or near-certain outcome of a provisional, revisable scientific theory?

Dawkins's insistence that atheism is the only legitimate worldview for a natural scientist is an unsafe and unreliable judgment. Yet my anxiety is not limited to the flawed intellectual case that Dawkins's makes for his convictions; I am troubled by the ferocity with which he asserts his atheism. One obvious potential answer is that the grounds of Dawkins's atheism lie elsewhere than his science, so that there is perhaps a strongly emotive aspect to his beliefs at this point. Yet in the course of my detailed reading of Dawkins's works, I have not come across anything that forces me to this conclusion. The answer has to lie elsewhere.

I began to find what might be an answer to my question while reading a careful analysis of the distinctive style of reasoning that we find in Dawkins's writings. In an important comparative study, Timothy Shanahan pointed out that Stephen Jay Gould's approach to the question of evolutionary progress was determined by an inductivist approach, based primarily on empirical data. Dawkins, he noted, "proceeded by elaborating the logic of 'adaptationist philosophy' for Darwinian reasoning." This being the case, Dawkins's conclusions are determined by a set of logical premises, which are ultimately—yet indirectly—grounded in the empirical data. "The very nature of a valid deductive argument is such that, given certain premises, a given conclusion follows of logical necessity quite irrespective of whether the premises used are true."[32] In effect, Dawkins uses an essentially inductive approach to defend a Darwinian worldview—yet then extracts from this worldview a set of premises from which secure conclusions may be deduced.

Although Shanahan limits his analysis to exploring how Gould and Dawkins arrive at such antithetically opposed conclusions on the issue of evolutionary progress, his analysis is clearly capable of extension to his religious views. Having inferred that Darwinism is the best explanation of observation, Dawkins proceeds to transmute a provisional theory into a certain worldview. Atheism is thus presented as the logical conclusion of a series of axiomatic premises, having the certainty of a deduced belief, even though its ultimate basis is actually inferential.

I have no doubt that Dawkins is persuaded of the case for atheism. Yet the case made is not publicly persuasive. Dawkins is obliged to make a leap of faith from agnosticism to atheism, corresponding to those who make a similar leap in the opposite direction. He dismisses those who point out the serious philosophical difficulties associated with scientific positivism—such as Karl Popper and Thomas Kuhn—as "truth-hecklers," seemingly unaware of just how corrosive their approaches are to his naïve scientism.

Conclusion

Dawkins is now firmly established as the leading luminary in atheism's firmament. Yet as a former atheist myself, I cannot help but wonder whether atheism may have made something of a misjudgment here. Dawkins seems to think that saying something more loudly and confidently, while ignoring or trivializing counterevidence, will persuade the open-minded that religious belief is a type of delusion. Sadly, sociological studies of charismatic leaders—both religious and secular—indicate that Dawkins may be right to place some hope in this strategy.[33] For the gullible and credulous, it is the confidence with which something is said that persuades, rather than the force of the actual evidence offered in its support. And what, one wonders, does that say about the present state of atheism—and above all, its unwise decision to link its fortunes with one particular (and highly contestable) way of interpreting the significance of Charles Darwin?

7

Intelligent Design and Evolutionary Psychology as Research Programs

A Comparison of Their Most Plausible Specifications

J. P. Moreland

The purpose of this chapter is to contrast intelligent design psychology (IDP), specifically, a Christian version of IDP (IDP_C), with its chief rival, evolutionary psychology (EP), specifically, the most plausible naturalistic version of EP (EP_N). After providing some preliminary remarks about scientific research programs and scientific theory assessment, I shall sketch out some of the details of IDP_C and contrast it with EP_N. Along the way, I shall draw out various explanatory or predictive issues relevant to comparing the two, and provide an occasional critique of EP_N.

Scientific Research Programs and Theory Assessment

Roughly, a scientific research program is a family of scientific theories existing through time that in one way or another are united; for example, by sharing a common domain of phenomena to be explained, a common metaphysical picture of what causes empirical phenomena, or a common form of scientific explanation deemed to be acceptable.[1] A commitment to atomism as opposed to field theory illustrates a research program.

So understood, two important things follow. First, a research program needs to be specified by a particular incarnation to be descriptively accurate, empirically testable, and explanatorily powerful. For example, atomism has been specified by various models throughout its history; for instance, inert Newtonian corpuscularianism, dynamic corpuscularianism, the Thomson atom, the Bohr atom. Second, research programs are generally harder to falsify than a particular theory that specifies it because if the specific theory is falsified, it does not follow that the research program is thereby falsified. It may well be that an alternative specification should be formulated.

By way of application, ID is properly understood as a research program with various ways of specifying it. In this essay, I shall provide a characterization of one version of a Christian specification of ID. Applied to psychology, I shall call this theory IDP_C. While I think that IDP_C is actually true, the reader should keep in mind that there are alternative formulations of IDP besides IDP_C. Similarly, I shall compare IDP_C with the most plausible naturalistic version of EP, namely, EP_N. Moreover, I shall assume a realist philosophy of science.

An important factor in scientific theory acceptance is whether or not a specific paradigm has a rival. If not, then certain epistemic activities; for instance, labeling some phenomenon as basic for which only a description and not an explanation is needed, may be quite adequate not to impede the theory in question. But the adequacy of those same activities can change dramatically if a sufficient rival is present. There are two issues involved in adjudicating between rival scientific theories relevant to the comparison of IDP_C and EP_N. The first is whether to take some phenomenon as basic or as something to be explained in terms of more basic phenomena. For example, attempts to explain uniform inertial motion are disallowed in Newtonian mechanics because such motion is basic on this view, but an Aristotelian had to explain how or why a particular body exhibited uniform inertial motion. Thus, what may be basic to one theory is derived in another.

Issue two is the naturalness of a postulated entity in light of the overall theory of which it is a part. A postulated entity should be at home with other entities in the theory. Some entity e (a particular thing, process, property, or relation) is natural for a theory T just in case it bears a relevant similarity to other entities, especially core, central entities, that populate T. An entity should fit in with and resemble naturally the other entities depicted as real by a theory.

Moreover, given rival theories R and S, the postulation of e in R is ad hoc and question-begging against advocates of S if e bears a relevant similarity to the appropriate entities in S, and in this sense is "at home" in S, but fails to bear this relevant similarity to the appropriate entities in R. For example, suppose theory S explains phenomena in terms of discrete corpuscles and action by contact, while R uses continuous waves to explain phenomena. If some phenomenon x was best explained in corpuscularian categories, it would be ad hoc and question-begging for advocates of R simply to adjust their entities to take on particle properties in the case of x. Such properties would not bear a relevant similarity to other entities in R and would be more natural and at home in S.

To illustrate, at the end of the nineteenth century, when J. J. Thomson discovered the electron, there was a debate between German and British scientists over the nature of electricity, the former favoring an aether wave theory and the latter a particle view. Now, certain phenomena discovered by Michael Faraday—namely, that in electrolysis experiments the amount of product liberated was proportional to the amount of electricity introduced into solution and that the same amount of electricity liberates masses of product proportional to discrete chemically equivalent weights—was easy to explain on a particulate view but not on a wave theory. It would have been ad hoc and question-begging in light of what was known at the time for German theorists simply to announce that for this particular phenomenon, waves suddenly exhibit particle phenomena.

Naturalness is relevant to assessing rivals by providing a criterion for identifying question-begging arguments or ad hoc adjustments by advocates of a rival theory. Naturalness can also be related to basicality by providing a means of deciding the relative merits of accepting theory R, which depicts phenomenon e as basic, versus embracing S, which takes e to be explainable in more basic terms. If e is natural in S but not in R, it will be difficult for advocates of R to justify the bald assertion that e is basic in R and that all proponents of R need to do is describe e and correlate it with other phenomena in R as opposed to explaining e. Such a claim by advocates of R will be even more problematic if S provides an explanation for e.

For example, suppose that R is neo-Darwinism and S is a version of punctuated equilibrium theory. Simply for the sake of illustration, suppose further that R depicts evolutionary transitions from one species to another to involve running through a series of incrementally different transitional forms except for some specific transition e which is taken as a basic phenomenon, say, the discrete jump from amphibians to reptiles. S pictures evolutionary transitions in general, including e, as evolutionary jumps to be explained in certain ways that constitute S. In this case, given the presence of S, it would be hard for advocates of R to claim that their treatment of e is adequate against S. Phenomenon e clearly counts in favor of S over against R.

These insights about basicality and naturalness may be used to enrich our understanding of recalcitrant facts and periods of paradigm crisis. Some purported fact is a recalcitrant one for a theory T if that fact resists being adequately described, explained, or predicted by the ontological and episte-mological resources central to T. In this sense, a recalcitrant fact is an anom-aly for a theory. Two signs that a theory is facing a set of recalcitrant facts are that (1) the theory deals with those facts by taking them as basic *sui generis* facts not at home with the central aspects of the theory and (2) advocates of the theory engage in a growing number of ad hoc, question-begging theory adjustments to save it from falsification by those recalcitrant facts.

When a theory faces a growing set of recalcitrant facts, it may be said to have entered a period of crisis. Typically, such a period is characterized by a multiplication of rival theories, none of which adequately deals with the recal-citrant facts. If these rival theories are all specifications of the same research program, then it is usually safe to say that the research program is a degenera-tive one and it may well be time to consider an alternative research program. As I hope to show below, a number of apparent facts about the nature of human persons are recalcitrant facts for naturalistic versions of evolutionary psychology. Thus it is time to consider an alternative research program and IDP, especially IDP_C, is the most reasonable candidate for that alternative.

The Central Features of IDP_C

In characterizing a research program or a theory that specifies it, one must lay out the core ontological and epistemological/methodological commitments of that program or theory. Space considerations do not permit a defense of the truth or rationality of these commitments, or a defense as to why they are included. Fortunately, such a defense has been given elsewhere (see refer-ences to follow) and, in any case, it is not required when one is simply laying out one's model. The following is a list of some of those commitments that characterize IDP_C:

IDP_C Ontological Commitments

1. The Christian God exists, is a necessary being, and is the creator/intelligent designer of the cosmos.[2] God's creative activity includes a combination of direct primary causal miracle and indirect secondary causality in which nat-ural entities such as processes or laws are employed to accomplish a divine purpose. Among other things, God's creative activity is an expression of a number of motives, for example, creative playfulness, and is not limited to efficiency.

2. God is a personal spirit and, as such, is an immaterial, spiritual substance who exemplifies mental properties, including different proper-ties of consciousness such as various sensations, thoughts, beliefs, desires,

and volitional choices that constitute the intrinsic nature of God's own conscious life. As an immaterial substantial person, God is a self-reflective center of conscious, an I, and knows things from God's own irreducible first-person point of view. Among other things, from (1) and (2) it follows that mental entities are more fundamental in reality than are physical entities. It also follows that spirit (for current purposes, mind or soul)/matter causal interaction is a basic, *sui generis* fact. There is no intellectual pressure to locate such interaction against a backdrop of naturalistic views of causation, for instance, singular causation is a possible model for divine and human mind/body causal interaction.[3]

3. God's free actions are to be characterized by agent causal versions of libertarian freedom. According to this account of divine or human free will, a person exercises free will when he or she has the power to act freely (such as to raise one's hand), exercises that power while retaining the ability to refrain from doing so, and is the ultimate cause and absolute originator of the act. Motives and other factors may influence a libertarian free act, but nothing can cause it to happen besides the agent's own exercise of freedom. A free act that is caused by something besides the agent him- or herself is a contradiction in terms.[4]

4. God exemplifies various intrinsically valuable properties; for example, various rational properties (wisdom, truthfulness, cognitive excellence), moral properties (fidelity, kindness, holiness, and so forth), and aesthetic properties (complexity and simplicity, integration of personality, artistic creativity). Among other things, from (1) and (2) it follows that value properties are more fundamental in reality than are physical properties. Humans exemplify these same properties.

5. Animals and humans have souls, but the human soul is unique in being created in the image and likeness of God.[5] Thus, humans bear a relevant similarity to God in so far as both are kinds of persons. Humans are therefore spiritual substances with bodies, they are unified, enduring I's, they possess libertarian freedom and exhibit teleological behavior, they have an essential nature—human personhood—that grounds membership in the natural kind "humankind." Various human conscious states—sensations, thoughts, beliefs, desires, volitions—are intrinsically constituted by irreducible, uneliminable mental properties. Humans have first-person points of view, including first-person introspective knowledge of their own selves and conscious states just as God has. Humans are classic substances, essentially characterized continuants. The self and its unity and continuity, free agency, and the nature of consciousness and its role in behavior are the central items of study. Finally, the most plausible view of time consistent with the existence of continuants is an A series or presentist view of time.

6. Animal and human bodies are ensouled physical structures such that (*a*) the macroparts (for example, organs, whole systems) are inseparable parts that gain their identity from the function they play in the ontologically prior whole organism; (*b*) the macroparts stand in internal relations to the organism as a whole; (*c*) the macroparts exhibit irreducible, literal function/teleology; (*d*) organicism is the proper view of the generation of animal and human bodies—it is the organism as a whole, for instance, the organism's soul, that is the first efficient cause of bodily development and that which contains genetic information (DNA is an instrument cause, it functions as a material supplier if it is told what to do and when to do it, and it requires the organism as a whole to function).

7. Information is a fundamental and irreducible feature of the world and it comes in at least two forms, mental and nonmental. Mental information, such as the contents of thoughts, beliefs, theories, and so forth is identical to propositions (a single thought) or various combinations of propositions (for instance, one's view of the Reformation).[6] In the basic sense, a proposition is the content of sentences/statements and thoughts/beliefs that is true or false. So understood, a proposition is not a physical entity, nor is it to be identified with a sentence or statement used to express it.[7]

Nonmental information is the irreducible or specified complexity exhibited by some whole in the internal relations among the parts, properties, or processes of that whole.[8] Roughly, irreducible complexity is a characteristic of some whole, such as an animal, that obtains just in case the parts, properties, or processes of that whole (*a*) gain their identity in that whole by the relations, especially functional relations, they stand in to the other parts of the whole or to the whole itself; and (*b*) cannot function without the others parts, properties, or processes of that whole. On an IDP_C model, information can neither be reduced to a combination of simple order and randomness nor generated by such a combination. As William Dembski says, "all reductionistic attempts to explain information in terms of something other than information will have to go by the boards. Information is sui generis. Only information begets information."[9]

On an IDP_C model, since God exists ontologically prior to the cosmos, mental information existed ontologically prior to nonmental information in the cosmos. More importantly, the structure of mental information in God's mind, and in human minds when they think God's thoughts after God, is isomorphic with the nonmental information that constitutes various wholes (such as human beings) in the cosmos. The intuitive notion of isomorphism is that two structures are isomorphic just in case their various aspects mirror or in some other way correspond to each other. For example, consider speaking into a tape recorder. For each distinguishable unit of sound, there is a distinct configuration of magnetized tape. Strictly speaking, the sounds are not literally in the tape, but there is a structure in the tape that is isomorphic to the structure of the sounds spoken into the tape recorder.[10]

Applied to information, IDP_C entails that there should be an isomorphism between divine and human theories, beliefs, and thoughts and the intentional objects and states of affairs in the world to which those theories and so forth refer. The correspondence theory of truth is one aspect of this isomorphism, and it finds a natural place in the ontology of IDP_C, as does the notion that human mental activity should be able to uncover the mind independent, deep informational structures in the world.

8. Given the characterizations above of divine/human libertarian freedom, a certain analysis of action, including moral action, is most at home in IDP_C. To clarify this analysis in the case of moral action, consider two people, Jack and Jill, who spend an afternoon with their grandmother. Jack, motivated by love for his grandmother, intends to show kindness to her by spending the afternoon visiting with her. As a result, Jack's grandmother is cheered by the company. Jill, motivated by greed, intends to secure a place in her grandmother's will by spending an afternoon visiting with her and Jill is successful in hiding her intention from her grandmother. As a result, Jill's grandmother is cheered by the company.

In these moral actions, an IDP_C model will distinguish four things relevant to their moral assessment: a motive, an intent, a means, and a consequence. A motive is why one acts. Jack's motive was a feeling of love, Jill's was greed. An intent is what act one actually performs. The intent answers the question, "What sort of act was it?" Jack's intent was to show kindness toward his grandmother and he performed an act of kindness. Jill's intent was to secure a place in the will and her act was one of attempting to secure that place. The means is the way an agent purposely carries out his or her intention. Jack and Jill each perform the same means, namely, each spends the afternoon visiting with the grandmother. Finally, the consequences are the states of affairs produced by the act. In each case, the grandmother was cheered up.

On an IDP_C model, the end does not justify the means and it is appropriate to assess the intrinsic moral worth of means as well as ends. The same thing may be said for motives and intentions, but according to IDP_C, the latter are more important than the former. Why? An intention is the key factor in deciding what sort of act a particular action is and thus the intention is what places the act in the relevant class of acts that is defined by a certain act type. Motives are also important, but they are more relevant to the assessment of the character of the moral actor than of the moral nature of the act itself.

Finally, while an IDP_C may appropriately take the consequences of an act to be among the relevant factors for assessing that act morally, nevertheless, consequences will be taken to be less important for such assessment than the intrinsic features of the act itself. Given this observation, along with the IDP_C claims that objective morality is a fundamental feature of reality and that humans were created to be holy, virtuous beings, IDP_C predicts the following regarding human moral action: Regardless of other purposes or consequences that moral action may procure for moral agents, humans will have a deeply ingrained, strong tendency to be preoccupied with the intrinsic value of their moral actions and their character, both in their own self-understanding as moral agents and in the way they desire others to take them as moral agents. Among other things, they will not be preoccupied with the reproductive advantages to themselves or to their group that they obtain as a consequence of their moral actions. Rather, they will be strongly inclined toward deontological and virtue ethics.

9. The world in not the way it was originally designed to be. Thus, there is evil, disteleology, and dysfunction in the world, and not everything is a reflection of the way things were designed to be.

IDP_C Epistemological/Methodological Commitments

10. The first-person point of view, including information gained about one's own conscious states and one's own ego from first-person introspection, is a generally reliable source of knowledge and justified beliefs. Moreover, there is no intellectual pressure to reduce or eliminate the first-person point of view in favor of the third-person perspective. Indeed, the first-person perspective is a primitive relative to the third-person perspective. In general, while not always infallible, humans have direct, private access to their own mental states and mental selves. Strictly material objects may be exhaustively described and known from a third-person perspective, but not humans. On the assumption that among the things psychology studies are the nature of mental states and the self, psychology will never be able to get away from relying on the first-person introspective reports of humans.[11]

11. There is no pride of place given to a bottom-up approach to scientific research according to which (*a*) macroproperties/behaviors of macrowholes supervene on, emerge from, and are dependent upon the physical-chemical parts, properties, and structures at the micro level; and (*b*) mechanistic explanations of macroproperties/behaviors are formulated in terms of factors at the micro level. According to IDP_C, living organisms, including humans, are substances and, as such, are primitive wholes and not mereological aggregates.

More generally, advocates of IDP_C will prefer the Great Chain of Being model of reality, according to which the world consists in a descending order of substances (God, angels, humans, various animals, plants, chemical elements, subatomic entities, and so forth). At each level, especially at and above the level of animals, entities are irreducible wholes constituted by their own essences (for instance, being human) with their own laws of development and functioning. Among other things, this implies that IDP_C practitioners will embrace a pluralistic, shopping-list ontology[12] and will embrace the epistemic value of phenomenological, descriptive accuracy over theoretical simplicity. By contrast, advocates of EP_N will embrace the standard complementarity model, according to which reality consists in an ascending order of wholes from subatomic entities to humans, with all wholes above the level of physics amounting to aggregates composed of separable parts at lower levels and with higher-level wholes depending on what happens at the level of physics for their existence, nature, and behavior. Thus, according to IDP_C, while bottom-up explanations may be appropriate on a case-by-case basis, holistic, top-down causal explanations will also be fruitful, especially at the level of psychology. EP_N advocates will eschew top-down causation. They will also embrace serious metaphysics[13] and, accordingly, will value theoretical simplicity over descriptive accuracy, especially if those descriptions express the first-person point of view.

12. Advocates of IDP_C will embrace both event causal/covering law explanations for phenomena as well as irreducible personal explanations for phenomena.[14] Event causation is a model of efficient causality widely employed in science. Suppose a brick breaks a glass. In general, event causation can be defined in this way: an event of kind K (the moving of the brick) in circumstances of kind C (the glass being in a solid and not liquid state) occurring to an entity of kind e (the glass object itself) causes an event of kind Q (the breaking of the glass) to occur. Here, all causes and effects are events that constitute causal chains construed either deterministically (causal conditions are sufficient for an effect to obtain) or probabilistically (causal conditions are sufficient to fix the chances for an effect to obtain).

Associated with event causation is a covering law model of explanation according to which some event (the explanandum) is explained by giving a correct deductive or inductive argument for that event. Such an argument contains two features in its explanans: a (universal or statistical) law of nature and initial causal conditions.

Because IDP_C employs divine and human libertarian agent causation, it is open to them to employ a form of personal explanation that stands in contrast to a covering law model. To understand this form of explanation, we need to look first at a distinction that is part of action theory: the difference between a basic and nonbasic action. To grasp the difference between a basic and nonbasic action, note first that often more than one thing is accomplished in a single exercise of agency. Some actions are done by doing others; for example, I perform the act of going to the store to get bread by getting into my car and by driving to the store.

Basic actions are fundamental to the performance of all others but are not done by doing something else. In general, S's X-ing is basic if and only if there is no other nonequivalent action description 'S's Y-ing' such that it is true that S X-ed by Y-ing. My endeavoring to move my arm to get my keys is a basic action. A nonbasic action contains basic actions that are parts of and means to the ultimate intention for the sake of which the nonbasic action was done. To fulfill a nonbasic intention, I must form an action plan: a certain ordered set of basic actions that I take to be an effective means of accomplishing my nonbasic intention. The action plan that constitutes going to the store to get bread includes the acts of getting my keys and walking to my car.

In my view, an action is something contained wholly within the boundaries of the agent. Thus, strictly speaking, the results of an action are not proper parts of that action. A basic result of an action is an intended effect brought about immediately by the action. If I successfully endeavor to move my finger, the basic result is the moving of the finger. Nonbasic results are more remote intended effects caused by basic results or chains of basic results plus more remote intended effects. The firing of the gun or the killing of Lincoln are respective illustrations of these types of nonbasic results.

With this in mind, a personal explanation (divine or otherwise) of some basic result (for instance, someone's finger pointing to an object) brought about intentionally by a person will cite the intention for the sake of which the person acted (for example, to locate a missing purse), the basic power the person exercised (such as the power to move one's index finger) and the reason why the person so acted (to help a friend locate her missing purse).

Again, suppose we are trying to explain why Wesson simply moved his finger (R). We could explain this by saying that Wesson (P) performed an act of endeavoring to move his finger (A) in that he exercised his ability to move (or will to move) his finger (B) intending to move the finger (I). If Wesson's moving his finger was an expression of an intent to move a finger to fire a gun to kill Smith, then we can explain the nonbasic results (the firing of the gun and the killing of Smith) by saying that Wesson (P) performed an act of killing Smith (I_3) by endeavoring to move his finger (A) intentionally (I_1) by exercising his power to do so (B), intending thereby to fire the gun (I_2) in order to kill Smith. An explanation of the results of a nonbasic action (like going to the store to get bread) will include a description of the action plan.

Because (but not only because) advocates of IDP$_C$ are free to employ both event causal/covering law and personal explanations, they will eschew methodological naturalism as a requirement for scientific explanation.[15]

13. Advocates of IDP$_C$ are free to employ irreducible teleological explanations and are under no pressure to provide etiological or other reductive accounts of functional explanations (see below). Among other things, providing a reason explanation will be taken to cite, not an efficient cause of action, but the end or goal for the sake of which the action was performed. Thus, in citing a reason to explain why someone performs some behavior, one is not citing the cause of the behavior—the agent himself is the cause—rather, one is citing the goal or teleological end for the sake of which the behavior was performed. In general, the "because of" locution in cases of the form "Person P did x because of y" will be taken in teleological, not efficient, causal ways such that y is an end, not an efficient cause.

Advocates of IDP$_C$ will also explore the world in light of their commitment to the existence of proper function understood in an irreducibly normative way. In general, to say that x properly functions to do y (the heart properly functions to pump blood, conscience properly functions to alert one to transgression of objective morality), is to say that x functions the way it ought to function. This, in turn, is to say that x functions the way it was intentionally, purposively designed to function by God. Moreover, to say that x is dysfunctional is to say either that x functions the way it ought not function and, in turn, the way it was not designed to function or that x fails to function the way it ought to function and, in turn, fails to function the way it was designed to function. In the explication of EP$_N$ below, it will become apparent that this notion of proper function is not available to advocates of EP$_N$.

14. For advocates of IDP$_C$, there is no need to seek current or ancestral adaptive functions in light of the demands for differential reproductive advantage, for various psychological properties, processes, and so forth. According to IDP$_C$, there is now, and has been since the fall, a struggle for survival, so there may well be a reproductive advantage to be found for some psychological properties or processes. But these will be the exception rather than the rule. In general, IDP$_C$ advocates will describe and analyze various aspects of human psychology in terms of the spiritual, moral, and familial purpose for the sake of which they were designed to function and in terms of the fall, and the sinful disruption it has brought. According to IDP$_C$, the need to transcend, express creativity, and exert will are among a small set of factors at the heart of human behavior and functioning, and pride and a desire to control/dominate others and God are near the very heart of human dysfunction. Thus IDP$_C$ predicts that factors at the heart of religious and moral issues, especially those revolving around creativity and will, will

be keys to human flourishing and dysfunction. According to IDP_C, it will be features that constitute the nature of divine and human persons, for instance, thoughts, beliefs, sensations, desires and volitions, especially as they figure into religious and moral aspects of life, that are the main driving force behind individual psychology and social, cultural development.

15. Because the fundamental being (God) is a spiritual substance with conscious mental states and humans are created in God's image, the fundamental categories of psychology—thought, belief, sensation, emotion, desire, purpose, volition—and various combinations thereof are taken to carve the world up at the joints (that is, to pick out really existing kinds of things in the world, just as being hydrogen or being oxygen do). These categories amount to genuinely existing, intrinsically describable natural kinds of properties that constitute the theory-independent world.

In this sense, IDP_C implies that psychology should be defined not primarily as a study of behavior, and certainly not primarily as a study of the brain and its mechanisms related to behavior, but as a study of the soul/self and the different aspects of consciousness intrinsic to it. The study of the brain and of behavior are relevant in the derivative sense that information derived from such study is an aid to the understanding of the self and its various conscious states. Thus, IDP_C implies a resistance to attempts to reduce or replace intrinsic descriptions of the self and its conscious states for functional, operational descriptions of the self and conscious states, though the latter may be helpful as tools for understanding the former.

In general, by an IDP_C approach, psychology is not reducible to nor replaceable by neuroscience and, indeed, the traditional, fundamental categories of psychology provide greater insights into the nature of humans than do the physical categories of chemistry, physics, biology, and neuroscience. These physical categories are most helpful in providing information about causal relations between the self and consciousness and the brain and body. As we shall see shortly, while there is great confusion among scientists about the precise nature of reductionism, EP most naturally implies either a reduction of psychology to neuroscience or a replacement of the former by the latter. Further, IDP_C implies that issues surrounding the unity and agency of the self will be prominent as keys for understanding human functioning and dysfunctioning.[16]

The Central Features of EP_N

In this section, I shall provide a sketch of some central features of EP_N as an expression of philosophical and methodological naturalism taken as a worldview.[17] So understood, EP_N combines a naturalist worldview and evolutionary theory with current formulations of psychology. EP_N is an entire approach to psychology, a way of thinking about the discipline such that principles and commitments derived from naturalism and evolutionary biology are put to use in doing psychological research. According to David Buss, four premises form the basis of EP_N:

1. Manifest behavior depends on underlying psychological mechanisms, defined as information-processing devices instantiated in brain wet-ware.
2. Evolution by selection is the only known causal process capable of creating such complex organic mechanisms.
3. Evolved psychological mechanisms are functionally specialized to solve adaptive problems that recurred for human ancestors over the vast expanse of evolutionary history.
4. Human psychology consists of a large number of these functionally specialized and integrated evolved mechanisms, each sensitive to particular forms of contextual input.[18]

These four premises were not formulated in a vacuum and, indeed, they may be properly understood only against the backdrop of the ontological and epistemological/methodological commitments of EP_N and its main rival, IDP_C. Since the main contours of IDP_C have already been presented, the broader EP_N backdrop remains to be characterized.

EP_N Ontological Commitments

1. The naturalist ontology must be consistent and at home with the naturalist story of how all things came to be. As naturalist Frank Jackson points out, the naturalist has a fairly standard story, told in the language of chemistry and physics, of how all things have come to be, and the naturalist must find a way of making a place for all entities he/she takes to be real by relating them to that story and showing how they are at home in it.[19] Call this story the Grand Story. The details of the Grand Story are not of importance here. Suffice it to say that, beginning with some big bang scenario and a contingent set of laws of chemistry and physics, the rest of the story will be related to these starting points.

Three features of the Grand Story are of importance for understanding EP_N. First, all change is to be understood in terms of efficient event causality according to which some causal event x is the cause of some effect y just in case there is a (probabilistic or deterministic) law of nature that subsumes x and y. Given x and that law of nature, y is the effect that follows. All causal transactions are mechanistic, not in the sense that they only involve action by contact and not forces, such as attraction and repulsion, but in the sense that they are nonteleological, efficient causal transactions. Moreover, all change must be understood to obey the Physical Causal Closure principle (PCC): Every physical event that has a cause has a physical cause. In tracing the causal ancestry of any physical event, one need never leave the level of the physical. As naturalist David Papineau correctly observes, PCC captures the naturalist commitment to the completeness of physics:

> I take it that physics, unlike the other special sciences [e.g., psychology], is *complete*, in the sense that all physical events are determined, or have their chances determined, by prior *physical* events according to *physical* laws. In other words, we never need to look beyond the realm of the physical in order to identify a set of antecedents which fixes the chances of subsequent physical occurrence. A purely physical specification, plus physical laws, will always suffice to tell us what is physically going to happen, insofar as that can be foretold at all.[20]

Second, the Grand Story must be understood as an expression of physicalism. While there are different versions of physicalism, naturalist Jaegwon Kim has stated three propositions that define minimal physicalism, the minimum ontological commitment to which all physicalists should subscribe:

1. The supervenience thesis: Mental properties supervene on physical properties, in that necessarily any two things (in the same possible world or in different possible worlds with the same laws of nature) indiscernible in all physical properties are indiscernible in mental properties.
2. The anti-Cartesian principle: There can be no purely mental beings (for instance, substantial souls, God) because nothing can have a mental property without having a physical property as well.
3. Mind-body dependence: What mental properties an entity has depend on and are determined by its physical properties.[21]

For our purposes, we may collapse proposition 3 into proposition 1. So understood, the supervenience thesis implies that the psychological properties that obtain in the world are fixed by and dependent on the physical properties of that world. Thus, bottom-up dependency characterizes the relationship between a human's physical and mental states. Further, the Grand Story results from combinatory modes of explanation in the atomic theory of matter and evolutionary biology according to which the nature and behavior of macro-objects is explained in terms of various structural arrangements of microparts. Thus, structural supervenient properties are allowed (for example, being water is a structural property—being H_2O) and unique, simple emergent properties are disallowed. This means that consciousness will be eliminated or identified with something physical.

Finally, the Grand Story is most naturally taken to imply that all wholes, from planets and galaxies to frogs and humans, are physical systems of separable parts standing in various external relations to one another and exhibit varying degrees of structural complexity. Human and animal bodies are ordered aggregates, and a special ordered aggregate, DNA, is the first efficient cause of an organism's characteristics and the container of genetic information.

2. From commitment 1, it becomes obvious that prior to the appearance of living things, there was no teleology, no agency, no value, no mental states and, arguably, no unified substances above the bottom level of the hierarchy. EP_N must analyze human persons in a way that is at home in the Grand Story and that is not ad hoc and does not beg the question relative to IDP_C. Six features of the ontology of humans relevant to our topic most naturally follow from these considerations, and they have been embraced by the vast majority of naturalists.

First, humans are not unified I's at a point in time or enduring I's through time. As naturalist critic Geoffrey Madell notes, "a conception of reality as comprising nothing but assemblies of physical elements must confront the materialist with the obligation to explain what it could be for some arbitrary element of that reality to be *me*."[22] This is one reason why notions such as the self or ego, especially when taken to express the unity and endurance of the person, tend to drop from sight on an EP_N view. Another reason will be EP_N's commitment to a relativistic ontology of time and a B series view of the nature of time. While logically possible, an ontology of enduring continuants is not plausibly harmonizable with a B series view. Thus Leda Cosmides and John Tooby speak for most advocates of EP_N when they claim that in keeping with a physicalist depiction of humans, psychology studies the brain and its relationship to behavior, and the human brain is a "collection of reasoning and regulatory circuits that are functionally specialized."[23]

Second, human action will be understood in compatibilist and not libertarian agent causal terms. Regarding the rejection of libertarian agent causation, naturalist John Bishop frankly admits that "the idea of a responsible agent, with the 'originative' ability to initiate events in the natural world, does not sit easily with the idea of [an agent as] a natural organism. . . . Our scientific understanding of human behavior seems to be in tension with a presupposition of the ethical stance we adopt toward it."[24]

Below we shall look at some of the epistemological/methodological commitments of EP_N. But an important point about those commitments should be mentioned here. Naturalist Thomas Nagel correctly observes that the naturalist rejection of libertarian agent causation derives not only from physicalism, but also from a naturalist commitment to the third-person point of view as the proper approach for gaining knowledge of reality:

> Something peculiar happens when we view action from an objective or external standpoint. Some of its most important features seem to vanish under the objective gaze. Actions seem no longer assignable to individual agents as sources, but become instead components of the flux of events in the world of which the agent is a part. . . . The essential source of the problem is a view of persons and their actions as part of the order of nature.[25]

According to compatibilism, human actions are happenings, parts of causal chains that lead up to them. While there are different versions of compatibilism, it is fair to say that, on an EP_N model, a free action is one that is governed by natural law and, in general, to say that some person performed an act freely is to say that the act (raising one's hand to vote) was caused in the right way by a chain of events leading up to it from the person's own relevant mental (that is, brain) state (the desire to vote and a belief that raising one's hand is a means of satisfying that desire) which was, in turn, caused by factors (environment, but especially, brain mechanisms selected for in the struggle for reproductive advantage) out of the person's own control.

Third, in the literal sense, human action is not teleological. Rather, human action turns out to be body movements that are the end-products of nonteleological, efficient causal chains of events that begin in the human organism's environment, run through the physical structures inside the organism and on to a bodily output.

It is sometimes thought that teleological and efficient causal descriptions of a sequence of events express complementary perspectives from different levels of description. But as naturalist critic William Hasker and naturalist John Bishop have shown, this is true in a fairly innocuous sense but false in an important sense.[26] Granting what an advocate of EP_N cannot deny—namely, that any particular bit of human emotion, thought, or behavior can be given an entirely mechanistic explanation in terms of sequences of physical, event causes—one can always adopt an "intentional stance" and describe that sequence "as if" it exhibited teleology.

But strictly speaking, such an intentional stance is false, especially when offered as a causal explanation of human action. For one thing, no event can be given more than one complete and independent causal explanation. If this were possible, then causal overdetermination would be required. In causal overdetermination, two causes are each completely adequate to produce an effect such that if one cause were absent, no difference would be made. Most scholars have taken causal overdetermination to be false and, indeed, unintelligible.

Second, given the EP_N principles of the causal closure of the physical and the supervenience of the mental on the physical, there is simply no work for a mental cause or a teleological cause. Since a human action is, in principle, capable of a complete causal explanation in mechanistic terms, the presence or absence of a complementary teleological explanation will make no difference at all to the causal history of the universe. The only way psychology can retain irreducible teleological explanations is to understand them in some sort of antirealist, noncausal way. In related fashion, truth construed according to some form of correspondence with reality will be eschewed in favor of some antirealist view of truth and a causal depiction as necessary and sufficient for capturing an organism's various relationships with its environment. As a result, EP_N advocates will have difficulty rebutting the claim that their theory is self-refuting.

Fourth, advocates of EP_N will reject both irreducibly teleological and normative understandings of human functioning because they do not harmonize with evolutionary naturalism. For example, naturalists Joshua Hoffman and Gary Rosenkrantz claim:

> Aristotle's account [of natural function and teleology] does *not* provide a naturalistic reduction of natural function in terms of efficient causation. Nor do characterizations of natural function in terms of an irreducibly emergent purposive principle, or an unanalyzable emergent property associated with the biological phenomenon of life, provide such a reduction. Theistic and vitalistic approaches that try to explicate natural function in terms of the intentions of an intelligent purposive agent or principle are also nonnaturalistic. Another form of nonnaturalism attempts to explicate natural function in terms of nonnatural evaluative attributes such as intrinsic goodness. . . . We do not accept the anti-reductionist and anti-naturalistic theories about natural function listed above. Without entering into a detailed critique of these ideas, one can see that they either posit immaterial entities whose existence is in doubt, or make it utterly mysterious how it can be true that a part of an organic living thing manifests a natural function. . . . [T]he theoretical unity of biology would be better served if the natural functions of the parts of organic life-forms could be given a reductive account completely in terms of nonpurposive or nonfunctional naturalistic processes or conditions.[27]

Accordingly, modern scientific descriptions of living organisms and their development offer reductive accounts of teleology and natural function that usually go something like this:

(1) The function of x is z.
(2) x does A in order to z.

So stated, (1) and (2) make reference to teleology and natural function, and this is as it should be according to the substance position. On the substance view we embrace, the function of the heart is to pump blood. The heart moves in such and such way *in order to* pump blood. Note that a heart is internally related to the other parts of the circulation system (a heart is whatever functions to pump blood in this system) and thus the whole system (and, eventually, the whole organism) grounds and defines the heart. Further, the heart does what it does in order to reach some end. Now a popular natural reductive account reduces (1) and (2) to something like this:

(3) x was a cause of z in the past and its having been a cause of z in the past causes x to be there now.
(3') x has the function of doing z if and only if item x is now present as a result of causing z.

(3) and (3') say the same thing, and they are examples of what is called the aetiological account of teleological notions such as design, purpose, and function. For example, the heart (x) was a cause of pumping blood (z) in the past and its having been a cause of pumping blood (z) in the past causes the heart (x) to be there now. This account gets rid of genuine function and teleology and replaces them with an evolutionary account of the existence of body parts and activities along with a reduction of final causality (that for the sake of which something happens) to efficient causality (that because of which something happens).

Fifth, on an EP_N view, there most likely is no such thing as human nature understood as the essentialist claim that there is some range of properties that all and only humans share and that grounds their membership in the natural kind "being human." Darwin's theory of evolution has made belief in, for instance, human substances with human natures, though logically possible, nevertheless, quite implausible. As E. Mayr has said, "The concepts of unchanging essences and of complete discontinuities between every eidos (type) and all others make genuine evolutionary thinking impossible. I agree with those who claim that the essentialist philosophies of Aristotle and Plato are incompatible with evolutionary thinking."[28] This belief has, in turn, lead thinkers like David Hull to make the following observation:

> The implications of moving species from the metaphysical category that
> can appropriately be characterized in terms of 'natures' to a category

for which such characterizations are inappropriate are extensive and fundamental. If species evolve in anything like the way that Darwin thought they did, then they cannot possibly have the sort of natures that traditional philosophers claimed they did. If species in general lack natures, then so does *Homo sapiens* as a biological species. If *Homo sapiens* lacks a nature, then no reference to biology can be made to support one's claims about 'human nature.' Perhaps all people are 'persons,' share the same 'personhood,' etc., but such claims must be explicated and defended *with no reference to biology*. Because so many moral, ethical, and political theories depend on some notion or other of human nature, Darwin's theory brought into question all these theories. The implications are not entailments. One can always dissociate '*Homo sapiens*' from 'human being,' but the result is a much less plausible position.[29]

The *sixth* feature of human persons that follows most naturally from EP_N is that both the existence and causal powers of the various states of consciousness should be denied. Regarding the existence of consciousness, naturalist Paul Churchland claims:

> The important point about the standard evolutionary story is that the human species and all of its features are the wholly physical outcome of a purely physical process. . . . If this is the correct account of our origins, then there seems neither need, nor room, to fit any nonphysical substances or properties into our theoretical account of ourselves. We are creatures of matter. And we should learn to live with that fact.[30]

Churchland puts his finger on two reasons why the naturalist should opt for strong physicalism—there is neither need nor room for anything else. Regarding need, I take it he means that everything we need to explain the origin and workings of human beings can be supplied by physicalist causal explanations. Regarding room, entities do not come into existence *ex nihilo*, nor do radically different kinds of entities emerge from purely physical components placed in some sort of complex arrangement. What comes from the physical by means of physical processes will also be physical. Thus, the sheer existence of consciousness is a problem for EP_N.

Moreover, if the existence of conscious states is embraced, then an advocate of EP_N will have a difficult time avoiding an epiphenomenal depiction of conscious states according to which they are caused by or emerge from the brain, but they are themselves causally impotent.[31] To see why this is so, consider a person getting a drink of water. Now, according to the causal closure principle, the cause of the person getting the drink is a relevant brain state. If so, what does the mental state of feeling thirst contribute? If it is a real mental state distinct from the brain state, there appears to be no room for it to affect anything, since the relevant brain state is the adequate cause. More generally, consider the following diagram (fig. 7.1):

Figure 7.1

The diagram depicts a sequence of two mental states and two brain states. Let us ask what the cause of M_2 is. If we wish to allow for mental causation, we may say that M_1 is the cause of M_2. According to the EP_N principle of supervenience, however, M_2 supervenes and is dependent upon P_2. Thus, if M_1 is to be the cause of M_2, it will have to cause M_2's subvenient base, P_2. But the EP_N principle of the causal closure of the physical requires that P_1 be the adequate cause of P_2. Moreover, M_1 itself exists in dependence upon it's subvenient base, P_1. Thus, assuming the falsity of causal overdetermination, we see that there is no room in EP_N for mental to physical causation (M_1 causing P_2) or mental to mental causation (M_1 causing M_2). The sequence of mental events running through a person's consciousness is like a series of causally impotent shadows.

While they may not be familiar with the argument just given, Cosmides and Tooby seem to grasp that epiphenomenalism follows from EP_N: "The brain is a physical system whose operation is governed solely by the laws of chemistry and physics. What does this mean? It means that all of your thoughts and hopes and dreams and feelings are produced by chemical reactions going on in your head."[32] The best way for an EP_N advocate to avoid the problem of epiphenomenalism is to identify conscious states with brain states. In this way, conscious states can retain causal power because they just are brain states. Unfortunately, this move amounts to a denial of consciousness, as it appears to first-person introspection.

3. The various brain mechanisms relevant to human behavior in general, and rational and ethical behavior in particular, are what they are because they aided (or at least did not hinder) their possessors in adapting to recurring problems over the long course of evolutionary history in feeding, reproducing, fighting, and fleeing, which in turn aided their possessors in the struggle for differential reproductive advantage. The details of his case cannot be presented here, but Alvin Plantinga has argued that securing true,

warranted beliefs is not relevant to the struggle for reproductive advantage and, in fact, EP_N is self-refuting because it provides a defeater for reason itself, including a defeater for any rational argument for EP_N.[33]

In my view, Plantinga's argument is a good one, but it is especially strong in those areas of rationality that are quite far removed from the demands of reproductive advantage. This may be why EP_N advocates often select phenomena that are closely tied to reproduction, such as male sexual jealousy, to generate and test their hypotheses. However, this selection of phenomena is itself question-begging against IDP_C. After all, it would be very difficult to offer anything besides a fairly simplistic just-so evolutionary story in attempting to relate to the struggle for reproductive advantage the sorts of epistemological, aesthetic, and ethical cognitive and intuitive faculties relevant to holding alternative views of the Enlightenment, doing abstract philosophy, ethics, and theoretical science, or to offering a defense of EP_N. So far as I know, no advocate of EP_N has performed a study or offered a hypothesis to address this question: Precisely how did the mechanisms that are involved in forming, testing, and evaluating EP_N vis-à-vis IDP_C address the specific, repeated long-term adaptive problems associated with successful reproduction?

In addition to rational behavior, EP_N would seem to imply a consequentialist evolutionary ethical understanding of moral action, specifically, a view of moral action as a means to reproductive success. As evolutionary naturalist Michael Ruse notes:

> Morality is a biological adaptation no less than are hands and feet and teeth. Considered as a rationally justifiable set of claims about an objective something, ethics is illusory. I appreciate that when somebody says 'Love thy neighbor as thyself,' they think they are referring above and beyond themselves. Nevertheless, such reference is truly without foundation. Morality is just an aid to survival and reproduction . . . and any deeper meaning is illusory.[34]

Thus, EP_N would seem to predict that human moral agents would not be interested in or preoccupied with the illusory intrinsic rightness or wrongness of intents, motives, virtues/vices, moral rules, and moral acts. Rather, those agents should be interested in and preoccupied with the reproductively advantageous consequences of intents, motives, and so forth. It could be responded that it may well be the case that, although illusory, objectivist deontological and virtue theory ethical beliefs on the part of moral agents would have more reproductive advantage than would accrue if those agents held to an evolutionary, consequentialist theory. Thus evolutionary processes may select those mechanisms that tend to produce (illusory) objectivist deontological and virtue ethical beliefs in moral agents.

However, such a claim would be difficult to prove and, in any case, it would have a disastrous implication for evolutionary ethics considered as a moral theory; namely, it would seem to suffer from what is called the publicity objection. To be adequate, a moral theory must provide moral principles that can serve as action guides that inform moral situations. Most moral situations involve more than one person and, in this sense, are public situations. Thus, moral action guides must be teachable to others so they can be publicly used principles that help us in our interpersonal moral interactions. According to the evolutionary consequentialist argument under consideration, it may be immoral to teach others to embrace evolutionary ethics because that would not promote reproductive advantage. It would promote reproductive advantage for people to believe (falsely) in objectivist deontological or virtue ethical theory. Thus, it could be immoral for one to go public and teach evolutionary, consequentialist ethics to others and, if so, this would violate one of the necessary conditions for a moral theory; namely, that it be teachable to others. It may be that EP_N advocates are unconcerned about the ethical implications of their view, but to the extent that they are concerned, the publicity objection would seem to present a serious problem for EP_N proponents.

There is another problem with the claim that evolutionary processes may select those mechanisms that tend to produce (illusory) objectivist deontological and virtue ethical beliefs in moral agents because those beliefs would be reproductively advantageous. Richard Swinburne has argued that if beliefs, and the mechanisms needed to form and sustain them, are the result of mere evolutionary processes, then organisms, including humans, would not be able to distinguish these two sorts of propositions: (P) All crocodiles are dangerous. (Q) Normally crocodiles are dangerous.[35]

This is because P (a genuine universal proposition) and Q (an approximate generalization) have the same behavioral implications regarding reproducing, fleeing, fighting, and feeding. Evolutionary processes would not be able to select mechanisms for distinguishing P-type from Q-type propositions (the distinction is invisible to processess that select discriminatory mechanisms solely with respect to reproductively advantageous behaviors). Moreover, since Q-type propositions contain less empirical content and do not apply as far beyond sensory stimuli as do P-type propositions, Q-type propositions are simpler and all that would be required for reproductive advantage. Thus, given EP_N, one would expect organisms to employ Q-type and not P-type propositions.

Now, argues Swinburne, a deontological moral belief is one that is universalizable, that is, it is a P-type proposition that applies to all relevantly similar cases. For example, all people in this circumstance should keep their promises. Only if an organism can form such universal judgments can it possess a deontological sense of moral duty and only then can it experience a conflict between moral duties or between a moral duty and a desire of some sort. By contrast, Swinburne uses the term *wanton* for an organism that has no sense of duty at all, but only acts to satisfy his own desires. The only conflict the wanton knows is that between two or more desires he cannot simultaneously satisfy (for instance, to eat more and lose weight). He knows nothing about duty.

If Swinburne's arguments are correct, then EP_N would seem to predict a world of wantons because creatures in such a world would lack a necessary condition (ability to employ P-type propositions) for understanding moral duty and conflicts involving moral duties. What is at issue is whether EP_N has the intellectual resources to avoid implying a wanton world. In my view, EP_N does not have those resources and it is both ad hoc and begs the question against IDP_C simply to readjust the most natural implications of EP_N when they tend to falsify EP_N and are nicely explained in light of IDP_C.

EP_N Epistemological/Methodological Commitments

4. It should be obvious that EP_N advocates will adopt methodological naturalism and seek event causal explanations either by starting with an adaptive problem and generating hypotheses about evolved psychological mechanisms considered as adaptive solutions or by starting with observed psychological phenomena and generating hypotheses about the adaptive problem they might have evolved to solve. Moreover, EP_N implies that the focus of study will be the brain, along with various processing mechanisms and their relationship to body movements. Among other things, this means that various mental phenomena such as agency, the subject/object relation, the relationship between one mental content and another mental content, and intentionality will be reduced to efficient causality. As John Post points out, "A scientific or naturalistic account of [human beings and their mental states] must be a causal account."[36]

Further, EP_N implies a third-person approach to research that will have little or no room for the first-person perspective. Speaking of the EP_N conception of objective reality, Thomas Nagel observes that if "one starts from the objective side, the problem is how to accommodate, in a world that simply exists and has no perspectival center, any of the following things: (a) oneself; (b) one's point of view; (c) the point of view of other selves, similar and dissimilar; and (d) the objects of various types of judgments that seem to emanate from these perspectives."[37] Because reality is objective, says the naturalist, the best way to study the mind (that is, brain) is to adopt a third-person perspective. The objectivity of science requires this approach.

Moreover, a complete, physical description of the world will only need to utilize third-person descriptions. This is because physical facts are able to be captured entirely from a third-person point of view without reference to any first-person perspective. Put differently, first-person descriptions do not express irreducible facts and thus are either reducible or eliminable.

5. It may come as a surprise to many psychologists, but on an EP_N view, the discipline of psychology itself should either be reducible to or eliminated in favor of biology and, ultimately, of chemistry and physics. As EP_N advocates Cosmides and Tooby admit, on an EP_N view, psychology becomes a "branch of biology that studies (1) brains, (2) how brains process information, and (3) how the brain's information-processing programs generate behavior. Once one realizes that psychology is a branch of biology, inferential tools in biology—its theories, principles, and observations—can be used to understand psychology."[38]

What Cosmides and Tooby apparently fail to realize is that the "theories, principle, and observations" of biology employ no distinctively psychological concepts whatever. Notions referring to beliefs, desires, introjection, having a self-representation, (and "being an inferential tool"!) and so forth simply drop from sight, especially when one notes that if evolutionary naturalism is correct, biology itself will increasingly be reduced to or replaced by chemistry and physics. On the basis of EP_N, philosophers such as Paul Churchland promote eliminative materialism; roughly, the view that in light of advances in neuroscience, the commonsense mentalistic categories of psychology, such as the ones just mentioned, will turn out to be like the notion of phlogiston, namely, discarded remnants of an abandoned theory.[39] This is not good news for those who think that mental notions are essential to the discipline of psychology. But it is precisely EP_N considerations that have lead Churchland and others to adopt eliminative materialism.

Of course, not all or even a majority of EP_N advocates accept eliminative materialism, and I suspect that Cosmides and Tooby would be among the dissenters. But many psychologists fail to grasp that, while EP_N may not require eliminative materialism, the only way to avoid it and stay squarely within the commitments of EP_N is to accept some form of reductionism regarding psychology. The reason many do not see this is that there is confusion about just exactly what reduction itself is.

There are six different forms of reduction relevant to our present concerns, five of which shall be listed here and a sixth shall be mentioned shortly: 1. *individual ontological reduction*: one object (a macro-object like the person) is identified with another object (for example, the brain). 2. *property ontological reduction*: one property (heat) is identified with another property (meaning kinetic energy); 3. *linguistic reduction*: one word or concept (*pain*) is defined as or analyzed in terms of another word or concept (*the tendency to grimace when stuck with a pin*); 4. *causal reduction*: the causal activity of the reduced entity is entirely explained in terms of the causal activity of the reducing entity; 5. *theoretical* or *explanatory reduction*: one theory or law is reduced to another by biconditional bridge principles, usually associated with Nagel-type reductions. Terms in the reduced theory are connected with terms in the reducing theory by way of biconditionals (if and only if) that serve as the grounds for identifying the properties expressed by the former terms with those expressed by the latter. For example, if one takes color terms to be coextensional with wavelength terms, then one can claim that colors are identical to wavelengths. In this way, explanatory reduction is the first step toward ontological property reduction.

EP_N requires individual ontological reduction because of its rejection of immaterial substances. It also requires causal reduction in virtue of its commitment to the causal closure of the physical, the supervenience thesis, and bottom-up approach implied by these two commitments.

When psychologists claim that they are nonreductive physicalists, they usually mean that they reject either property ontological reduction that follows from explanatory reduction or linguistic reduction. Property ontological reduction—for example, identifying a mental property such as being in pain with a physical property such as having such and such C fibers firing—is widely believed to have failed because of the problem of multiple realization: Several different organisms (humans, dogs, Vulcans) could all be in a pain-type state while being in very different sorts of brain-type states, so a pain-type state cannot be identified with a brain-type state. Given this problem, the argument goes, neither explanatory nor property reduction succeeds.

Does the argument from multiple realizability save psychology from property reduction on an EP_N view? Probably not. One can still formulate mental/physical biconditionals to serve as the grounds for property identity that are relativized to different species. Such biconditionals would take on this form:

$$S_1 \longrightarrow (M_I \longleftrightarrow P_1)$$

Figure 7.2

This proposition expresses a species-relative biconditional that can be read as follows: For some species S_I (a Vulcan, dog, human), if something is a member of that species, then it will be in mental state M_I if and only if it is in brain state P_I. This means local, species reductions will be possible. Human psychology will be reducible to human neurophysiology, dog psychology to dog neurophysiology, and so forth.

A different way to deal with mental states is to treat them as functional states. In this way, a mental state, such as pain, is defined totally independently of the state's intrinsic features made evident to first-person introspection (being hurtful, throbbing) and, instead, is defined as the property of having some property that plays a certain functional role. For example, being painful could be defined as having some brain state or other that is caused by pin sticks and that causes a sense of self-pity and the body movements of grimacing and shouting "Ouch!" As with behaviorism, functionalism is consistent with the denial of consciousness and, indeed, the intrinsic features of mental states are simply irrelevant as far as their functional characterizations are concerned.

This functionalist move appears to be the favored strategy for EP_N advocates, and while it does prevent a linguistic reduction of psychology to neuroscience, it does so at a price, and the cost can be made clear by describing a sixth form of reduction called *functional realization reduction*. This reduction is accomplished in two steps:

Step 1: Functionalize the mental property. For example, the mental property of being in pain is identified with a property of having some physical property or other that plays the right role in the organism; for example, by being that physical property that is caused by pin pricks, toothaches, and so forth, and which causes the organism to grimace and desire relief.

Step 2: Identify the property that plays the correct role mentioned in step 1 with a physical property. Step 2 requires that the only properties that realize functional roles are physical properties. This is similar to requiring that only some sort of physical hardware can be the realizer of functional roles specified in computer software. In this way, the functionalist requires that each time a human, Vulcan, dog, or turtle is in pain, that particular pain event must be taken as identical to a physical event in the brain and nervous system. Thus, pain is reduced to/identified with some physical event or other, even though it remains impossible to state necessary and sufficient conditions for the type of brain event to which the type of mental state is reduced. Moreover, what makes the individual physical event a pain event is not the physical event's intrinsic features. Rather, it is a pain event because it plays the right role in the organism.

In this way, functionalism prevents the linguistic reduction of psychological terms to neuroscience terms because psychological terms such as "introjection," "having a self-concept," and so forth, are mere artifact terms such as "being a table" that neither carve the world up at the joints nor play a role in causal explanations. The causal behavior of an organism will be fixed by its distinctive chemical and physical properties, not by the functional interpretations placed on that organism. As Kim has argued, this sort of functional reduction of psychology implies an epiphenomenal view of the mental precisely because it is the intrinsic physical features of the brain that cause an organism's body to move, not some second order extrinsic functional description of the organism.[40]

The simple fact is that consciousness and mental properties and states, along with the psychological categories used to describe and explain them, are just not at home in an EP_N view. If EP_N is correct, the only way to save psychology from elimination or various forms of reduction is to take its explanatory categories as arbitrary, functional notions that are causally impotent. As Geoffrey Madell notes,

> The explanatory categories we use in describing human action and experience seem to be irreducible to the categories employed in the physical sciences. If the materialist is right to claim that reality consists in assemblies of elementary particles, we should naturally expect that the explanatory categories employed in the physical sciences should prove adequate to deal with the whole of reality, including that of human experience. Yet it seems clear, on the face of it, that intentional notions don't correspond to physical categories, that they don't pick out natural physical kinds, and that they betoken a mode of understanding quite distinct from that of the physical sciences.[41]

What Madell observes is at home in and, in fact, predictable from IDP_C. This is what we would expect if human persons are made in the image of an Immaterial Substantial Spirit. Many facts about human persons should be recalcitrant facts for EP_N, and anyone who is familiar with the last sixty years of philosophy of mind should understand the claim that physicalism is in a period of paradigm crisis.[42] But if EP_N is correct, then psychology itself may well have to go. Thus it is more than ironic that EP_N advocate David M. Buss triumphantly proclaims that evolutionary psychology is a fulfillment of Darwin's dream that his theory would place psychology on a new foundation and open up to it new fields of research.[43] In fact, it may well be that Darwinism and EP_N are the cure that killed the patient.

8

Because "Cause" Makes Sense

The Anthropic Cosmological Principle and Quantum Cosmocausality

Hal N. Ostrander

Since the very structure of the universe is seen to be remarkably amenable to the existence and continued sustenance of the human race, the question thus becomes one of whether such a state of affairs can be explicated in theistic terms, more specifically, in relation to a theistically instantiated anthropic cosmological principle (ACP).

In order to pursue this line of thinking, a number of provisional definitions must be supplied. The ACP itself comes in four basic versions, but only two are dealt with here—the weak and strong anthropic principles,[1] each defined as follows:

1. The *weak anthropic principle* (WAP): "The observed values of all physical and cosmological quantities are not equally probable but they take on values, restricted by the requirement that there exist sites where carbon-based life can evolve and the requirement that the Universe be old enough for it to have already done so."
2. The *strong anthropic principle* (SAP): "The Universe must have those properties which allow life to develop within it at some stage in its history."[2]

Granted, these are technical definitions,[3] but a veritable plethora of such fine-tuned items exists, most of which are categorized as elementary lengths and times, fundamental constants, masses of elementary particles, physical fine structure constants, and even cosmic coincidences.[4]

In addition, a working definition of *quantum cosmocausality* (QC) is required. According to Stanley Jaki, the search for such an all encompassing, *a priori* definition of cosmic cause has always been with us historically, but a contemporary restatement of it is sorely needed. As Jaki explains:

> A broad awareness among cosmologists is still to arise concerning the very real possibility of knowing conclusively the intrinsic impossibility of knowing that the universe can only be what it is. The latter knowledge implies the necessary and exclusive character of the existing universe and can have therefore its source only in *a priori* considerations. To know the universe in such a way is not only very different from knowing all its quantitative correlations. . . , but also rigorously impossible. The ambition to formulate an explanatory framework in which the world appears to be a necessary form of existence is not new. It is as old as physics.[5]

Hence, the definition of QC is a synthesizing one; it must attempt conceptually to consolidate the six types of causality previously posited, utilized, and modified throughout the history of philosophy: material, formal, efficient, final, instrumental, and sufficient.[6] Although there is undoubtedly some overlap in meaning among these six accounts of cause, the tension between the demand for complete clarity and the conceptual inadequacy of existing causal terminology is especially marked in attempting to define QC.

The barest definition possible, then, is that QC is the all-encompassing conglomeration of the various strains of causal meaning, each of which is potentially involved in the creation of the universe as instantiated by God in all of its quantum-to-macro world particulars. With this in view, the present chapter will follow various theological, philosophical, and scientific leads into the universal "cause" of human beings, that is, an anthropic cosmological cause, if viewed *in toto*. Accomplishing this lends itself to several areas of study:

1. the fact that the universe and human beings are so propitiously and compatibly structured;
2. the relation of the supernatural to the concept of discontinuity:
3. the dilemma faced by empiricists who disregard metaphysics;
4. the ACP in relation to God as the mechanism for cosmic cause, something intrinsically involving a theoretical leap from the micro- to macro-world as well as an ontology of law;

5. the notion that the ACP serves as God's principle for regulating a created cosmos;

6. the defining of a theistic QC in light of the weak and strong versions of the ACP; and

7. an exploratory look at omnicausality with the universe as the product of a theistic QC whose six types of causation establish the ACP as God's regulative principle for creating and sustaining the universe.

With these seven items in mind, the ACP is ripe for a QC harvest. As anthropic theorist Nicola Dallaporta maintains, the ACP holds the key to a better scientific understanding of the universe, stating, "The recognition of the anthropic principle should be considered as a turning point in the development of science, opening new roads towards the unknown aspects of the universe."[7]

The Propitious Nature of Cosmic/Anthropic Compatibility

Many scientists uphold the fact that a singular compatibility of sorts is at work between human beings and their cosmic environment. While permeating the cosmos as a whole, the known laws of physics seemingly zenith to standards of near-perfection for the sake of humanity's presence on this planet, Earth. Because it is a match so propitious in nature, philosophers of science and cosmologists alike often voice their beliefs concerning this remarkably fine-tuned, cosmic/anthropic compatibility. On occasion, their words are characterized by tacit religious interference. At other times, they seem to preach words of straightforward theological appeal.[8]

In view of these cosmic/anthropic structural compatibilities, it is important to note that the ACP perspective most often endorsed by cosmic/biological evolutionary theorists is one devoid of any attached religious overtones. On the other hand, such compatibilities may also be reasonably expressed in terms of a divinely energized principle, one in complete accord with more historically pervasive explanations of creation wherein supernatural involvement is taken seriously.

Supernatural Involvement and Discontinuity

The question of supernatural involvement in the creation of the cosmos is, at bottom, as all-encompassing an inquiry as there can be. All the same, naturalistic scientists find it difficult to accept concepts of supernatural involvement in the creation of the universe because they are allegedly unsupported by accumulated evidence. The crux of the matter is whether the evidence, rightly interpreted, points either to some form of external supernatural engagement or to some internal chance process operative from within.

Naturalists presume that succumbing to notions of supernatural creativity introduces a measure of discontinuity into the cosmological quest; it interrupts their vision of nature as a seamless web of causal connections.[9] Moreover, anxiety over supernatural discontinuity seems to manifest itself regularly in the field of evolutionary biology.[10] Even so, a proportionally fewer number of scientists tends to question whether the ontological status of "chance" creative processes is even a valid notion. Atheists, agnostics, and theists alike come under the influence of varying philosophical assumptions about what roles contingency and determinism should play in their respective investigations of cosmic cause.[11] This is best illustrated via the empiricist approach to knowledge gains.

The Empiricist Dilemma

Concerning empiricism, the tendency of scientists to isolate empirical issues from metaphysical concerns must be interpreted in terms of a false dichotomy.[12] Such an approach only serves to confirm empiricism's epistemological weakness. Deriving its coherence as a theory of knowledge solely from a sensory base, its openness to truths beyond the range of its own methodology is critically held captive. Furthermore, since empiricism is incapable of incorrigibly proving that factual truths beyond the sensory realm do not exist, and since the scientific method has traditionally relied too heavily on empirical measures alone for its advancement, whatever elements are said to compose *the* scientific method must not only be supplemented definitionally but also restructured procedurally. To the extent that scientific laws are arrived at through empiricist methods, to that same extent benefits provided by truths lying beyond the five senses (metaphysical truths) are forfeited, resulting in the loss of a more comprehensive metascientific perspective with respect to whatever metaempirical elements of created reality can be shown to exist.[13]

Philosopher of science Philip Gasper suggests a methodology similar to this, but concedes only partially a source for scientific law beyond empirical confines. Agreeing that causal relations seem to be scientifically necessary *and* irreducibly metaphysical in the face of nontheistic empiricist standards, Gasper analyzes how the traditional Humean interpretation of causal relations[14] continues to be applied by contemporary philosophers of science:

> Instead of offering a verificationistically unacceptable metaphysical explanation of appeals to theoretical considerations in identifying causal relations (according to which knowledge of unobservable causal

mechanisms is being applied), the empiricist offers a conception according to which reference to laws of nature is part of the conventional definition of causal relations and the theory-dependence of methods is simply a manifestation of scientists' efforts to identify those laws.[15]

Here Gasper expresses dissatisfaction with the Humean notion of causality in which a determinate relation between events is left unspecified, except in the most general, unexplained way: a law of nature. He argues further that Hume mistakenly incorporates "the notion of a law of nature into the very definition of causal relations," and by contemporary philosophy of science standards this generates a deficient account of what "causation" actually means philosophically. References to unobservable causal relations are problematical by definition, Gasper affirms, but science is leading the way beyond the difficulties introduced historically by the Humean acausal interlude so as to reconstruct a more philosophically satisfying notion of causation.[16]

Further, Gasper's contemporary, Nancy Cartwright, also critiques the same timeworn meanings for cause that gave rise to the skepticist tradition, extending the impact of Gasper's censure of Hume while voicing her own position that empiricism's approach to causality is both misguided and unsubstantiated. It is not only possible, she maintains, but essential as well to seek out and apply explanatory causes to various physical phenomena in contradistinction to mere explanatory laws. To go beyond law to the cause of law is the real issue. Consequently, science, as an enterprise rightly concerned with methodology, must always be wary of confusing causal claims with theoretical accounts of phenomena based on natural law; superior causal explanations must eventually supersede inferior empiricist theories.[17] In brief, Cartwright's philosophy of science, like Gasper's, is non-Humean in its particulars and eager to achieve a philosophically corrected account of causality no longer encumbered by Humean frames of reference.

In response, a logical question arises: What is it that supersedes cause? All in all, such a question must be permitted on at least three counts: the fact that it is never directly asked; the inadequacy of naturalistic, cosmic/biological approaches to bring a genetically diverse mankind/*anthropos* into corporate being; and empiricism's past failures to examine sufficiently the philo/scientific side of causality in relation to a larger cosmic causality.

God as Cosmocausal Mechanism

According to Norman Newell, "Natural processes operating in accordance with natural laws do indeed represent 'supreme power,' the power of the universe, and the existence of this power is beyond dispute. Whether it is called Nature or God is a matter of personal preference."[18] In other words, What is the creative power lying back of the universe? And the questions persist. For example, In what sense is the universe itself a cause-and-effect sequence and, as such, may it be delimited in terms of God himself? If so, Should God be considered as the actual causation agent of this cause-and-effect universe—or better, its anthropic causation agent, however difficult to explain or easy to devalue something so causally deterministic appears to be?[19] Thus, To what extent does God render precise the ostensibly deterministic, scientific/mathematical parameters of the cosmos for the sake of God's chief creation—humanity?[20]

In reply, the very framing of the questions involves totaling up a number of theo/philosophical integers: created *ontos*, plus a designing/intentioning *telos*, plus a sentient *bios*, plus a divinely imaged *anthropos*, plus a humanly habitable *cosmos*, plus the underlying cause-and-effect sequences operational within each, all adding up to a quantum-to-cosmos causal sum that points toward a duly evidenced theism. If God, then, is hypothesized to own a threefold creative role as (1) the *a priori* cause of the universe; (2) as its actual existence/sustenance mechanism; and (3) as humanity's anthropic causation agent, then God's existence and interaction with the cosmos and human beings themselves suddenly become reasonable assumptions. For cosmic/biological evolutionary forces to accomplish the same three-point task, while devoid of intelligence and empowered by chance alone, does not add up coherently.[21] Beyond this, a foray into the quantum world helps to illustrate this need for coherence.

A Metalevel Below

Conditions at the microcosmic level of reality are usually described as chaotic, random, and nonteleological in nature. In view of this, as reality moves from the quantum world up to the macroworld, the physical systems and processes operative throughout appear to involve teleological outworkings—those of "design" and "purpose." To "jump up" from the micro- to the macroworld is to acknowledge the existence of thermodynamic forces working at or below the quantum level. Yet these forces must necessarily and simultaneously be involved in some as-yet-unknown macrotransformational process; they must in some way be transformed into the more explicitly teleological processes so characteristic of the Newtonian macroworld. And all this, it should be stressed, is somehow accomplished while in seeming opposition to the renowned second law of thermodynamics, one of the most basic of natural laws.[22] This *chaos*-to-*telos* move, against the grain of the second law's stated purpose, is, for all intents and purposes, an outwardly inexplicable event.

Theorist F. David Peat, however, carefully addresses this very issue by suggesting that something akin to a "gentle action for a harmonious world" is functioning throughout the microworld environs.[23] What Peat proposes here is technically unsatisfying, but the very fact that he alludes to the existence of possible subprocesses and structures lying behind, or prior to, the chaos-to-order reality jump is significant in itself; it is scientific theory *au naturel* pushing the categories-of-reality envelope.

From another direction, Ilya Prigogine and Isabelle Stengers are also committed to finding workable answers to the chaos-to-order conundrum. One of their main conclusions reads, "At all levels, be it the level of macroscopic physics, the level of fluctuations, or the microscopic level, *nonequilibrium* is the source of order. *Nonequilibrium* brings 'order out of chaos.'"[24] In other words, some lack of thermodynamic equilibrium, a negative entropy of sorts, is essential to this quantal megaleap into the large-scale universe. Moreover, they try to reinforce their conclusions in terms of what they call "active matter," precisely the kind of matter needed to help speed along chaos and randomness to arrive at some semblance of macroworld order. In doing so, active matter not only transforms means to ends but also becomes engaged in an intrinsically irreversible process capable of negating the second law's entropic effects on the energy levels of the universe.[25]

The accuracy of these theories aside, the speculative efforts of Peat, Prigogine, and Stengers, as well as others,[26] grant future promise to the order-out-of-chaos enigma. Their labors may at least be interpreted as the search for some sort of mechanistic dialectic between chance and regularity within the cosmos. In essence, it is the search for a metalevel below, or behind, the quantum microworld, that is, an as-yet-undiscovered level of reality wherein the quantum-to-macro world puzzle is solved.[27] Moreover, such approaches help to provide a framework for reinterpreting the regularity side of this tricky dialectic equation. If asserted as a theistic framework, the regularity of the macrocreation must in some sense be predicated as God's cosmo-causal mastery over (or negation of) the so-called instrumentalizing power of chance, with such lordship itself defined in terms of God's ongoing interactivity with both the quantum microcreation and the hypothesized metalevel just below it.[28] Although further warrant is needed, such a state of creative affairs is linked to the search for an ontology of law.

Ontology of Law

Venturing to construct an omnicomprehensive ontology of law for the created order is also important in understanding how God can be regarded as the cosmocausal mechanism at work within the cosmos. As the metaphysical parallel to twentieth-century grand unified theories (GUTs) and theories of everything (TOEs), J. H. Lambert set forth precisely this kind of scenario, at least in nascent form, as far back as 1760.[29] Contemporary thinker Ted Peters also explores an ontology of law's cosmocausal possibilities, but articulates them in far more theistic terms than Lambert:

> Law is the one form of divine activity within the cosmos. Laws are the result of the intersection of God's faithfulness with the course of otherwise contingent events. God in the God self is *a se*, not bound to the cosmic order. What we experience as governing principles are ordinances freely invoked by God to keep the world in being—to keep it organized as a cosmos—for a given duration.[30]

Peters's definition here takes seriously the laws of nature and their implementing power, albeit derivatively by God, to keep the universe under theistic control.[31]

Howard J. Van Till also expresses a similar notion when, in speaking of the entirety of created things, he says: "Every category of structure, creature and process was conceptualized by the Creator from the beginning but actualized in time as the created material employed its God-given capacities in the manner and at the time the Creator intended from the outset."[32]

It is evident, however, that Peters and Van Till fall short of specifically connecting their views to the ACP itself, but their corporate philosophizing about ontological law in theistic terms has cosmocausal import insofar as, in their views, God ordains such a lawlike nexus in order to create and sustain the universe.

The Anthropic Cosmological Principle as God's Regulative Principle for Creation

The data gathered by exploring the quantum-to-universe domains may be interpreted scientifically and mathematically in terms of sheer anthropic parameters, but also in overtly theistic terms. In view of this, if the ACP is highlighted as the focal point of God's creative process (that is, as the regulative principle God employed to bring the universe into existence and maintain it as such), then it may be construed as having a significant cosmocausal role to play—that of the cosmocausal drive responsible for giving intelligibility to design/intentionality and mechanism/*telos*,[33] perhaps even as the connecting point between earthly physics and divinized metaphysics. As Friedrich Cramer asserts, "There are no physics without metaphysical basis, but it is of utmost importance to define precisely the connecting point between physics and meta-physics in order to avoid a confusion of categories."[34]

True to his own premises, Cramer is referring here to a naturalistic ACP in the context of cosmic/biological evolutionary forces. For purposes of instituting a theistic QC, however, if Cramer's connecting point between physics and metaphysics is cosmically expressed in terms of a theistically wrought ACP, then it is simply a substitution of contexts that enables the universe to become God-organized as opposed to self-organized, with theory and metatheory cosmocausally linked within the ACP itself. Such a hypothesis is at least in keeping with what some anthropic theorists have themselves already concluded. For example, George Schlesinger remarks, "Over an extended period science has kept providing results that the adversaries of religion have been able to use as their ammunition. The anthropic principle seems to redress the imbalance, since for a change it offers at least a prima facie argument supporting the theist."[35]

Summary

In summary, a full-bodied theistic QC must be cognizant of the compatibility structures now existing between the universe and the human species, in which case it may be couched in terms descriptive of a supernatural discontinuity at work over against the continuous forces of cosmic/biological evolution. Positing a creator-God as the mechanism responsible for a cosmos consummately fit for humanity involves a limited understanding of the micro-to-macroworld transformation process intrinsic to creation. The hypothesis of a reality mechanism existing below the quantum world that both undergirds and assists it in bringing the macroworld to present order is seemingly a necessary one. In addition, an ontology of law of sorts, based on theistic premises, is at work cosmocausally throughout the created order in connection with this metalevel below. Then, over time, God utilizes the ACP itself—intrinsically comprised of a body of numerous, unchanging constants and parameters—as the regulative principle for instantiating and organizing created reality at all levels. How the ACP in its weak and strong versions fits into this overall picture of a theistic QC is addressed next.

The Anthropic Cosmological Principle—Weak and Strong

The Weak Anthropic Principle

Concerning empiricism, the WAP seems to underscore the empiricist dilemma noted earlier, that a strictly empirical approach to the acquisition and interpretation of knowledge is by definition hindered from probing into knowledge realms that are metaphysical in nature. As a consequence, the scientific enterprise today embodies elements of skepticism with respect to how reality should not be interpreted apart from an empirical *modus operandi*.[36] Furthermore, empiricism's lack of metaphysical perspective cultivates an atmosphere of unfamiliarity with respect to the cosmos, that is, the harmonious intricacies revealed in the very structures of the micro- and macro-universes are often overlooked in the pursuit of rigorously amassing facts.[37]

Empirical approaches to knowledge are undoubtedly efficient at accumulating experimental facts but seemingly ineffectual when it comes to modeling them into constructive interpretational frameworks, a task requiring a metaphysical point of view if it is to operate productively. And if the WAP's straight numbers and coincidental relations are, in fact, placed within a metaphysical framework—one that upholds the viability of anti-chance operations—then a basis for constructing a theistic QC is partially established. Insofar as the shaping of the anthropic "facts" (constants and parameters) into a theistic paradigm is accomplished, the survivability of the explanatory power of theistic ACP arguments is assured. According to John Polkinghorne:

> It is fair to inquire whether [the anthropic parameters] will . . . survive the advance of knowledge. . . . [W]hile correlations in the structure of the world may be revealed to us which are currently hidden and which may explain naturally what now seems to be coincidental, there is likely to remain a degree of balance necessary for life and irreducibly given in scientific terms, which will call for a deeper explanation.[38]

Hence, a WAP backed by theistic concerns confirms the need for constructing a quantum cosmology that takes God's role seriously as the cosmo-causal impetus for the creation of the universe.

The Strong Anthropic Principle

Concerning those who deny the relevance of the SAP and what Brandon Carter calls its "anthropic enigma," many theoretical physicists are still optimistic about undermining its influence as a principle. To accomplish this, however, the "underlying physical mechanisms fixing" the WAP's "independent fundamental constants" would have to be discovered, documented, and unquestionably recognized by everyone concerned. Such measures would provide the means for theorists to argue that "at the [SAP's] deeper theoretical level" the WAP constants could have no other set of values than what they presently exhibit.[39] In deciphering Carter's meaning here, it seems that he is simply stating that if the SAP can demonstrate a strictly physical reason for how and why the WAP's constants/parameters have the numerical values they do, then it is unnecessary to resort to some metaphysical source to explain these already existing values. In essence, it is the search for why we are here; it is the propagating of a formal naturalistic cause over against the acknowledgment of a possible supernatural cause that Carter and others are trying to advance.

From another direction, other anthropic theorists strive to sidestep the obstacle of cause altogether so that troubling deliberations about how and why a supernatural cause brought the universe into existence (especially for divinely created human beings to inhabit!) are either ignored or suppressed in favor of a bare cosmic/Darwinian teleology. As anthropic theorist Livio Gratton phrases it:

> The inconsistency of SAP is that it is not a causal but a *teleological* argument. . . . In fact, after Darwin, every sensible man is aware that plants and animals have evolved in order to adapt themselves to environmental conditions and not, on the contrary, that these conditions have been expressly planned to make their life possible.[40]

Hence, Gratton's approach here is not truly cosmocausal in scope, siding instead with a cosmic/bioevolutionary version of teleology as opposed to a scientifically causal teleology wherein the cosmos first and humanity second were "genesised" into being, only to take up their divine *telos* from that point onward in accordance with God's planned initiative.

As its name implies, the strong anthropic principle goes beyond the effectiveness of the WAP in its attempt to give cosmocausal impetus to the creation and maintenance of the universe. As George Ellis asserts, "I understand the Anthropic Principle's primary role as being to enable us to comprehend causal links we would not otherwise realize existed."[41] Paul Davies contends more strongly than Ellis that the very laws of nature governing the cosmos function as they do because of the universal, regulatory potential of the SAP: "The strong anthropic principle can therefore be regarded as a sort of organizing meta-principle, because it arranges the *laws* themselves so as to permit complex organization to arise."[42] In other words, the forces of cosmocausality at work in the universe take on aspects considerably more powerful than what the blind nonteleological forces of cosmic/bioevolution are able to support. Sheer cosmocausal forces, then, may be examined more perspectively than what the prevailing ACP literature allows for; that is, they may be scrutinized with all due fairness through the lens of a pan-causal framework, a theistic quantum cosmocausality.

Toward a Theistic Quantum Cosmocausality

The idea that theistic causal powers are at work in the universe and are conversant with it on both quantum and cosmological scales is a reasonable one inasmuch as other origins mechanisms are proving to be increasingly incapable of producing the desired result, namely, a cosmos inhabited by human beings.[43]

Omnicausality

So does the ACP cause cosmocausality to function, or does God allow the ACP to run on its own power, derivatively granted? Further, does God cause the ACP to cause such things as existence, design, and intentionality? And how far back do theology, philosophy, and science have to go, logically and temporally, to differentiate between God himself and the cosmocausal mechanism at work to create a universal environment fit for human beings? And, if no such distinction can ever be formulated by finite human minds, is it entirely beyond the realm of possibility for God as Creator to be in control of every quantal movement, in charge of the quantum machinations of the roughly 10^{80} atoms estimated to comprise the cosmos—a determinate omnicausality, if you will?[44] Some argue that if God is only responsible for having caused or directed even a single quantum, space-time event throughout the history of the universe, then God is omnicompetent, such that God can have controlled every quantum space-time event up to the present moment.[45]

It is doubtful whether any theologian, philosopher, or scientist knows the definitive answer to questions like these. But that is not to say that a Christianized version of the ACP—serving as the basis for a theistic QC, while desiring to explore deeply the finely tuned constants and parameters built in to the universe—is merely theo/philosophical sophistry.[46] Nor does it mean that if God chose voluntarily to use an instantiating-of-created-reality principle such as the ACP to manufacture and support a universe requiring a minimum of divine intervention to work, then "God Himself, if he really created the world, must have been an extremely lazy creator."[47]

The truth of the ACP matter is this: the instantiating into *ontos* of a cosmological *telos* to work on God's behalf as the regulatory creative principle of the universe is a difficult-to-define proposition. On the other hand, it is *not* very hard to differentiate its intent and purpose from the premises lying behind a naturalistic ACP; namely, that some evolutionary force is operative categorically, yet entirely wrought by chance.[48] Considering such omnicausal matters, the potential for assimilating the six types of cause mentioned earlier into an all-inclusive causal framework functioning in connection with the ACP itself will now be investigated.

The Canonical Conjugates of Cause[49]

In distinguishing the six types of cause, it is first necessary to note that the very idea of a first cause for the universe has fallen out of favor on many different levels. If Stanley Jaki is correct, however, the contemporary philosophical scene rejects the concept because it is too much in league with a more scientifically unacceptable class of causal theories—those dealing with the God of the Bible. As Jaki candidly remarks:

> One may . . . suspect that belief in the "scientific" overthrow of the principle of causality would not have become a tone of thought of our age, had this scientific age of ours not already parted with belief in the First Cause which makes all other causation possible. . . . Those who know something of the remorseless law of logic will not be surprised on finding that if reality or objective coherence fails to be accepted, any analysis of knowledge becomes a celebration of incoherence."[50]

For the sake of coherence, the six types of causes are summarized below in relation to how the ACP may be said to function cosmocausally within the universe via God's unfolding plan (see figure 8.1).[51]

Type of Cause	Definition	ACP Cosmocausal Function
Material cause	That out of which something is made	Quantum particles
Formal cause	The design or idea followed in the process of making something	Created reality's design as it existed in God's mind
Instrumental cause	The means or instrument by which something is made	ACP-design instantiated as space-time reality
Final cause	The purpose for which something is made	Cosmos for *anthropos*
Efficient cause	The chief agent causing something to be made	God
Sufficient cause	A cause equal to the task of causing something to be made	Only God

Figure 8.1

Expanding on this panoply of the ACP's cosmocausal capacities, the ACP itself is not the material cause of the universe, but it functions as God's regulatory, instrumentalizing causal principle for existencing atomic/sub-atomic materials into space-time being *ex nihilo*, creating them at or below a quantum level of reality in order to instantiate ontologically the formal design of the cosmos as originally conceived by God. On its way to God's *final* cause for the universe, a home for *anthropos*, the quantum materials are instrumentalized and configured mathematically by the ACP into whatever constants and parameters are absolutely necessary for forming and sustaining a universe of macroproportions through *creatio continua* means, a universe intentioned as it is for the sake of human beings from the very first moment of creation. And God, of course, is both the efficient cause and only sufficient cause of the entire ACP process—cosmocausal in its God-scope—as opposed to a nonteleological, cosmic/bioevolutionary force somehow unfolding itself so propitiously for humanity's sake on the basis of sheer chance events alone.

Conclusion

Somewhere Francis Bacon has said, "Inquiry into final causes is sterile, and like a virgin consecrated to God, produces nothing."[52] In like manner, this may be one's immediate reaction to a notion as ambitious as developing a theistic QC—that it will produce nothing of real consequence. On the other hand, many believe it to be a fruitful endeavor, whether on theological, philosophical, or scientific grounds. Further work is in the offing, granted, but even to conceptualize causation itself is an exceedingly difficult proposition. Nevertheless, as one theorist puts it, "The centrality of the concept, both to ordinary practical discourse and to the scientific description of the world, is difficult to deny."[53]

This, then, is a provisional rendering of what could be called theistic quantum cosmocausality, one in which both versions of the anthropic cosmological principle—the WAP and the SAP—serve constructively as its very basis. Future efforts are sure to improve upon this stated conclusion, but one can do no better than appeal to Stanley Jaki's seasoned insights once again:

> Once one truth, the truth of knowing reality is not let in. . . , no truth whatever about reality is any longer forthcoming and certainly not the most important truth, about the totality of real things, namely, that a specific, consistent, thoroughly one universe cried out for a necessary Being as its sole *raison d'être*. Only such a Being can call into existence the universe, a process called creation out of nothing. Such a process

is the deepest, though most luminous mystery which alone can shed light on anything else and prevent rational discourse from relapsing into irrational reversals of its progress. That modern science displays with astonishing effectiveness, the specificity, consistency, and unity of the universe, . . . can certainly reassure the theist that in addition to philosophy, science too is on his side and not on the side of atheists.[54]

In other words, the cause of the universe is, at the very least, vitally related to truth and the reasonable expression of truth. Further, if God is characteristically true and simultaneously relates to the universe as its Creator and Sustainer, then it follows reasonably that God is also the one who cosmocausally instantiated it into being for a divine purpose—that purpose being, in one sense, for the sake of scientists themselves, whether Christian, agnostic, or atheistic. Moreover, such a viewpoint may be seen as the basis for establishing the very concept of scientific explanation in the first place, and, once established, such explanations as finely tuned anthropic principles may serve to elevate and empower the status of whatever scientific methods and procedures are eventually used to study creation's mysteries productively.

As Ernan McMullin maintains, appealing to God as the Creator and Preserver of the universe is not really an "appeal . . . to a 'gap' in scientific explanation" so much as it is "to a different order of explanation that leaves scientific explanation intact, that explores the conditions of possibility for there being *any* kind of scientific explanation."[55] To say that God creates and sustains the universe cosmocausally via anthropic principles fine-tuned for our existence as human beings is to offer up more than a mere declaration of the fact. Instead, if God himself instantiates a universe into being via the sixfold, ACP-delineated causal package already examined, then such a proposition goes beyond what any naturalistic analysis of causation/causality could ever hope to accommodate. Why? Because in the very defining of these causes, there obtains a theo/philosophical richness that naturalism categorically rejects, an aliveness to God's awesome majesty that might otherwise go undeclared except for the disclosures that the ACP and a theistic QC bring to our rapt attention, in turn, taking something of the edge off of the mystery that God's created order poses to our given yet truncated framework of reality.

In closing, then, when it comes to God's action in the world via anthropic cosmological principles and their required linkage to theistic quantum cosmology, the words of Isaiah 55:9 ring all the more true: "For as the heavens are higher than the earth, so are My ways higher than your ways, and My thoughts than your thoughts" (NASB). Thus, in moments of God-given clarity: intelligent cause makes sense![56]

9

Science, Divine Action, and the Intelligent Design Movement

A Defense of Theistic Evolution

Nancey Murphy

This essay is an attempt to flesh out my suspicion that the conflicts among Christians regarding evolutionary biology are rooted in differing assumptions about the nature of divine action. I first explore a bit of the history that created the modern problem of divine action. I claim that the idea of the natural world as a closed causal order governed by the laws of nature left Christian theologians with two major options for understanding God's relation to nature: either God is to be understood as the immanent, but noninterfering, ground of nature, or else as the sovereign creator and sometimes violator of the laws of nature. The immanentist strategy is almost exclusively associated with the liberal tradition, and interventionism with the conservative.

Next, I compare the options of progressive creationism (PC) and theistic evolutionism (TE), noting that PC is clearly a version of interventionism (as is the intelligent design movement), but claiming that TE is ambiguous. TE is the thesis that God creates through the evolutionary process, but the essential question is whether God guides the process or not. If not, there is no difference here from the liberals' immanentism. If God does, then must it not be by interventionism, and so is it any different from PC?

In the third section, I introduce contemporary theories of divine action that have developed since the demise of the Newtonian worldview; in particular, the theory that God performs special, intentional, but noninterventionist acts at the indeterminist quantum level. I end by endorsing Robert J. Russell's use of this theory of quantum divine action to produce a clear and stable account of TE.

The Problem of Divine Action

In the medieval period, especially after the integration of the lost works of Aristotle into Western thought, God's action in the world could be explained in a way perfectly consistent with the scientific knowledge of the time. Heaven was part of the "physical" cosmos. God's agents, the angels, controlled the movements of the "seven planets," which in turn gave nature its rhythms. But modern science has changed all that, primarily by its dependence on the concept of the laws of nature. The notion of a law of nature began as a metaphorical extension of the idea of a divinely sanctioned moral code.[1] For early modern scientists, as well as for medieval theologians, the laws of nature provided an account of how God managed the physical universe. In fact, Descartes took the laws of motion to follow from a more basic principle, explicitly theological: "God is the First Cause of movement and . . . always preserves an equal amount of movement in the universe."[2]

After a century or so, however, the metaphorical character of the term "law of nature" had been forgotten. The laws were granted some form of real existence independent of God, and it is one of the ironies of history that they later came even to be seen as obstacles to divine purposes. Whereas for Newton, a complete account of the motions of the solar system had required both the divinely willed laws of motion and God's occasional readjustment, for Laplace it was no longer necessary for God to make adjustments and, finally, the question was raised of whether it was even conceivable that God should intervene. First, if God acts, this requires that God violate, override, or suspend the laws of nature, which otherwise would have brought about some different event. Many have argued that this is an unacceptable view of the nature of God. If God created the laws in the first place, then God's violation of them is irrational; Jewish philosopher Baruch Spinoza argued that, in such a case, God would be involved in self-contradiction. Second, if action in the material world requires a force, then to conceive of God making things happen in the world is to conceive of God as a force among forces. This, too, is theologically problematic since it reduces God to the level of a demiurge.

The simplest reconciliation of divine action with the modern conception of the clockwork universe was Deism, a very popular option in the eighteenth century. The Deists concluded that while God was the creator of the universe and author of the laws of nature, God was not at all involved in ongoing natural processes or in human affairs. They maintained a notion of God as the source of moral principles, but the most extreme rejected all the rest of positive religion, including the notion of revelation.

Modern theologians who would stay within the Christian fold have found only two strategies for reconciling their accounts of divine action with the Newtonian-Laplacian worldview. Liberal and conservative Protestants divide rather neatly into two camps here. Conservatives take an interventionist approach to divine action—God is sovereign over the laws of nature and is thus able to overrule them to produce special divine acts. Liberals take an immanentist approach, emphasizing God's action in and through all natural processes.

Interventionism

Most conservative theologians hold that in addition to God's creative activity, which includes ordaining the laws of nature, God occasionally violates those very laws in order to bring about extraordinary events. God makes something happen that would not have happened in the ordinary course of nature. According to nineteenth-century theologian Charles Hodge, there are three classes of events when regarded from the perspective of divine action:

> In the first place, there are events . . . due to the ordinary operations of second causes, as upheld and guided by God. To this class belong the common processes of nature; the growth of plants and animals, the orderly movements of the heavenly bodies; and the more unusual occurrences, earthquakes, volcanic eruptions, and violent agitations and revolutions in human societies. In the second place, there are events due to the influences of the Holy Spirit upon the hearts of men, such as regeneration, sanctification, spiritual illumination, etc. Thirdly, there are events which belong to neither of these classes, and whose distinguishing characteristics are, First, that they take place in the external world, *i.e.,* in the sphere of the observation of the senses; and Secondly, that they are produced or caused by the simple volition of God, without the intervention of any subordinate cause. To this class belongs the original act of creation, in which all coöperation of second causes was impossible. To the same class belong all events truly miraculous. A miracle, therefore, may be defined to be an event, in the external world, brought about by the immediate efficiency, or simple volition of God.[3]

In response to the question of how God relates to the laws of nature, Hodge writes:

The answer to that question, as drawn from the Bible is, First, that He is their author. He endowed matter with these forces, and ordained that they should be uniform. Secondly, He is independent of them. He can change, annihilate, or suspend them at pleasure. He can operate with them or without them. "The Reign of Law" must not be made to extend over Him who made the laws. Thirdly, as the stability of the universe, and the welfare, and even the existence of organized creatures, depend on the uniformity of the laws of nature, God never does disregard them except for the accomplishment of some high purpose. He, in the ordinary operations of his Providence, operates with and through the laws which He has ordained. He governs the material, as well as the moral world by law.[4]

So it is a mistake to think that the laws, once "created," are immutable; they merely reflect God's ordinary way of working, and they can be suspended on occasion for some higher purpose. The important point for present purposes is that to assume that an event is an act of God only if it cannot be explained by natural laws is a degenerate view of divine action by Hodge's standards. God works in the regular processes just as much as in miraculous interventions.

Immanentism

The liberals' immanentist view of divine action was a reaction both against Deism, with its view that God is not active at all within the created world, and against the conservative theologians' view that God performs special, miraculous acts. The liberal view emphasizes the universal presence of God in the world, and God's continual, creative, and purposive activity in and through all the processes of nature and history.[5] This view made it possible to understand progress, both evolutionary progress in the natural world and human progress in society, as manifestations of God's purposes.

A primary motive for emphasizing God's action within natural processes was the acceptance of the modern scientific view of the world as a closed system of natural causes, along with the judgment that a view of divine activity as intervention reflected an inferior grasp of God's intelligence and power. That is, in addition to Spinoza's point regarding self-contradiction, it suggested that God was unable to achieve all of the divine purposes though an original ordering; the higher view of divine action is one in which God does not need to intervene. Thus, the interpretation of divine activity in terms of miracles tended to disappear in the liberal tradition.

We find variations on these themes from Friedrich Schleiermacher up through the present. Schleiermacher claimed that divine providence and the operation of causal laws entirely coincide; the word *miracle* is just the religious word for "event." Furthermore, he argued that it can never be in the best interests of religion to interpret an event as a special act of God in opposition to its being a part of the system of nature, since to so interpret it works against the sense of the absolute dependence of the whole upon God.[6]

Contemporary theologian Gordon Kaufman sees the problem of divine action as still critical to theology, saying that unless it can be resolved "we are condemned either to live in an intolerable tension between our religious language and life and the rest of experience . . . or to give up Christian faith and talk as outmoded and no longer relevant to the actual structures of our lives and the world."[7]

Kaufman claims that particular acts of God performed from time to time in history and nature are not just improbable or difficult to believe, but "literally inconceivable."[8] For this reason, if we are to understand the phrase "act of God," we should use it to designate the "master act" in which God is involved, namely, the whole course of history. God's action consists in giving the world its structure and giving history its direction. This concept of divine action provides a "more austere" account of providence than is often found in Christian circles: "This is no God who 'walks with me and talks with me' in close interpersonal communion, giving his full attention to my complaints, miraculously extracting me from difficulties into which I have gotten myself by invading nature and history with *ad hoc* rescue operations from on high."[9] Instead, the paradigm of divine action is the story of a man praying that this cup might pass from him, "that prayer answered not with legions of angels to rescue him but with lonely suffering on a cross"; but this is followed by the birth of faith and hope in a new community after his death.

> The God who works in this fashion to turn the darkest despairs and defeats into further steps toward the realization of his beneficent ultimate objectives, without violently ripping into the fabric of history or arbitrarily upsetting the momentum of its powers, is one who can also be conceived as working within and through the closely textured natural and historical processes of our modern experience: this is a God who acts, a living God, the adequate object for a profound faith, and his action is not completely unintelligible to a mind instructed and informed by modern science and history.[10]

Kaufman's language gives evidence of a measure of scorn for Christians with more robust views of divine action, and also a sense (somewhat surprising for a pacifist) that God's involvement in particular events could only be violent.

I believe that no other single factor has had such thoroughgoing consequences for theology; the divide between liberals and conservatives on this issue opens a veritable chasm between their theological outlooks. It is of fundamental importance in determining their views on theological method and Scripture: immanentism requires an experiential foundation for theology, since scriptural foundationalism is dependent upon an interventionist view of revelation. One's view of revelation in turn affects one's theory of religious language and the positions available regarding the relations between science and religion. For the immanentists, religious language, understood as expression of human religious awareness, is so different in kind from scientific language that there is no possibility of either consonance or conflict between the two. This is often called the two-worlds view of science and religion.

Divine Action and the Creation-Evolution Issue

It is common to think of a spectrum of positions on the relations between creation and evolution—running from none to none! At one end are the six-day creationists, for whom evolution plays no role. Then there are the day-age creationists, progressive creationists, theistic evolutionists and, finally, the two-worlds theorists for whom, again, there is no relation.

The concern of this essay is with PC and TE. PC is the view that much of the development of the universe took place according to natural law but, particularly in the creation of life, God intervened at points along the way. TE is the view that God has created life entirely though the evolutionary process. So defined, these sound like sharply distinct categories, but consider the following thought experiment from Owen Gingrich.

Gingrich asks us to imagine three scenarios for God's involvement in creation, and to make it specific, takes as an example the trilobite *paradoxides*—an interesting case, it being so named because it seemed to have no obvious ancestor in the Cambrian strata. One scenario is that "at one time there was no *paradoxides* and the next moment it was there, like the magician's rabbit pulled from an empty hat. Perhaps *paradoxides* came slithering up out of the mud, full grown, female, and pregnant. . . . The second scenario starts with a creature similar to *Paradoxides*, but with a mechanism that is considerably more detailed. A few cosmic rays zoom through the DNA of the parent creature's germ cells; mutations occur, and its offspring is different. After one, or perhaps a series of steps, a *paradoxides* is born. . . ."[11]

These cosmic rays are sent by God to achieve a definite goal. Gingrich notes that scenarios 1 and 2 are observationally indistinguishable, and both agree with the fossil record. Option 3 is that "God's plan and design for the universe prepares for living beings to arise without further immediate intervention according to preordained rules of order."[12]

Which category listed above fits each of these scenarios? Doesn't scenario 3 represent the two-worlds view? Is this not what Kaufman would say if asked how God created humans? Then is not scenario 2 an instance of theistic evolution—God is creating through the evolutionary process by using and guiding it? This means that scenario 1, the magical appearance, must be what is envisioned by the progressive creationists.

While it might be technically correct to call Kaufman a theistic evolutionist, this would not be sociologically correct; the liberal approach to divine action was intended specifically as a means to opt out of the kind of debate upon which this volume is focused. In fact, Gingrich goes on to attribute scenario 3 to Howard Van Till, a self-avowed theistic evolutionist, and one often criticized by intelligent-design theorists. So they are right that some of the TE advocates have not made their differences from the classical liberal position clear enough. One issue is whether God guides the evolutionary process at all. (If it is entirely guided by God, then this is the position sometimes called evolutionary creationism.) So at issue is whether God guides it subtly or occasionally. But then the question is, How? If by means of interventions, even small ones like Gingrich's cosmic rays, then this is just a less obvious kind of PC.

The ID movement is an instance of PC, and rejection of TE is one of its distinctive characteristics.[13] But I believe that the arguments between TE and PC are at a stalemate. The problem for TE, as already suggested, is that it is an unstable category. If evolution is unguided, the position collapses into immanentism; if guided, it collapses into PC. In the latter case, if it shares the same space on the spectrum as ID, then one wonders what the disagreements are about.

Phillip Johnson concurs that TE "is not easy to define," but he goes on to say that "it involves making an effort to maintain that the natural world is God-governed while avoiding disagreement with the Darwinist establishment on scientific matters."[14] So the real issue is whether one does or does not see defeat of evolutionary explanations as providing evidence for divine (or some other designer's) action.

The opposing of divine action to natural causation, however, is objectionable for both practical and theological reasons. The practical matter is that science will never be at a total loss for explanations. Ironically, this is due in part to the fact that, since the demise of the Newtonian worldview, philosophical accounts of causation have not kept pace with science. It is not clear what answer is to be given today to the question of what it is that causes cause. It is common now to speak of events or states of affairs, rather than objects, as the effects of causes. Suppose we describe an event as a change from one state of affairs (S_1) to another (S_2). Then, is it S_2 or the change from S_1 to S_2

that requires causal explanation? And is S_1 the cause, or merely a necessary condition? Scientific language is not consistent here. When there is a regular connection between states of type 1 and states of type 2, we are inclined to speak of S_1 as the cause of S_2. If there is no such regularity, however, we have two options. The first is always to look for an additional factor to label as the cause. If none can be found, we speak of S_2 as a chance event.

Another complication: it is also possible to treat the laws of nature as the most significant factor in a causal explanation, in which case S_1 is designated as the set of initial conditions. This tendency has been furthered by Carl Hempel's influential nomological account of explanation, wherein a causal explanation takes the form of a law and a set of initial conditions from which the explanandum can be deduced.[15]

So with current physics and cosmology having displaced the simple clockwork model of the universe, we are left without a clear scientific answer to the question of the causal nature of matter. Neither do we seem to have an agreed-upon philosophical analysis of causal concepts. Jaegwon Kim concludes that given the vast diversity in the ways we use causal language "it may be doubted whether there is a unitary concept [of causation] that can be captured in an enlightening philosophical analysis."[16]

With all of these possibilities, a new creation such as a bacterial flagellum would indeed have to pop into existence like Gingrich's *paradoxides* out of a magician's hat; furthermore, it would have to do so under the microscope of a scientist who is intelligent, well educated, evidently honest, in a position of having something to lose if the account proves false, and operating publicly in a well-known part of the world (Hume's criteria for the credibility of a witness) in order to begin to be considered beyond the scope of science.

Much more important, however, is the theological inadequacy of any account of God's relation to the world that opposes divine action to natural causation. John Hedley Brooke, in an account of the development of TE, observes the salutary effect that Darwinism had on subsequent theology, leading to an emphasis on God's continuous participation in nature.[17] In 1889, British theologian Aubrey Moore wrote that "one absolutely impossible conception of God, in the present day, is that which represents him as an occasional visitor. Science has pushed the deist's God further and further away, and at the moment when it seemed as if He would be thrust out all together, Darwinism appeared, and, under the disguise of a foe, did the work of a friend."[18]

So my conclusion is that ID should not be pursued because of its defective understanding of divine action. TE, however, *would* be the ideal position if it could be kept from sliding into either PC or two-worlds thought—either interventionism or immanentism.

New Directions for Divine Action

I have been careful to specify that theologians in the modern era have found only two options for understanding divine action, interventionism versus immanentism. A number of theologians and philosophers, however, claim that the end of modern physics means that new options are open for understanding God's action in the world that splits the difference between intervention and a two-worlds approach. The goal is to give an account of divine action that is noninterventionist and yet still allows for the recognition of some events in the world as specially attributable to God's intentions—noninterventionist special divine action.

These discussions have been ongoing at least since 1953, when Karl Heim noted that, since Laplacean determinism had been overturned by quantum indeterminacy, God could be thought of as acting at the quantum level.[19] Great impetus for the research came from an initiative of the Vatican Observatory, a century-old astronomical research institute. In 1979, Pope John Paul II had called for scholarly study of the relations between science and faith. In response, the Observatory, beginning in 1990, sponsored (along with the Center for Theology and the Natural Sciences in Berkeley) a series of six conferences on divine action in light of recent developments in science.[20]

Three major strategies have been considered. One was Arthur Peacocke's proposal, beginning with the recognition that God is both immanent and transcendent. Thus, God is in the world but, in a sense, the world is in God. He then developed the concept of whole-part constraint, whereby a complex system is capable of affecting the behavior of its parts. By analogy, he argued that the transcendent God is able to affect the behavior of the constituents of creation.[21]

John Polkinghorne has been the main sponsor of the proposal that God works in chaotic systems. These are systems in which future states are highly sensitive to earlier states, and thus can exhibit extreme fluctuations. Because differences that make a difference in these initial conditions are too small to measure, the systems are inherently unpredictable. Polkinghorne goes on to argue that these systems may hint that the universe is not basically deterministic, but instead open and flexible and therefore amenable to noninterventionist divine action.[22]

The third strategy, and the one that has best withstood criticisms, is divine action at the quantum level—quantum divine action (QDA). My own argument begins theologically. If God is present and active in all of creation, then necessarily this includes the smallest, most basic creatures. Tradition holds that God's action includes sustenance, cooperation, and governance. Sustenance and cooperation come easily with an immanentist account; at the quantum level, it is possible to describe governance as well—and without intervention.

Quantum theory, developing since the beginning of the twentieth century, describes a world of the very small in which matter is ambiguously wavelike and particlelike depending on circumstance; in which no definite location and trajectory of a particle can be measured at the same time; in which events happen when they happen only within statistical averages.

I understand QDA as follows: God is immanent in all of the entities and processes at the quantum level, sustaining them in existence. This is the mode of God's sustenance of the entire physical creation. God's cooperation consists in God's participation in all deterministic processes, and in not interfering with the basic natures of the creatures God has made. For example, electrons by nature are negatively charged; God never causes an electron to carry a positive charge. God's governance consists in determining the otherwise indeterminate processes—actualizing one of the potentials of the system in question. This is no violation of natural laws because a statistical law is not, strictly speaking, a law; it is a generalization that does not forbid any particular event.[23]

This provides a very subtle account of God's special divine action, according to which God has chosen to act in the natural world only in such a way that does not override the intrinsic behavior of the various creatures he has made—just as he does not override human freedom. But this subtlety is an advantage of the theory: if God's ordinary way of acting were more like what Cecil B. DeMille imagined, then how to account for the ghastly evils in the world that God has *not* acted dramatically to prevent?

A Stable Account of Theistic Evolution

I believe that Robert Russell is the ablest defender of QDA[24]; in addition, he has used the theory to solve the problem with TE that I have called its instability. In "Special Providence and Genetic Mutation: A New Defense of Theistic Evolution," Russell points out that liberal defenders of TE often end up meaning that God does nothing distinctive in the natural world "since nature does what it does entirely by law." Conservative defenders of TE are willing to speak of interventions but "this often threatens to undercut the conversation with science and minimize their credibility in a scientifically informed culture; at worst, it can move them in the direction of scientific creationism."[25]

Russell's argument first addresses the issue of the interpretation of quantum indeterminacy. From the beginning, there has been a debate about whether the indeterminacy is only a matter of lack of human knowledge or whether it reflects an actual feature of reality. Currently, the latter is the more common interpretation. Russell presents as an example the decay of an atom of uranium. In a sample of uranium, a particular atom may decay into a thorium atom by emitting an alpha particle. The probability of the event can be calculated, but no explanation can be given as to why this particular uranium atom decayed when it did and why its neighbors did not. Russell follows Werner Heisenberg's interpretation of the nature of quantum phenomena, which has the following consequences:

> We can characterize a quantum system in terms of potentialities and actualities. The system starts off in a superposition of "coexistent potentialities": a variety of distinct states are simultaneously possible for the system, but none of them are fully actual. Suddenly one of them becomes realized or actual at a specific moment in time, though we cannot attribute the process of actualization to interaction with other processes. The uranium atom moment by moment comes to be what it has been, uranium, and then it comes to be something else, something which it could always have been, thorium.[26]

The consequence for divine action is that nature is "genuinely open to God's participation in the bringing to actuality of each state of nature in time."[27]

The next step of Russell's argument is to specify the role of quantum phenomena in the evolutionary process. Evolution proceeds by means of variation and selection. The variation that matters is that which occurs in the hereditary material, which can be passed on to future generations. Variation, in turn, is a product of mutation and sexual reproduction. Mutations in DNA involve either point mutations, that is, changes of one or a few pairs of the nucleotides making up the genetic code of one gene, or chromosomal mutations that change the number or arrangement of genes on a chromosome.

While earlier authors (such as Heim) have noted generally that QDA might offer an account of God's action in the evolutionary process, Russell carefully catalogues the sorts of mutations that are known to involve quantum, as opposed to classical (deterministic), processes, as well as a list of still-open questions. The known sources of mutations involving quantum effects are "point mutations, including base-pair substitutions, insertions, deletions; spontaneous mutations, including errors during DNA replication, repair, recombination; radiative physical mutagens (including x-rays and ultraviolet light); and crossing over."[28] Note that the inclusion of radiative physical mutagens provides a fourth category of cause for *paradoxides*: not God sending in (intervening with) cosmic rays to produce mutations, but God immanent in the quantum mechanical processes during the interaction of cosmic rays and DNA, thereby directing these processes to their intended goal. Such divine action is noninterventionist because, following Heisenberg's interpretation, there is no sufficient natural cause for these quantum processes.

The conclusion of Russell's argument is that God can be understood theologically as acting within the process of evolution without disrupting the process or violating any laws of nature. Indeed, it is these very (quantum) laws that point to the insufficiency of natural causality (ontological indeterminism). God's special action results in specific, intentional consequences, different from what would have otherwise resulted. Yet, because of the irreducibly statistical character of quantum physics, these results would be entirely consistent with science,[29] and (my point) these would be invisible to science *qua* science.

Conclusion

I endorse Russell's emphasis on the importance of this theory in synthesizing the strengths of both liberal and conservative approaches to divine action, especially in the evolution debates. It answers the ID theorists' legitimate criticism of TE as often paying only lip service to divine creation. At the same time, it explains why ID goes astray in opposing divine action to science. I hope that Russell's and related work might serve as a happy meeting place for all Christians who believe that the Creator is still at work in the wonderful world of nature.

10

The Universe as Creation

John Polkinghorne

Scientists are motivated by the desire to understand what is happening in the world. Their quest has been remarkably successful, extending its scope far beyond those everyday processes whose comprehension might plausibly be explained by evolutionary necessity having shaped our brains to be apt for this purpose.[1] Science helps us understand the realm of subatomic physics and the nature of cosmic space-time, regimes remote from direct impact upon us and with a character whose understanding calls for modes of thought quite different from those required to cope with mundane necessity. Yet science's success has been purchased by the modesty of its explanatory ambition. It does not attempt to ask and answer every question that one might legitimately raise. Instead, it confines itself to investigating natural processes, attending to the question of how things happen. Other questions, such as those relating to meaning and purpose, are deliberately bracketed out. This scientific stance is taken simply as a methodological strategy, with no implication that those other questions, of what one might call a why kind, are not fully meaningful and necessary to ask if complete understanding is to be attained.

Yet, even in relation to its own self-limited field of enquiry, science cannot function as a wholly freestanding discipline, capable of answering fully its how kind of questions. Considering causal issues illustrates this point. The consideration of causality is certainly constrained by what science has to say, but the outcome of that discussion is not fully determined by science alone. Understanding the nature of causality calls also for acts of metaphysical decision. Quantum theory makes the point clearly enough.[2] The quantum world is necessarily characterized by the presence of intrinsic unpredictabilities, and epistemic access to it is restricted by Heisenberg's uncertainty principle. So much physics can say. But do these facts arise from an unavoidable ignorance of certain fine details relating to a physical reality whose underlying nature is actually fully deterministic, or are they signs of the intrinsically indeterministic character of the quantum world? It turns out that either answer is compatible with the empirical evidence that physics can offer. While most physicists follow Niels Bohr in giving the second answer, there is an ingenious theory due to David Bohm[3] that demonstrates that the first answer is also a possibility. The choice between these two options cannot be made on purely scientific grounds, but appeal has to be made to metascientific criteria, such as judgments of economy, elegance, and naturalness (the absence of contrivance).

Those who have a thirst for understanding will not find it quenched by science alone. While many scientists exhibit a kind of professional distrust of the notion of metaphysics, the truth is that no one can do without a wider view than the strictly scientific. The scientistic reductionist who proclaims that scientific knowledge is all we have, or need to have, is making a statement that has not been derived from science itself, properly understood. Human beings think metaphysics as naturally and as unavoidably as we speak prose.

Nothing comes of nothing, and any metaphysical scheme must rest on an underived and unexplained basis, which then serves as the foundation for subsequent explanatory development. In the Western tradition there have been two fundamentally distinct kinds of metaphysical starting points. One takes as its basic brute fact the existence of the material world, treating the laws of nature as the given basis for all further explanation. David Hume was a notable proponent of this kind of materialistic metaphysics. The other approach takes the brute fact of a self-subsistent divine agent as its basic foundation, seeing the world as being ordered according to that agent's will and its history as expressive of that agent's purpose. Theism is the metaphysical stance that seeks to understand the universe in terms of its being a divine creation.

Arguments for and against these two great explanatory traditions have raged for many centuries. Recently a new kind of defense of the theistic position has been proposed—or perhaps one might better say an old kind of defense has reappeared dressed in novel intellectual clothing. Under the rubric of ID, this new movement claims to be able to discern scientific aspects of our knowledge of the living world whose existence cannot be understood without appeal to the direct action of a designing intelligence at work within the course of history. While the proponents of this view are very discrete about saying anything definite concerning the nature of this active intelligence—it is a tactic of their discourse to eschew the use of words such as *God* or *Creator*—it seems pretty clear that the underlying agenda of the ID movement is to offer a particular kind of tacit defense of theistic metaphysics. Before attempting to evaluate this approach, it is necessary to make a preliminary survey of the scientific and theological contexts within which it has to be considered.

Science

We have seen that physics does not determine metaphysics, but it certainly constrains it, rather as the foundations of a house do not determine the edifice that will be erected on them, but they do constrain its possible form. Five aspects of science's view of reality are particularly relevant to the present discussion.

1. *Fragmentary Accounts.* Physics proceeds by the detailed investigation of particular domains: subatomic physics, condensed matter physics, continuum mechanics, and so on. Within each domain, considerable understanding can be gained of the processes involved, but the relationships between the different domains are often far from being properly understood. To be perfectly frank, physics' contribution to an account of the causal nexus of the world is distinctly patchy.[4]

A striking example of the fragmentary nature of physical understanding is provided by the perplexities that are still unresolved concerning how quantum physics and classical physics should be thought to relate to each other. This problem remains challenging even after eighty years of highly successful calculational achievement. We know how to do the sums, but we do not fully understand what is happening. The most notorious difficulty relates to the measurement problem. Quantum physics is based on the superposition principle, permitting the combination of states that Newtonian thinking, or common sense, would say were strictly immiscible. An electron can be in a state that is a mixture of being here and being there. Not only does this possibility reflect the unpicturable strangeness of the quantum world, but it also relates to the probabilistic nature of quantum physics. If the position of an electron in such a superposed state is actually measured, sometimes the result will be here and sometimes it will be there. The formalism enables one to calculate with impressive accuracy the relative probabilities of obtaining these two answers, but there is no widely agreed upon and satisfactory theoretical explanation of why a particular result is found on a particular occasion. This scientific aporia is the measurement problem. In other words, it is embarrassing for a physicist to have to confess that he or she does not understand how the cloudy quantum world and the clear classical world are joined to each other by the bridge of measurement. As a result, there is a yawning gap in physics' account of causal structure.

A second example of patchiness is the failure to combine quantum theory and chaos theory in a coherent manner. Chaotic systems possess such exquisite sensitivity to the smallest detail of their circumstances that prediction of future behavior would soon require a degree of accurate knowledge that Heisenberg uncertainty forbids. This implies that there should be an intertwining of quantum theory and chaos theory but, in fact, the two formalisms as they now stand are incompatible with each other. Quantum theory has a scale, given by Planck's constant, but the fractal character of chaotic dynamics means that it is scale-free, having the same characteristics whatever size is sampled. The two just do not fit together.

Physics is unable to offer a seamless account of what is going on in the world. It is clear that it has failed to establish the causal closure of the universe on its own physicalist terms.

2. *Unpredictability.* Twentieth-century science discovered the existence of intrinsic unpredictabilities in physical process. They first came to light at the subatomic level of quantum physics, and then later more were discovered at the macroscopic level of chaos theory. It is important to give full weight to the word *intrinsic.* We are not referring to situations where better measurement techniques, or more powerful means of calculation, could remove the unpredictabilities. Unpredictability is an epistemological property, referring to what we can or cannot know about future behavior. There is no logically necessary link between epistemology and ontology (what is actually the case). As we have seen already in the case of Heisenberg uncertainty, a metaphysical decision is required concerning what kind of ontological interpretation to espouse (determinism or indeterminism?). It is a perfectly coherent and acceptable strategy to interpret physical unpredictabilities as signals of the presence of a causal openness, permitting the operation of causal influences over and above those resulting from the exchange of energy between constituents that has been the traditional story told by science. An obvious candidate for such an additional causal principle would be the willed acts of intentional human agents. Another possibility would be divine providential action, continuously operating within the open grain of nature.[5] An honest science is not in the position to forbid either of these possibilities.

3. *Relationality.* Newtonian thinking thought of physical process in terms of the collisions of particles moving in the container of absolute space and in the course of the unfolding of absolute time. The twentieth century replaced

this picture with something altogether more intrinsically relational; Einstein's theory of general relativity combined space, time, and matter in a single integrated account. Matter curves space-time, and the curvature of space-time influences the paths of matter. In the quantum world, once two particles have interacted, they remain mutually entangled, effectively becoming a single system so that, however far they separate, acting on one will produce an immediate effect on the other. (This is the celebrated "EPR effect.") Even the subatomic world, it appears, cannot be treated atomistically.

4. *Evolving and Emergent Complexity.* The universe 13.7 billion years ago was just a small, almost uniform, expanding ball of energy. Today it is a vast cosmos, populated by rich and diverse structures. That ball of energy has become the home of saints and scientists. The processes that have brought about this astonishingly fruitful transformation have been evolutionary in character, whether one is considering early cosmic history, in the course of which the universe became lumpy and grainy with stars and galaxies, or the 3.5-billion-year story of the development of life on earth. Evolutionary process is the result of the fertile interplay of two contrasting tendencies that one may label "Chance" and "Necessity." Necessity stands for the lawful regularity of the world. Chance stands for contingent particularity, the happenstance that this occurs rather than that. The range of possible events is so vast that even in 13.7 billion years only a small fraction of what might have happened has actually happened. Many illustrations could be given of the symbiotic interplay of these two tendencies.

Science has learned to recognize that true novelty can only emerge in regimes that may be said to be at the edge of chaos, a realm where order and contingency interlace to constitute the domain of chance and necessity. Pure necessity would correspond to a world too rigid in its nature to permit anything really new to emerge. Pure chance would correspond to a world too haphazard in its nature to allow anything really new to persist. Without a degree of genetic mutation, there would be no new forms of life. Without a degree of stable genetic transfer between the generations, there would be no metastable species established on which the sifting process of natural selection could operate.

The powerful fertility of the universe is made apparent by the punctuated emergence of wholly new forms of complexity, whose natures were unforseeable in terms of what had preceded them: life from inanimate matter; consciousness from life; human self-consciousness (the very means by which the universe became aware of itself, thereby making science an eventual possibility).[6] However, it is not clear that conventional evolutionary thinking is the complete scientific account of how this has come about. It is just becoming possible to study the behavior of moderately complex systems, treated in their entirety rather than being decomposed into constituent parts. Presently, most of this work is at the natural-history stage of simply looking at specific instances, often computer-generated models. However, it is already clear that complex systems frequently manifest astonishing powers of spontaneous self-organization, resulting in the generation of novel patterns of structure and behavior. It is entirely conceivable that the emergence of novelty is partly influenced by holistic pattern-forming laws of nature, of a kind not previously considered by science and as yet far from being fully understood.[7]

5. *Fine-tuned Potentiality.* Much discussion of evolutionary significance has concentrated on the chance half of the duality, but necessity should not be taken as being in any lesser degree significant. A surprising development in scientific understanding has been the recognition that lawful regularity had to take a very specific, quantitatively precise form, if it were to be possible for carbon-based life to evolve anywhere at all in the course of cosmic history. A universe capable of being the home of life is a very special kind of universe indeed. While life only seems to have developed after about ten billion years of cosmic history, our universe was pregnant with this possibility from the big bang onward, in the sense that its given physical fabric had just the right character to permit this to happen. The collection of scientific insights that led to this remarkable and unanticipated conclusion has been given the name of the Anthropic Principle.[8] One example must suffice to indicate the kind of thinking that underlies it.

Because the very early universe is very simple, it only produces very simple consequences. The only chemical elements it can generate are the two simplest, hydrogen and helium. For life, one needs much more diversity of chemical resources. In particular, one needs carbon, whose capacity to generate long chain molecules lies at the basis of all living beings. There is only one place in the whole universe where carbon can be made: in the interior nuclear furnaces of the stars. We are people of stardust, made out of the ashes of dead stars. The person who first understood this process was Fred Hoyle. In a moment of great insight, he saw that stellar carbon production was just possible, in a beautiful and delicate way, because there was an enhancement effect (a resonance, as we say) at just the right energy to permit what would otherwise have been a forbidden process. Hoyle also realized that if the nuclear forces had been only slightly different, there would have been no suitable resonance and so no carbon-based life. Despite a lifelong commitment to atheism, he is reported to have said that the universe is a "put-up job." In other words, Hoyle could not believe that the existence of carbon was just a happy accident. Because he did not care for the word *God*, he said there must be some intelligence that had fixed the laws of nature to make it so. We could say that Hoyle felt he had perceived intelligent design present in the fabric of the world. This would, of course, be quite different from the ID movement's claim to discern a different kind of intelligent design, present in the actual detailed structures of some living beings. The former relates to the rules of the cosmic game; the latter refers to specific moves in that game.

Theology

The foregoing discussion has concentrated on scientific insights concerning which there would be widespread agreement in the competent community. But full understanding of the implications of these remarkable discoveries requires locating them in the deeper context of intelligibility afforded by an overarching metaphysical point of view. We have already noted that there will be no logical inevitability or necessary uniqueness about such a move and, consequently, there will not be universal agreement about which metascientific scheme to adopt. The thesis of this essay is that seeing the universe as a divine creation provides the most intellectually satisfying context of understanding. Exploring that claim requires identifying some of the resources of insight that theism can offer. Three concepts are of particular relevance.

1. *Creation.* To see the world as creation is to believe that the mind of God lies behind its marvelous order and the will of God behind its fruitful history. The astonishing power of the human mind to understand the deep structures of the world—the very fact that has made science possible, but which science itself is unable to explain—can be rendered intelligible by the ancient belief that humans are made in the image of God (Gen. 1:26-27). The rational beauty disclosed in fundamental physics, which affords scientists the reward of wonder as a recompense for all the labor of their research, is not then seen as some happy accident, but it is recognized as a true reflection of the mind of the Creator, encountered through the marvelously ordered fabric of creation. The anthropic fine-tuning of that fabric, which has been necessary to enable the astonishing fertility of cosmic and terrestrial history, is understood from a theistic point of view to be the endowment given by the Creator to enable creation to fulfill the divinely willed purpose of its creative history.

These insights all refer to aspects of the laws of nature that a materialistic metaphysics would have to treat as mere brute fact, but whose significant character seems to call for an explanation if the thirst for understanding is truly to be quenched. To see the universe as creation is to discern intelligent design built into its physical fabric. In this perspective God is not pictured as the great Artificer, contriving ingenious and particular structures, but as the grand Ordainer of inherent potentiality and order without which the world would be a chaos rather than a cosmos. This understanding meets Hume's criticism of the physico-theologians of the eighteenth century, people like John Ray and William Paley, whose appeal to the functional aptness of living beings was an argument at the level of organisms similar to the arguments now being made by the ID movement at the level of molecular mechanisms. Hume said that the picture of God offered by the physico-theologians was too anthropomorphic, treating the act of creation as if it were comparable to a carpenter making a ship. But bringing into existence a world endowed with inherent potentiality is quite different from manipulating existing material in order to produce new forms. In Hebrew terminology, the former is *bara* (a distinctive word used only of divine creativity) rather than *'asah* (the ordinary word for any form of making).

2. *Kenosis.* Christian theology understands love to be the nature of God. In consequence, it can neither picture the Creator as an indifferent deistic Spectator, who having set it all going just lets it all happen, nor as the cosmic Puppet Master pulling every string in the theatre of creation. The gift of love must always include some due degree of independence granted to the object of love. Recognizing this has led many contemporary theologians to understand the act of creation to be an act of creatorly kenosis, involving a divine self-limitation in order to permit the created other truly to be itself and, indeed, to make itself.[9]

The thought of creaturely self-making (as old as Charles Kingsley's initial response to the publication of the *Origin of Species*) is the theological way to interpret evolution, seen as the shuffling explorations of chance by which the divinely given potentiality of the universe is brought to specifically realized actuality. It can be claimed that a world of that kind of evolving fruitfulness is a greater good than a ready-made creation would have been. Yet that goodness has a necessary cost. There is an inevitable shadow side to evolutionary process, as contingent exploration results not only in new kinds of fruitfulness, but it also leads to ragged edges and blind alleys. In an evolving world, the death of one generation is the necessary cost of the new life of the next. We know that biological evolution has been driven by genetic mutation, but if germ cells are to be able to mutate and produce new forms of life, then somatic cells will also, by the same process, be able to mutate and sometimes they will then become malignant. Some help is offered here to theology as it struggles with the deep perplexities of theodicy. The anguishing fact of cancer is not something gratuitous, as if a Creator who was a bit more competent or a bit less callous could easily have eliminated it. It is the necessary cost of creation in which creatures are allowed to make themselves.

3. *Providence.* We have seen that an honest evaluation of science's actual knowledge of the causal nexus of the world is compatible with understanding its process to be more subtle and more supple than the picture of creation

as a gigantic piece of cosmic clockwork. There are no adequate scientific grounds requiring us to exclude a metaphysics of agency, including the possibility of divine providential interaction in the course of unfolding history.[10] The idea of a universe of becoming, open to its future, permits an understanding of divine providence as operating within the open grain of created nature, rather than as acting against that nature, whose character, after all, is itself an expression of the Creator's will. It was suggested earlier that the locus of the necessary causal flexibility might lie in those cloudy domains of intrinsic unpredictability that have been discovered by science. If that is the case, it follows that the process of the world cannot be taken apart and exhaustively itemized, as if one could assert that nature did this, human will did that, and divine providence did the third thing. There is intrinsic entanglement. Acts of providence may be discernible by faith, but they will never be demonstrable by experiment.

What, then, about miracles? Christianity has to face the issue, since at the heart of its belief is the resurrection of Christ, and no one could pretend that a man rising from death to a transformed life of unending glory came about through clever exploitation of quantum or chaotic unpredictabilities. Here there must have been a direct act of God of a completely unprecedented kind. Since science is concerned with what usually happens, it cannot logically forbid the possibility of unique occurrences. Yet theology itself forbids thinking of God as a kind of whimsical celestial conjurer, doing an occasional trick just to astonish people. If unprecedented events like miracles actually happen, it can only be because unprecedented circumstances have made that a possibility, which is consonant with the consistency of divine will.[11] If Jesus was the incarnate Son of God, as Christians believe, then his resurrection can indeed be seen as a consistent form of divine action, and also understood as the signal and seal within history of what God intends to do for all humanity beyond history (1 Cor. 15:22). This approach to the question of miracles sees them as events that open windows onto deep levels of the divine nature, affording more profound insight than is revealed by everyday experience. It corresponds to ways in which John's Gospel calls them signs.

Intelligent Design

The concept of providence just proposed is one that pictures God as ceaselessly interacting with creation by means of continuous action taking place within the divinely ordained open grain of nature. Special divine acts in special circumstances of revelational disclosure are not excluded, but the expectation is that these acts will be comparatively rare and that they will occur for highly significant reasons. If the purpose of miracles is truly to be signs of deep significance, they will not be rashly and prodigally scattered throughout history. In fact, consideration of the biblical miracle stories shows that they concentrate around times of particular importance in salvation history: the exodus, the dawn of prophecy in Israel, the life of Jesus Christ, and the foundation of the church.

Although the carefully chosen language of the ID movement recoils from using the word *miracle*, its picture of the developing history of life carries the clear implication that it is seeded with numerous miraculous interventions, discontinuous acts in which new entities are specially created. How else could one suppose complex designed systems to have sprung into being, other than through a direct act of intervention by an intelligent designing agent? And to be perfectly frank, what credible designing agent could there be other than God? One has to ask what evidence could be offered to support this extremely strong claim.

William Dembski set out to discuss what would be the kind of evidence that could be held to point in a logically persuasive manner to the presence of intelligent design.[12] His key concept is what he calls the *complexity-specification criterion*. Three elements are identified as necessary for the satisfaction of the criterion: contingency, complexity, and specification. *Contingency* means that the entity is not something that was bound to be formed through processes of inexorable necessity. When using a personal computer, if you click on "print," the resulting text will inevitably correspond to the words that were already on the screen. Whatever intelligence went into the original composition, no further intelligence was involved making an automatic copy. *Complexity* means that the entity is not so simple that its formation by mere chance is perfectly likely. If you type four letters at random, occasionally they will correspond to an English word and this is sufficiently likely that, when it does happen, no great significance attaches to the event. However, if you type a hundred letters at random and find that they can be split up into a sequence of English words, one may rightly think that this occurrence calls for some further explanation. *Specification* is the most elusive of the conditions to define. It requires the presence of a pattern whose character is such as naturally to suggest a role for intelligence in its formation. If those hundred letters are found to correspond to the words of a Shakespearean sonnet, then surely something is going on of a highly significant kind. A problem with the specification condition lies in the identification of the presence of significance. If the hundred letters formed the translation of the sonnet into Urdu, that would also be a significant fact, but one that would be likely to be overlooked by a monoglot English speaker.

It seems reasonable to agree that an act of intelligent design would be expected in some way to fulfill the complexity-specification criterion. What is much more controversial is the assertion that fulfilling that criterion is a sufficient condition for establishing intelligent design. After all, the Darwinian thesis of natural selection specifically suggests a way in which the winnowing effects of environmental sifting and preservation, continuously operating on small random differences and accumulating over long periods of time, can bring about consequences for the adaptation of living entities to their environments that are contingent and complex, and which can be considered to fulfill specification, not in a preset sense, but in the sense that the results are functionally effective to a high degree. It was precisely the ability of evolutionary thinking to explain the appearance of design without needing to invoke the direct intervention of a designer that subverted the arguments of the physico-theologians. On both sides of the argument, however, more is needed than highly generalized argument. What will be persuasive is the careful investigation of particular cases.

Here, the ID theorists turn to a concept that has been discussed extensively by Michael Behe. It is the idea of irreducible complexity, which Behe defines as meaning "a single system composed of several well-matched, interacting parts that contribute to the basic function, wherein the removal of one of the parts causes the system to effectively cease functioning."[13] It is clear that the evolution of such a system, at least if treated as being isolated, could not be explained by the Darwinian notion of gradual incremental development, at each stage of which some further degree of survival efficiency is supposed to be gained. Behe believes that he can identify several such irreducibly complex systems. One of his favorite examples is provided by the cilia that enable organelles to swim. This argument is the molecular counterpart of the difficulties raised soon after the publication of the *Origin of Species*, concerning how complex organs such as the eye could have evolved. Darwin himself was troubled about this, though later thinking has been able to propose plausible evolutionary pathways, and the fact that eyes have developed several times independently in the course of evolutionary history is suggestive that there is not a real problem. Are matters at the molecular level really that different?

I do not think that Behe has established the irrefutable existence of irreducible complexity. It is not sufficient to consider a single system as if it were simply an isolated system. Evolutionary process is entangled in complex ways, and it is characterized by the improvising cooption of subsystems, developed for one purpose and then appropriated for an entirely different purpose. It would be very difficult to prove that there was no pathway by which what was claimed to be an irreducibly complex structure could have evolved, just as it would be difficult to establish for certain the actual route of its evolutionary development. At the present stage, an open verdict is the utmost that might be claimed. Yet, since the ID claim is of such potential significance, the burden of proof must surely rest with those who assert it. I do not think that burden has been discharged.

If irreducible complexity could be established, it would be a *scientific* achievement of substantial magnitude. In fact, one might think it to be a discovery of Nobel caliber. The frequent criticism made of the ID movement—that it is not at all scientific because its proponents perform no experiments—is unfair. Historical-observational sciences do not have ready access to direct experimental verification. Their argument must depend upon proposing the best explanation of a complex set of processes, whose details are only fragmentarily known. Darwin's account in the *Origin* has just that character. The ID people are asking an important scientific question. The trouble is that they do not as yet know the answer.

A significant criticism of ID is that its covert theological program is based on a mistaken strategy. The God who is the ordainer of nature can be understood to act as much through the processes of nature as in any other way. There is no distinction that has to be enforced between natural explanation and the work of the Creator. God's will is as much expressed in the evolutionary process that results in the continuous exploration of potentiality as in any supposed events of direct divine intervention. God is present both in the chance and in the necessity of creation.

Theistic Evolution

The latter way is exactly how theistic evolution interprets the doctrine of creation. The anthropically fine-tuned necessity of the universe is seen as a manifestation of the will of its Creator, while divine providence is believed to be at work within the contingencies of cosmic history, according to the picture already given of continuous providential action operating within the open grain of nature. To use a musical metaphor employed by Arthur Peacocke,[14] the fugue of creation is not the performance of a fixed score already written in eternity, but it is a grand unfolding improvisation in which Creator and creatures both participate. This collaborative process is made possible by the Creator's kenotic love for creation, according to which creatures are allowed to be themselves and to make themselves. The grand fugue of creation will come to its final resolution, for it is an entirely coherent belief that God will achieve determinate purposes along contingent paths.[15] Meanwhile, the present counterpoint accords with the intentions that the divine Musician has for the shape of its development, even if there is significant creaturely influence on the harmonic details. It was not decreed from all eternity that *homo sapiens* should appear in our contingent five-fingered specificity, but the emergence of self-conscious beings able to know and worship their Creator was ordained by the divine will.

The balance struck between creatorly guidance and creaturely independence is a delicate matter, not open to clear specification. This is a familiar theological problem, for it is simply the issue of grace and free will, now written cosmically large. We have seen already that acknowledging the independence granted to creatures offers theology some help in its wrestling with the perplexities of disease and disaster. God does not directly will either a murder or an earthquake, but both are allowed to happen in a creation that is something more subtle and flexible than a divine puppet theater. The concept of theistic evolution also helps us understand the apparent imperfections of design observed in evolved beings. Vestigial organs such as the human appendix, serving no currently useful purpose, are simply leftovers from earlier functional necessities, rather than otiose features of an imperfect design. Anyone who has suffered from back pain will be aware that the human skeleton is not perfectly intelligently designed for bipedal motion.

An irritating feature of some contemporary religious discourse is the way in which important words have been hijacked in an attempt to make them the private property of a minority. Like other theists, I am a creationist in the true sense of believing that the divine will is the source of the universe's being and the divine purpose is expressed in its history, but I am certainly not a "creationist" in the curious North American sense of believing in a flat-footed literal interpretation of the first two chapters of Genesis. I believe also in intelligent design, built into the physical fabric of the world and finding its emergent expression through processes that are guided, but not solely determined, by God, but I do not believe that the Creator has chosen to act by episodic acts of direct intervention, as if the great act of creation needed continual reconstructive tinkering in its details.

11

Intelligent Design

Some Critical Reflections on the Current Debate

John C. Lennox

The intelligent design debate is part of a wider discussion about the relationship of science to religion that is often felt to be one of deep hostility and antagonism as, for instance, encapsulated by Richard Dawkins's recent popular book *The God Delusion*.[1] The inadequacy of this conflict thesis is reflected in the equally recent book *The Language of God*[2] by Francis Collins, director of the Human Genome Project, and has been admirably documented by John Brooke.[3] Indeed, the fact that there are eminent scientists who believe in God and eminent scientists who do not shows that the real conflict is not between science and religion at all but between the diametrically opposed worldviews of materialism and theism, and there are scientists on both sides.[4] The central issue at stake, therefore, is which worldview is supported by science? It is in that context that I wish to reflect on the matter of intelligent design.

At a 2006 discussion in Oxford, I asked a group of scientists and theologians whether it was legitimate to look for scientific evidence of the involvement of intelligence in the origin of the universe and in its laws of operation. The response was overwhelmingly positive. However, protest was elicited when it was suggested that this question lay behind the notion of intelligent design. The ensuing discussion revealed that now ID is freighted with very different connotations, namely, that of a stealth creationism that concentrates solely on attacking evolutionary biology and is antiscience in spirit.[5]

This semantic shift spawns unfortunate consequences. It obscures the long and distinguished philosophical and theological pedigree of the idea of intelligent causation. It fails to do justice to the divergence of scholarly interpretations of the Genesis account, even among those who ascribe final authority to the biblical record, and shifts the focus away from the fact of creation to the timing of creation. Finally, concentration on evolutionary biology alone can lead to failure to take account of wider evidence for intelligent causation from other sciences such as physics and cosmology and, importantly, from the philosophy of science.

It may be helpful to distinguish between a broader theory of intelligent design that deals with that wider evidence and a narrower theory that concentres on biology. For example, William Dembski says, "Intelligent design is the field of study that investigates signs of intelligence. It identifies those features of objects that reliably signal the action of an intelligent cause"[6] (the broader perspective) whereas Dembski and Michael Ruse define intelligent design as "the hypothesis that in order to explain life it is necessary to suppose the action of an unevolved intelligence"[7] (the narrower perspective).

The term *intelligent design* is intended to separate the recognition of design from the identification of the designer with a view to regarding the first issue as falling within the remit of science. However, this attempt can be misunderstood in that highlighting the first issue has led to accusations of avoiding the second in order to conceal a theistic or even a creationist agenda. Now it is, of course, difficult to think of design at the big-picture level of the universe and life without thinking of God as the putative designer and many if not most of those people espousing intelligent design are theists. Perhaps it would be best if worldview commitments, since we all have them,[8] were made explicit so that we could then concentrate on the arguments themselves and avoid the all-too-common genetic fallacy: "you believe X only because you are a Y."

The other danger of too forced a separation between the recognition of design and the identification of the designer is the inadvertent communication of the erroneous impression that the former question is strictly scientific whereas the latter, not being strictly scientific, is nonrational and the sciences (of whatever kind) can contribute nothing to it.[9]

Nevertheless, it is surely clear that the two questions are logically separate. If the first Earth visitors to Mars were to see a sequence of thousands of piles of titanium cubes where each pile contained a prime number of cubes and the piles were arranged in ascending order—2, 3, 5, 7, 11, 13, 17, 19, and so forth—they might well conclude that intelligent life had been there before them but they would not be able to say anything about the identity of the intelligence involved.[10] SETI raises the same issue and is discussed in detail in Dembski's *The Design Inference*.[11]

Is ID Science?

This question can be somewhat misleading. Consider the parallel questions: Is theism science? Is atheism science? Most people would probably give a negative answer to both. But if we interpret the question as: Is there any scientific evidence for theism or atheism, then the answer might well be positive. For instance, E. O. Wilson holds that "scientific humanism" is "the only worldview compatible with science's growing knowledge of the real world and the laws of nature."[12] Incidentally, atheists of his persuasion can scarcely object to Christians using science to support the New Testament claim that there is evidence of God in the created universe.[13] We deal below with the related question as to whether ID is science in the sense of making testable predictions.

Why Is ID Perceived to Be Antiscience?

For context we need to consider design arguments in general. They come in two levels. Level I consists of arguments that the scientific laws by which the universe operates are designed (in the sense that they are the result of intelligent input) and the phenomena of the universe are the evidence of their fruitfulness. Level II consists of arguments that the phenomena themselves involve direct input from a designing intelligence rather than emerging as a consequence of the (designed) laws.

The arguments at each level fall into two types: Type I are arguments from the history, philosophy, and methodology of science; and Type II are arguments from the detailed results of the sciences—cosmology, physics, biology.

Crucial for our understanding of the ID debate is the observation that Type II arguments split into two very different kinds. Type IIA are arguments that flow from an acceptance of mainstream science; and Type IIB are arguments that involve challenging mainstream science. Obviously IIB arguments are much more controversial than IIA arguments and inevitably attract more (media) attention.

Now, Type IIB arguments are not unimportant—indeed, science in general is kept healthy and advances as a result of being challenged, sometimes even resulting in a paradigm shift that leads to great advance (Galileo's questioning of Aristotle and Wegener's work on plate tectonics, to give but two examples). It is understandable, however, that arguments of Type IIB are not likely to be taken seriously unless they are supported (and preceded) by other arguments of Types I and IIA.

Type I Arguments: The History, Philosophy, and Methodology of Science

At the heart of all science lies the conviction that the universe is rationally intelligible. For Albert Einstein this was something to be wondered at:

> You find it strange that I consider the comprehensibility of the world . . . as a miracle or as an eternal mystery. Well, a priori, one should expect a chaotic world, which cannot be grasped by the mind in any way . . . the kind of order created by Newton's theory of gravitation, for example, is wholly different. Even if man proposes the axioms of the theory, the success of such a project presupposes a high degree of ordering of the objective world, and this could not be expected a priori. That is the "miracle" which is being constantly reinforced as our knowledge expands.[14]

Sir Roger Penrose, whose understanding of the depth and subtlety of the relationship between physics and mathematics is unquestioned, writes:

> It is hard for me to believe . . . that such SUPERB theories could have arisen merely by some random natural selection of ideas leaving only the good ones as survivors. The good ones are simply much too good to be the survivors of ideas that have arisen in a random way. There must be, instead, some deep underlying reason for the accord between mathematics and physics.[15]

Now science itself cannot account for this resonance. "Science does not explain the mathematical intelligibility of the physical world, for it is part of science's founding faith that this is so."[16] What does account for it? Our answer will depend not so much on whether we are scientists or not, but on our worldview. From a theistic perspective, the rational intelligibility of the universe makes perfect sense in light of the rationality of God the Creator. Indeed, it would seem that this was the driving force behind the rise of science. Melvin Calvin, Nobel Prize-winner in biochemistry, writes:

> As I try to discern the origin of that conviction [that the universe is orderly], I seem to find it in a basic notion discovered 2000 or 3000 years ago, and enunciated first in the Western world by the ancient Hebrews: namely that the universe is governed by a single God, and

is not the product of the whims of many gods, each governing his own province according to his own laws. This monotheistic view seems to be the historical foundation for modern science.[17]

More recently, Peter Harrison has made a strong case that a dominant feature in the rise of modern science was the Protestant attitude to the interpretation of biblical texts, which spelled an end to the symbolic approach of the Middle Ages.[18] We are not, of course, suggesting that there never has been religious antagonism to science. T. F. Torrance points out that the development of science was often "seriously hindered by the Christian church even when within it the beginnings of modern ideas were taking their rise." He nevertheless supports Melvin Calvin: "In spite of the unfortunate tension that has so often cropped up between the advance of scientific theories and traditional habits of thought in the Church, theology can still claim to have mothered throughout long centuries the basic beliefs and impulses which have given rise especially to modern empirical science, if only through its unflagging faith in the reliability of God the Creator and in the ultimate intelligibility of his creation."[19]

It is sometimes claimed that notions of intelligent design fail to be scientific because they make no testable predictions. But this is surely as far from the truth as it could be if one of the major impulses behind the rise of science is the confirmation of a prediction, based on biblical texts, of the rational intelligibility of the universe. Putting it a different way, Richard Swinburne writes: "Note that I am not postulating a 'God of the gaps', a god merely to explain the things that science has not yet explained. I am postulating a God to explain why science explains; I do not deny that science explains, but I postulate God to explain why science explains. The very success of science in showing us how deeply ordered the natural world is provides strong grounds for believing that there is an even deeper cause for that order."[20]

The Reductionist Alternative

The alternative, indeed, the only possible option under atheistic assumptions, is ultimately to ascribe the rational intelligibility of the universe to purely material causes. An example of this extreme kind of (ontological or conceptual) reductionism is given by Francis Crick: "You, your joys and your sorrows, your memories and ambitions, your sense of personal identity and free will, are in fact no more than the behaviour of a vast assembly of nerve cells and their associated molecules."[21] The telltale words that reveal such reductionism are "no more than" or "nothing but." Remove them and usually something unobjectionable remains—our memories certainly involve the behavior of nerve cells. Add the words "nothing but" and we have changed a scientific statement into a statement of materialistic belief—and nothing more.

If Crick's thesis is true, we could never know it, as John Polkinghorne shows when he describes such a reductionist[22] program as containing the seeds of its own destruction:

> Ultimately it is suicidal. Not only does it relegate our experiences of beauty, moral obligation, and religious encounter to the epiphenomenal scrap-heap. It also destroys rationality. Thought is replaced by electro-chemical neural events. Two such events cannot confront each other in rational discourse. They are neither right nor wrong. They simply happen. . . . The very assertions of the reductionist himself are nothing but blips in the neural network of his brain. The world of rational discourse dissolves into the absurd chatter of firing synapses. Quite frankly, that cannot be right and none of us believes it to be so.[23]

Indeed. None of us believes that a Rembrandt painting is nothing but a distribution of molecules of paint on canvas. Any adequate explanation of the painting both involves the materials and mechanisms involved—the canvas, the paint, and the tools by which it is applied—and the intelligent agent Rembrandt. The fundamental point at issue in intelligent design (in the broad sense) is the same: Is a mechanistic description of the universe adequate as explanation in the fullest sense?

Type IIA Arguments in Physics and Cosmology

A complete explanation of a Rembrandt painting involves both mechanism and agency seen as complementary levels of explanation. They neither compete nor are they the same kind of explanation. Rembrandt will not be found in a minute analysis of the chemistry of the paint: it is rather the organization and execution of the whole painting that points to him. Similarly, when Kepler made his brilliant observational deduction that the planets move in ellipses 'round the sun as focus and Newton later explained these motions in terms of his law of gravity, they did not conclude that their discoveries of law or mechanism obviated God. Kepler said: "The chief aim of all investigations of the external world should be to discover the rational order which has been imposed on it by God, and which he revealed to us in the language of mathematics." Sir John Houghton has captured the idea well: "Our science is God's science. He holds the responsibility for the whole scientific story. . . . The remarkable order, consistency, reliability and fascinating complexity found in the scientific description of the universe are reflections of the order, consistency, reliability and complexity of God's activity."[24]

Thus, the two explanations, the first in terms of law and mechanism, the second in terms of agency (God), run in parallel and, far from the second inhibiting work on the first, it was, certainly for many of the pioneers of science, their central motivation. Similar things may be said for the fine-tuning arguments from cosmology that have been discussed by many authors.[25] Arno Penzias, who won the Nobel Prize for discovering the microwave background radiation that indicated a finite age to the universe, sums up his position: "Astronomy leads us to a unique event, a universe which was created out of nothing, one with the very delicate balance needed to provide exactly the right conditions required to permit life, and one which has an underlying (one might say 'supernatural') plan."[26] It needs to be emphasized that these design arguments flow out of mainstream science, in this case the Standard Model in cosmology. They do not arise out of ignorance of science but out of knowledge of science.

At the heart of the majority of the fine-tuning arguments lies the conviction that space-time had a beginning some thirteen to fifteen billion years ago,[27] which is of interest in connection with the question mentioned earlier of whether intelligent design theories make testable predictions. For centuries the Genesis account has been available with its magisterial opening words: "In the beginning God created the heavens and the earth." It must be fairly obvious, surely, that if these words had been taken seriously by scientists, the attempt to find scientific evidence for such a beginning, and thus challenge the Aristotelian paradigm of an eternal universe, would have started long before it did. In the event, when evidence began to pile up that the cosmos had a beginning, ironically it was fiercely resisted by prominent scientists (like Sir John Maddox, then editor of *Nature*) because they thought it would give too much leverage to those who believed in creation! It is particularly apposite that it was Penzias who wrote: "The best data we have [concerning the big bang] are exactly what I would have predicted, had I nothing to go on but the five books of Moses, the Psalms and the Bible as a whole."[28] Note the word *predicted*.

Type IIA Arguments in Biology

Type IIA arguments are not restricted to physics and cosmology. They are used to question the notion that evolutionary biology demands atheism (a Type IIA anti-intelligent design argument). For instance, chapter 4 of Dawkins's recent book, *The God Delusion*,[29] titled "Why There Is almost Certainly No God," is devoted to showing: "Far from pointing to a designer, the illusion of design in the living world is explained with far greater economy and with devastating elegance by Darwinian natural selection." For Dawkins, God and evolution are alternative, mutually exclusive explanations. However, he commits the category mistake of failing to distinguish agency from mechanism. Dennett does the same, but in such a way that the reader thinks he has dealt with the matter of agency, when he has not even addressed it: "Love it or hate it, phenomena like this [DNA] exhibit the heart of the power of the Darwinian idea. An impersonal, unreflective, robotic, mindless little scrap of molecular machinery is the ultimate basis of all agency, and hence meaning, and hence consciousness in the universe."[30] Leaving aside the question of whether Dennett's grandiose claim for DNA is true, DNA as a molecular machine may well be impersonal, unreflective, robotic, and mindless. Most machines are. But that says absolutely nothing about whether they have been designed or not—in fact, most machines have been.

To quote Sir John Houghton once more: "The fact that we understand some of the mechanisms of the working of the universe or of living systems does not preclude the existence of a designer, any more than the possession of insight into the processes by which a watch has been put together, however automatic these processes may appear, implies there can be no watchmaker."[31]

On this view, the evolutionary viewpoint, far from invalidating inference to intelligent origin, simply backs it up one level—from primary to secondary causation. On seeing a car for the first time a person might suppose that it is made directly by humans, only later to discover it is made in a robotic factory by robots which, in turn, were made by machines made by humans. It was not the inference to intelligent origin that was wrong but the concept of the nature of the implementation of that intelligence. Direct human activity was not seen in the factory because it is the existence of the factory itself that is the product of that activity.

In this vein Charles Kingsley wrote to Darwin suggesting that his theory of natural selection provided "just as noble a conception of Deity, to believe that He created primal forms capable of self-development . . . as to believe that He required a fresh act of intervention to supply the lacunas which He Himself had made." Though Kingsley was not a scientist, Darwin was so impressed by his words that he cited them in the second edition of *The Origin of Species*, possibly with an eye to influencing his more skeptical clerical readers.

The fine-tuning arguments from physics and cosmology are, of course, independent of evolutionary theory, yet it is important to note that the theory demands the existence of a fine-tuned universe producing exactly the right kind of materials and operating according to complex laws that are consistent with supporting life. Such anthropic fruitfulness could then be regarded as evidence of creative intelligent activity. Keith Ward speaks of evolution as "having been chosen by a rational agent for the sake of some good that it, and perhaps it alone, makes possible."[32] John Polkinghorne speaks of creation as "realising the inbuilt potentiality with which the Creator has endowed it."[33] Theistic evolution has thus commended itself to many scientists, from Asa Gray[34] and Richard Owen in Darwin's day to the present.[35]

Even the late Stephen Jay Gould thought that regarding Darwinism as necessarily atheistic was going beyond the evidence: "Either half of my colleagues are enormously stupid, or else the science of Darwinism is fully compatible with conventional religious beliefs—and equally compatible with atheism."[36] However, Dawkins and Dennett think not. Dennett regards Darwin's idea as a kind of corrosive acid, which "threatens to destroy all pre-Darwinian views of the world; in that, instead of the universe's matter being a product of mind, the minds in the universe are a product of matter. They are nothing more than the results of an undirected, mindless, purposeless process."[37] He claims that "natural selection somehow designs without either itself being designed or having any purpose in view" characterizing it as "mindless, motiveless, mechanicity."[38] In the language of Aristotle, Dennett's claim is that it is the very nature of the efficient cause (evolution) that rules out the existence of a final cause (divine intention).

Type IIB Arguments in Biology

It is, in part, this kind of assertion that leads to the Type IIB question whether the evolutionary mechanism will bear all the weight that is put on it, for instance, by Richard Dawkins: "Natural selection, the blind, unconscious, automatic process which Darwin discovered, and which we now know is the explanation for the existence and apparently purposeful form of all life, has no purpose in mind."[39]

Does natural selection really account for the existence of life as distinct from its variations?[40] Surely it cannot be quite so straightforward for the simple reason that, until life exists, there is no mutating replicator on which natural selection can operate. Theodosius Dobzhansky, one of the pioneers of evolutionary biology, who said that "nothing makes sense in biology except in light of evolution," also said that "prebiological evolution is a contradiction in terms."

This question of what accounts for life's existence is at the heart of the (narrower) ID debate, a debate that received an unexpected stimulus when eminent philosopher Antony Flew gave as the reason for his conversion to theism after over fifty years of atheism that the investigation of DNA by biologists "has shown, by the almost unbelievable complexity of the arrangements which are needed to produce life, that intelligence must have been involved. . . . It has become inordinately difficult even to begin to think about constructing a naturalistic theory of the evolution of that first reproducing organism."[41]

It will be objected that this is an antiscientific God of the Gaps solution of the sort "there is no plausible material process for X, therefore X must involve the input of intelligence." We must take this objection seriously, though we first of all record a warning by an expert on the origin of life, Nobel laureate Robert Laughlin, of the danger of an evolution of the gaps:

> Evolution by natural selection which Darwin conceived as a great theory has lately come to function as an anti-theory called upon to cover up embarrassing experimental shortcomings and legitimize findings that are at worst not even wrong. Your protein defies the laws of mass action—evolution did it! Your complicated mess of chemical reactions turns into a chicken—evolution did it! The human brain works on logical principles no computer can emulate—evolution is the cause![42]

The origin of life has not been observed, so scientists use the historical methods appropriate to the investigation of unrepeatable past events and make inferences to the best explanation. It is therefore clear how an evolution of the gaps could be just as metaphysically motivated for an incautious atheist as a God of the Gaps could be for an incautious theist. For materialists there simply must eventually be a solution in terms of material processes alone, so they might as well call it evolution, filling in the details as they are found—for they must be found.

Now many scientists who are theists and all who are atheists insist that science restricts its explanation to material processes. They therefore reject Level II arguments. The theists among them often use Level I arguments for the existence of God. To warn of the dangers of Level II God of the Gaps arguments, they might cite Newton's letter in which he said that his law of gravitation could explain the motion of planets around the sun but not their motion around their own axes, which needed a "divine arm." Progress in physics, they might well add, has removed the need for this kind of divine intervention and has led us to a seamless scientific understanding of the evolution of the cosmos in terms of material processes involving cause and effect, chance and necessity. There are no singularities—except (for many) at the beginning. We can see all of this cosmic development as the fruit of mathematical and physical laws that express the Creator's mind. So why can the same not hold for the origin of life?

As a scientist, the author takes such reasoning and the concomitant charge of intellectual laziness that is often leveled at God of the Gaps-type arguments very seriously indeed but, nevertheless, thinks there is more to be said both from a scientific and from a theological perspective. Let us take the theological perspective first. If there is a God who does anything in the world indirectly, then, as Alvin Plantinga argues, logic would tell us that God must do something directly. What is that direct something? Most theists would agree that it was causing the universe to exist, creating it originally, and maintaining it throughout its history. The initial act of creation would then appear as a singularity to any scientific analysis based on purely material processes.

Cosmology speaks of precisely such a singularity and is not embarrassed to do so. Its understanding of physics leads back to the big bang singularity where, according to Stephen Hawking: "the laws of physics break down." Once we admit that God has acted directly at least once in the past to create the universe, what is there in principle to prevent God acting directly more than once, whether in the past or in the future? For nature's laws are not independent of God. From a Level I perspective, they are mathematical formulations of the regularities with which God has endowed the physical universe and so, as C. S. Lewis has argued,[43] it would be absurd to think that they constrained God so that the Divine could never do anything special: "Could we not sensibly conclude, for example, that God created life, or human life, or something else specially?"[44]

Apparently not, says Paul Davies: "There's no need to invoke anything supernatural in the origins of the universe or of life. I have never liked the idea of divine tinkering: for me it is much more inspiring to believe that a set of mathematical laws can be so clever as to bring all these things into being."[45] So Davies assumes that if God created life specially, it would demean God into a kind of cosmic magician who constantly interferes with the universe. However, this reaction is surely unwarranted. After all, if the claim that God created and upholds the universe is not demeaning, why should the claim that God created life, especially if human life bears the Divine image, be demeaning?

1. It is not as if claims were being made (from a biblical perspective, now) that God was constantly tinkering with the universe. For instance, in the Genesis creation narrative it is interesting that the number of special commandments—"And God said . . ." is relatively small and the series of such commandments (however long it took) came to an end. Indeed, the surprise is how few such special actions of God are claimed in the Bible as a whole.

2. To say that the universe and life have been brought into existence by mathematical laws is astonishing. Apart from begging the question of where the laws came from, such laws are abstract mathematical formulations that by their very nature (laws are not material), far from bringing anything into existence, cannot even cause anything. Newton's laws of motion will tell you a billiard ball's trajectory once it has been hit and the fact that it will remain at rest if it is never hit—but the laws will never move the ball. Or, more simply, $2+2 = 4$, but this fact has never put any money in anyone's pocket.

3. Davies says that he does not "like the idea of divine tinkering" to which one might respond, first, that it is perhaps unwise to decide the nature of reality by our likes or dislikes but rather on the basis of evidence and, second, that the pejorative word *tinkering* scarcely does justice to a God who has the power to created the universe and life.

David Hume has persuaded many scientists that special activity by God (miracle) involves a breaking of the laws of nature and is therefore ruled out *a priori* as scientifically impossible. However, C. S. Lewis[46] and others have shown that Hume's objection involves the misunderstanding of the nature of law mentioned in my second point above. The laws are a description of what normally happens in the universe, but God the Creator can do something special directly without breaking the laws. For example, at the heart of Christianity is the claim that Jesus was raised from the dead by a direct injection of the power of God.[47] It is noteworthy that a mathematical physicist of the eminence of Sir John Polkinghorne does not think that his position as a scientist is compromised by his belief in the resurrection of Jesus, even though, from the perspective of explanation in terms of unguided material processes, the resurrection is a singularity.

Thus, scientists who are Christians would appear to be committed to at least two singularities, (1) creation itself, the beginning of space-time, and (2) the resurrection of Jesus within space-time. There is therefore, surely, no in principle reason not to consider the origin of life as a potential third singularity, provided, of course, if the evidence warrants it.

This is the key question. However, since many scientists will feel that we have long since left the realm of science for fairyland, it is important first to discuss what kind of scientific evidence we might expect if the origin of life has a supernatural dimension and is not explicable solely in terms of purely material processes.

First, we should expect that explanations in terms of material processes fail at certain points. This logical observation, however, is the focus of a major objection, hinted at earlier: Is it not an intellectually lazy, antiscientific attitude simply to give up the attempt at material explanation after the first few tries and say God did it?

Our response is that it might well be. However, pure mathematics has something to teach us here. If mathematicians have tried to prove a conjecture in pure mathematics for a long time, like the anciently posed task of trisecting an angle with straightedge and compasses, and they fail, there will come a time when they will try to mount an attack in the opposite direction and try to *prove* that the conjecture is false. This was done after many centuries in the case of angle-trisection by Pierre Wantzel in 1836. Consequently, no one tries to do it any more.

Now, origin-of-life research burst on the world in 1953 with the announcement of the results of the Miller-Urey experiment—the production of some of the amino acid building blocks of protein in a simulated primeval soup bombarded by electricity. However, over the subsequent fifty-four years, it has been realized that the real problem was not obtaining the building blocks of life (although that problem is still with us) but getting those building blocks in the right order as revealed by the genetic code whose discovery ranks as perhaps the greatest ever scientific achievement.

Subsequent research has produced several emergent[48] and self-organizing scenarios that, although of great interest, seem rather to highlight and intensify this problem rather than solve it, as is, somewhat ironically, very well expressed by Paul Davies:

> Life is actually *not* an example of *self*-organisation. Life is in fact *specified*, i.e. genetically directed, organisation. Living things are instructed by the genetic software encoded in their DNA (or RNA). Convection cells form spontaneously by self-organisation. There is no gene for a convection cell. The source of order is not encoded in software; it can instead be traced to the boundary conditions in the fluid. . . . In other words, a convection cell's order is imposed *externally*, from the system's environment. By contrast, the order of a living cell derives from *internal* control. . . . The theory of self-organisation as yet gives no clue how the transition is to be made between spontaneous, or self-induced organisation—which in even the most elaborate non-biological examples still involves relatively simple structures—and the highly complex, information-based, genetic organisation of living things.[49]

This brings us to the meat of the problem—to explain the genesis of the specified computer-language-like structure of DNA that Dennett calls a "mindless scrap of molecular machinery." Now it may justifiably be said that fifty-four years is not a very long time in science. So why not simply keep on trying to establish the truth of the conjecture that the origin of biological information is a purely material process and not give in to a God-of-the-Gaps thinking? Well, that might be the thing to do provided that, to use mathematical terminology, the conjecture is not provably false.[50]

But is this not to fall afoul of the "impossibility of proving a negative" dictum? Not in principle, as is seen from my mathematical example. More importantly, physics gives us more relevant examples. Take, for instance, the law of conservation of energy that prohibits the existence of certain material things, such as perpetual-motion machines. It is therefore pointless to argue that, although people have failed to construct perpetual-motion machines in the past, it would be against the spirit of science to give up on the construction of such a machine. Physics itself says they are impossible constructions. Any machine will use more energy than it produces.

Of immediate relevance to our discussion are the following parallel observations. The first is due to a pioneer of information theory, Leonard Brillouin: "A machine does not create any new information, but it performs a very valuable transformation of known information."[51] The second comes from the brilliant mathematician Kurt Gödel, who proved certain far-reaching impossibility theorems in mathematics, like the incompleteness of arithmetic:

> The complexity of living bodies has to be present in the material [from which they are derived] or in the laws [governing their formation]. In particular, the materials forming the organs, if they are governed by mechanical laws, have to be of the same order of complexity as the living body. . . . More generally, Gödel believes [Gödel sometimes expressed himself in the third person] that mechanism in biology is a prejudice of our time which will be disproved. In this case, one disproval, in Gödel's opinion, will consist in a mathematical theorem to the effect that the formation within geological times of a human body by the laws of physics (or any other laws of a similar nature), starting from a random distribution of the elementary particles and the field, is as unlikely as the separation by chance of the atmosphere into its components.[52]

Nobel Laureate Sir Peter Medawar thought there might be some kind of law of conservation of information[53] and, more recently, William Dembski argues for a nondeterministic law of conservation of information along the lines suggested by Brillouin to the effect that, although natural processes (involving only chance and necessity) can effectively transmit complex specified information, they cannot generate it so that information is not reducible to physics and chemistry.[54]

Now there is clearly a great deal at stake here—in particular a radical challenge to materialistic philosophy and, if we add in the fact that the concept of information, especially information with a semantic dimension is notoriously difficult to define, it is not surprising that the question of the validity of such a law of conservation of information is still a topic of hot debate. Making due allowance for this fact, however, just as we can test the plausibility of the law of conservation of energy by finding the energy flaw in a putative perpetual-motion machine, we can test the plausibility of a theory of information conservation. If information is conserved in some meaningful sense, then we would expect that any scenario that claimed to get information for free (by chance and necessity) was flawed and that information had to be smuggled in somewhere. That seems to be exactly what is found in all scenarios hitherto offered, for instance, by Dawkins and others.[55]

To put it another way, there seem to be two kinds of gaps; bad gaps and good gaps. The bad gaps are those that are targeted in God-of-the-Gaps accusations, those that science will eventually fill. The good gaps are those that are revealed by science, such as the information gap discussed just now. We emphasize that it is science that reveals the good gaps, and not theology. However, theology can help illuminate where they are likely to be (witness creation). We would therefore argue that, just as the beginning of space-time is a good gap in the explanatory power of physics, the origin of life is a good gap in the explanatory power of molecular biology. Biology is not reducible to physics and chemistry.

John Polkinghorne also suggests a similar differentiation:

> We must never rest content with a discussion in such soft-focus that it never begins to engage our intuitions about God's action with our knowledge of physical process. . . . If the physical world is really open, and top-down intentional causality operates within it, there must be intrinsic "gaps" ("an envelope of possibility") in the bottom-up account of nature to make room for intentional causality. . . . We are unashamedly 'people of the gaps' in this intrinsic sense and there is nothing unfitting in a "God of the gaps" in this sense either.[56]

These arguments amplify work by scientist and philosopher Michael Polanyi,[57] who asks us to think of the various levels of process involved in constructing an office building with bricks. First, there is the process of extracting the raw materials out of which the bricks have to be made. Then there are the successively higher levels of making the bricks—they do not make themselves; bricklaying—the bricks do not self-assemble; designing the building—it does not design itself; and planning the town in which the building is to be built—it does not organize itself. Each level has its own rules. The laws of physics and chemistry govern the raw material of the bricks; technology prescribes the art of brickmaking; architecture teaches the builders; and the architects are controlled by the town planners. Each level is controlled by the level above. But the reverse is not true. The laws of a higher level cannot be derived from the laws of a lower level; although what can be done at a higher level will, of course, depend on the lower levels. For example, if the bricks are not strong, there will be a limit on the height of the building that can safely be built with them.

The same is true of a printed page. As Nobel laureate Roger Sperry has said: "The meaning of the message is not to be found in the physics and chemistry of the paper and ink."[58] We are suggesting here that information and intelligence are fundamental to the existence of the universe and life and, far from being the end-products of an unguided natural process starting with mass energy, they were involved from the very beginning. Interestingly, Paul Davies writes:

> The increasing application of the information concept to nature has prompted a curious conjecture. Normally we think of the world as composed of simple, clod-like, material particles, and information as a derived phenomenon attached to special, organised states of matter. But maybe it is the other way around: perhaps the universe is really a frolic of primal information, and material objects a complex secondary manifestation.[59]

However, the proposal that information be regarded as a fundamental quantity has been around for centuries. "In the beginning was the Word . . . all things were made by him" wrote John, the author of the fourth Gospel. The Greek for "Word" is *Logos*, a term used by Stoic philosophers for the rational principle behind the universe and subsequently invested with additional meaning by Christians to describe the Second Person of the Trinity. The term *Word* itself conveys to us notions of command, code, communication, meaning, and thus information, as well as the creative power needed to realise what was specified by that information. The Word, therefore, is more fundamental than mass energy. Mass energy belongs to the category of the created. The Word does not.

It is surely very striking indeed that at the heart of the biblical analysis of the creative acts, so readily dismissed by many, we find the very concept to which science has shown to be of paramount importance—the concept of information. Perhaps if these profound biblical ideas had been taken more seriously by scientists they would have concluded more rapidly that information is important. Just as with the fact of the beginning, a scientific prediction could have been theologically informed in this way.

I have spent a relatively long time on these arguments of Type IIB, not because they are more important—although I believe that the last point is of immense significance—but because they are the most controversial and the most misunderstood. I would conclude, however, by recalling once more that the main arguments to intelligent causation are of Types I and IIA. The evidence of God is to be seen mainly in the things that we do understand and not in the things we don't. If those of us who favor such arguments keep this perspective, we can then evaluate and use some arguments of Type IIB without giving the impression that all our eggs are in the God of Bad Gaps basket.

12

Flat or Round?

The Sixth-Century Debate over the Shape of the Earth

Ken Keathley

Do intelligent design proponents give away the farm to Darwinists? Many creationists think so. Secular media dismisses ID as closet creationism, but card-carrying creationists are often equally dismissive. Traditional creationists such as Ken Ham and Kurt Wise are quick to warn about the dangers of ID—an approach they view as a useless hybrid that is neither fish nor fowl.[1]

To see why creationists have such an intense dislike and distrust of ID, one must note the four distinctives of the Christian doctrine of creation: God created the universe out of nothing (*creatio ex nihilo*); God freely chose to create without any sense of need or necessity; the universe is contingent and depends upon God for its continued existence; and God created the universe with a goodness that was lost at the fall. It is this last component— the original goodness of creation—that creationists believe ID compromises. They see ID's acceptance of an ancient earth in which disease and death exist from the beginning as an abandonment of a key nonnegotiable aspect of biblical teaching.

There is a precursor in church history to the dispute between traditional creationists and ID proponents on the best way to defend the doctrine of creation. In the sixth century, one of the greatest intellectual challenges to the Christian faith was the neo-Platonic belief in an eternal universe. This clearly was contrary to the first tenet of creationist doctrine—that the world had a beginning when God created it out of nothing. Neo-Platonism, as it developed into a distinct and predominant philosophy, incorporated much of Aristotle's physics, including his arguments that the world had no beginning. Certain neo-Platonic philosophers used this hypothesis to attack the credibility of Christianity. Proclus (ca. 411–485), for example, gives eighteen arguments against the Christian doctrine of creation in favor of an eternal universe.[2] John Philoponus (ca. 490–570), a Christian philosopher in Alexandria, rebuts the arguments both of Proclus and Aristotle and, in so doing, he begins the process of dismantling Aristotelian physics. Historians of science credit Philoponus with establishing the unified principles of dynamics necessary for the formation of modern science.[3]

In many respects, there is nothing new about the debate between Darwinism and intelligent design. Many see it as a continuation of an ongoing dispute between faith and science that previously occurred most prominently between Galileo and the Roman Church in the seventeenth century. At the time, the Roman Curia perceived Galileo's advocacy of the Copernican cosmology over the Ptolemaic system as a threat to Church dogma. The Roman Church's dogged support of Ptolemy must be seen as ironic, especially when one considers the issues concerning his cosmology that the Church faced in its early days. In the sixth century, the question at hand was whether or not Ptolemy's cosmology was acceptable to Christians, since it was based on pagan presuppositions. John Philoponus and Cosmas Indicopleustes took opposite positions, and their debate shows that the relationship of faith and science is complex and symbiotic, and not simply one of conflict.

Trained under Ammonius at the academy in Alexandria, Philoponus was in many ways the pagan philosopher's worst nightmare—an academically astute Christian equipped to answer the Aristotelian on his own terms. Throughout his life, Philoponus's writings progressed from strictly philosophical works to primarily theological texts. In his early years, he wrote only commentaries on Aristotle. Midway in his career, Philoponus penned *Against Proclus on the Eternity of the World* and then later *Against Aristotle on the Eternity of the World*, which approach the debate by answering the philosophers on their own turf. He makes no appeal to the Christian Scriptures, but rather bases his arguments on accepted grounds of reason and evidence. Not until late in life, and in response to Christian opponents, did Philoponus write any texts overtly based on the Bible.

Philoponus's refutation of Aristotle not only answered the criticisms leveled against the doctrine of creation, but also would pave the way for a new understanding of physics. Galileo depended heavily on the views of Philoponus, and cited him more often than Plato, Albert, or Scotus.[4] Sorabji stated that Philoponus's alternative theories would help fuel the Renaissance's rejection of Aristotle, while Thomas Kuhn credited Philoponus's theory of impetus as a paradigmatic scientific revolution.[5]

As one would expect, the philosophers within the Academy reacted to Philoponus with critiques of his position, most notably the neo-Platonic philosopher Simplicius (ca. 490–ca. 560).[6] As Pearson notes, the severe and extensive way in which Simplicius responded indicates that Philoponus had struck a nerve.[7]

The strongest attacks on Philoponus did not come from pagan philosophers, however, but from other Christians. A Nestorian monk who also lived in Alexandria, Cosmas Indicopleustes (ca. sixth century), wrote a rebuttal that rejects Philoponus's work on the grounds that it subscribes to the notion of a round earth, a thoroughly pagan idea in Cosmas's estimation. As his surname indicates ("Indian Voyager"), Cosmas was a widely traveled merchant-sailor prior to becoming a monk, and he journeyed the Indian Ocean as far south as Sri Lanka. Cosmas was unsurpassed in his day in his firsthand knowledge of the geography of the world, and historians consider him to be a premiere source for information concerning sixth-century customs and cultures and plant and animal life in both Africa and India. Cosmas uses this eyewitness information frequently in his rejection of Philoponus's round earth. In a text he titled *Christian Topography*, Cosmas offers an alternative he considers to be more in keeping with the biblical record and the physical evidence.

As Cosmas saw it, either one can be a true Christian who accepts the biblical account of creation and its description of the cosmos, or one can be a pagan, filled with the self-confidence of worldly wisdom, and ascribe a circular motion to the heavens by the use of geometry and the observation of phenomenon such as solar and lunar eclipses. That certain "professing" Christians would advocate the compromise of accepting both the Ptolemaic cosmology and the doctrine of creation motivated him to write his work. "It is against such men my words are directed . . . ," Cosmas declares, and he denounces them as "two-faced" because they wished to "occupy a middle position." They "laugh at everyone, and are themselves laughed at by all."[8]

Philoponus responded to Cosmas with a commentary on Genesis, *On the Creation of the World*, which he wrote with two aims in mind. First, he wished to demonstrate that the doctrine of creation as presented by Moses is compatible with the "phenomena" as understood by the natural philosophers. He wanted to provide an explanation of creation that is reasonable both to educated Christians and to any pagan who might be considering Christianity. Second, Philoponus considered Cosmas's arguments to be the braying of an ignorant ass and he was concerned that Cosmas's views might be received as the standard Christian position. His advice to Cosmas and to those like him: be quiet. "If some people . . . cannot understand what has been said because of a lack of training . . . [let] silence cover their ignorance."[9] Cosmas and Philoponus may have lived in the same city at the same time, but they were worlds apart.

The debate between Philoponus and Cosmas was actually a disagreement about how to establish a Christian basis for science, and for this reason alone their conflict has real lessons for today. Like Philoponus, many in the ID movement endeavor to answer the prevailing worldview on its own terms without an appeal to biblical authority. And like Cosmas, many creationists believe that such a task is impossible, because knowledge of creation is available only by revelation. They believe a purely empirical investigation to be at best misguided, and that ultimately such an approach will do more damage than good. This chapter will demonstrate that though Philoponus presents a much better model for the Christian engaged in scientific pursuits, Cosmas's concerns should not be ignored.

Philoponus's Arguments against Aristotle

Philoponus disposes of some of Aristotle's arguments rather quickly. For example, Aristotle argues that the circular nature of the orbits of the spheres demonstrate their eternal nature, since a circle has no beginning or end. Philoponus replies that, in this regard, the characteristics of a circle are no different from that of a straight line, since a straight line on a Euclidian plane also has no beginning or end.[10] Aristotle claims that the heavens were not generated because they have no contrary. Philoponus replies that, indeed, anything that exists has a contrary, namely, privation.[11]

Philoponus's key insight, however, is to see that Aristotle's two main arguments for an eternal earth contain inherent contradictions. An eternal cosmos requires infinite time and infinite motion. Yet, according to Aristotle's own logic, both are impossible.

First, Aristotle rejects the possibility that an actual infinite existed in the physical world due to the paradoxes and logical contradictions that would result. Namely, adding a finite number to infinity results in the annihilation of the finite number. Infinity plus any finite equals infinity, which means that the finite would be simply absorbed. Basic arithmetic grinds to a halt when infinity is brought into the equation, and for this reason, among many, Aristotle dismisses the notion that anything of infinite quantity exists.

Philoponus points out that adherence to an eternal cosmos assumes an infinite regress of time, and therefore commits the very error Aristotle meant to avoid. If the world were infinitely old, then every twenty-four hours would be the addition of a finite day to an infinitely long past. Aristotle had already proven this impossible, so the universe must have had a beginning.[12]

The second Aristotelian fallacy Philoponus exposes is the notion of the eternal revolutions of the heavens. In so doing, Philoponus dismantles Aristotle's theory of motion altogether. In order to have an eternal and unchanging heaven, Aristotle must hypothesize that they consist of an element—the aether—which is different from the elements found on earth. He presents the sublunar world as made up of four basic elements (earth, water, air, and fire), with each element possessing a distinct nature and corresponding density. Aristotle understands motion to result from the elements attempting to return to their respective natural or proper places. Earth is densest, so it falls to the center, while fire rises since it is the lightest. All motion is explained in terms of this vertical sorting of the elements to their respective natural levels. He explains elemental movement in almost psychological terms.

Aristotle reasons that the celestial sky consists of a fifth element—the quintessence, or aether—that is perfect and everlasting. Celestial motion is different from the motion of the mundane elements, for the quintessence already resides at its proper level. The circular and unending motion of the heavens is seen as evidence of its eternal nature. The second-century astronomer Ptolemy (ca. 90–168) codifies Aristotle's paradigm with his famous cosmology of concentric spheres surrounding a spherical earth.

Philoponus has a great deal of fun highlighting the problems Aristotle's system has in explaining lateral motion. If movement is caused by the elements seeking their proper vertical level, then why does a javelin move forward when it is thrown? Aristotle is forced to posit that somehow successive pockets of air continue pushing the javelin, even after it leaves the thrower's hand.[13] Philoponus ridicules his answer by pointing out that if Aristotle were right, then an army would no longer need to launch projectiles at its enemies, but simply have bellows blow behind the arrows and let the air do the rest.

At this point, Philoponus presents a crucial insight. He suggests an alternative to Aristotle's physics by suggesting that a thrower implants a force or impetus into the javelin when he throws it. Later, Galileo and others will further refine Philoponus's innovative concept into the law of inertia.[14]

Aristotle, because he holds that the heavens are made of a fifth element, does not believe that the sun consisted of fire or contained heat. He had argued that the stars and the sun could not be made up of fire, or else they would have already burned up. He accounts for the heat from the sun by claiming it was the result of friction caused by its revolving sphere.[15]

Philoponus replies that just because the celestial bodies have not burned up yet, it does not mean that they never will.[16] He also argues that the reason we do not feel the heat of the stars is because they are so distant.[17] Philoponus reasons that if the heavens had a beginning, then they also can have an end. And if the heavens are perishable, then there is no need to believe that they are made up of a fifth element. The heavens are made up of the same elements as the Earth[18] and the same principles of motion apply to both.[19]

Philoponus presents a powerful case against the neo-Platonic doctrine of an eternal world, and in so doing, discredits much of the Aristotelian physics underlying it. Historians of science see Philoponus as providing two crucial steps toward the formation of science as a discipline: the concept of impetus and a unified concept of dynamics.[20] His primary motive was to supply a reasonable apologetic for creation. Not all in the Christian community, however, are impressed with Philoponus's efforts.

Cosmas's Attack on Philoponus

As far as Cosmas is concerned, when Philoponus accepts the Ptolemaic cosmology, he throws the fight before the match begins. The pagans base their belief in an eternal universe on a spherical world, so to concede this point is to give up the debate. Cosmas asks Philoponus, "Is it not evident that you argue against the hope held out by the Christian doctrine? For [your] views cannot be consistently held except by pagans, who have no hope of another and better state, and who consequently suppose the world is eternal. . . ."[21]

Cosmas warns Philoponus that his inflated view of his own intellectual abilities has caused him to attempt to do what cannot be done: reconcile pagan and Christian beliefs. After reminding

Fig. 12.1.

him that no man can serve two masters, Cosmas chides Philoponus: "How great is your knowledge! How great your wisdom! How great your intelligence! How great your inconsistency!"[22]

From Cosmas's description of the exchanges that occur between the flat-earth advocates and the round-earth adherents, it is apparent that Cosmas is not a solitary gadfly. As we will see, a sizable faction in Alexandria agrees with his position and is ready to carry the flat-earth banner.

After denouncing Philoponus's compromise, Cosmas presents his description of the true shape of the world. The heavens form a vault over the earth, and the universe has the shape of a chest.[23] The earth is flat, because it acts as the floor of the chest. Cosmas provides illustrations (see fig. 12.1).

The inhabited world is one giant continent indented with various seas and is surrounded by an unnavigable ocean that acts as an impassable moat.[24] The ocean is held in place by an oblong ring of land making up the perimeter of the cosmos. Paradise lies on the east side of this boundary (see fig. 12.2).[25]

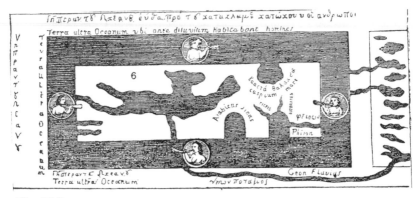

Fig. 12.2.

The heavens are attached to the earth by giant walls at the perimeter, and these walls give the cosmos a rectangular shape.[26] A firmament at the top of the walls separate heaven into two parts, and this is why the Bible speaks of two heavens.[27] The realm below the firmament is the celestial heaven; the vaulted region above is the eternal heaven where God and the saints abide.[28]

Cosmas presents a threefold argument for a flat earth. First, he selects certain proof-texts from Scripture, and second, he contends that Moses' tabernacle in the wilderness is a model of the world. For the third part of his argument, he contends that the current understanding of geography proves the earth is a flat rectangle.

First, in building his case from the Bible, Cosmas appeals to several passages that portray the heavens either as a vault, a canopy, or a tent.[29] He interprets certain texts to teach that the heavens and the earth are fastened at the edges. To consider such expressions as poetic figures of speech never occurs to Cosmas.

Cosmas notes that the earth is said to have extremities, which cannot be said of a sphere. Jesus himself taught that Africa is the world's southernmost edge, since he describes the Queen of Sheba as having come from the ends of the earth (Matt. 12:42).[30] As for the northern part of the world, Cosmas claims biblical warrant for believing that the sun travels through the north each night on its return journey (Eccles. 1:5-6).[31] We do not see the sunlight as it returns because the light is blocked by a giant northern mountain (see fig. 12.3).[32]

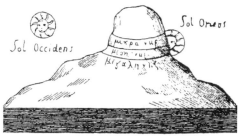

Fig. 12.3.

There can be no one living on the underside of the earth, Cosmas deduces, because the Bible speaks only of those on the earth (that is, the living) and in the earth (meaning the dead), but never under the earth (Phil. 2:10).[33] Cosmas lampoons the absurdity of Antipodes with his depiction in figure 12.4.

Cosmas lists a litany of theological problems posed by a round earth. He argues that the spherical cosmology has no place for a coming kingdom of heaven. In fact, if the spherical model is right, then the pagans "are therefore justified in denying the resurrection of the body."[34] He states: "For the famous sphere of the pagans does not harmonize at all with what Christian doctrine proclaims; but is adapted rather for those who hope neither for a resurrection of the dead nor for another state after it, but assert that the whole world is in an endless process of generation and corruption."[35]

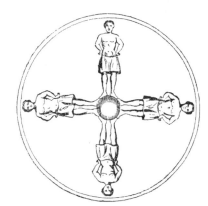

Fig. 12.4.

Cosmas accepts the standard explanation for the cause of eclipses, but he rejects the possibility that the heavens revolve because it is "a theory subversive alike of all divine scripture both of the Old and the New Testament, and of Christian doctrine." In other words, Cosmas rejects, in principle, the idea that the heavens move.[36] If the heavens are moving around the earth, then there is no hope of ascending to God, no watery firmament separating the heavens exists, and there will be no end of the world.[37] In addition, there cannot be eight or nine heavens consisting of solid spheres. How, then, would it be possible for Christ to have ascended through them?[38]

A spherical earth is just as problematic for Cosmas as a spherical heaven. He declares that a round earth renders impossible Noah's universal flood and the creation account of the earth originally covered in water.[39]

Moses' tabernacle in the wilderness as a model of the world is Cosmas's second line of reasoning, and he justifies his position by referring to the description of the tabernacle in the book of Hebrews (Heb. 8:2).[40] The author of Hebrews, according to Cosmas, depicts heaven as the true tabernacle, of which the earthly tabernacle is a replica (Heb. 8:1-2; 9:11-12, 21-24; 10:1).[41] Cosmas gives his unique, detailed interpretation of the tabernacle. The veil models the distinction between heaven and earth.[42] The twelve loaves of the showbread stand for the twelve months of the year. The seven lamps of the candlestick represent the sun, moon, and stars, while the table pictures the earth. The waved molding around the table represents the ocean. The crown around the waved molding represents the land beyond the ocean. The rectangular shape of the table—two cubits long and one cubit wide—reveals the shape of the earth (Exod. 37:10).[43]

Third, Cosmas makes an extensive argument for a flat, oblong earth based on the contemporary depictions of geography of his day. He notes that the biblical description of the distribution of Noah's offspring indicates a rectangular shape to the inhabited world.[44] Cosmas appeals to various ancient historians such as Ephorus, whose map of the earth has the Indians in the East, Celts in the West, Ethiopians in the South, and the Scythians in the North.[45]

Cosmas argues from firsthand knowledge acquired through his personal travels. Few in his day had journeyed as extensively as he had, so after giving a travelogue of the inhabited world, he claims, "I have written thus with the advantage of possessing exact knowledge, and I cannot therefore have fallen much short of the truth. For the facts I am indebted partly to what I observed in the course of my voyages and travels, and partly to what I learned from others on whose accuracy I could depend."[46] He concludes that the length of earth,

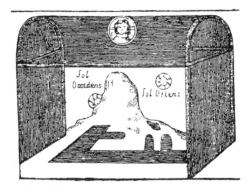

Fig. 12.5.

from east to west, is about twelve thousand miles, while the width of the earth is six thousand miles (see fig. 12.5 for Cosmas's summary illustration).[47]

In an appendix added to later editions, Cosmas answers opponents who argued that the sun, since it was larger than the earth, could not possibly be hidden at night behind a great northern mountain range. He quotes them as asking, "How can the sun possibly be hidden, as you hold, by the northern parts of the earth, which according to you are very high, while he is many times the earth?"[48] Cosmas rejects the premise of the objection and sets out to prove that, in fact, the sun is much smaller than the earth. He states that, during his travels as far south as Ethiopia and as far north as Asia Minor, he had noticed that on the same day of the year the sun casts shadows at different angles depending on the latitude. Calculating from the change in shadows, Cosmas believed the sun to be 42 miles in diameter and to travel a course 4,400 miles above the earth. "And from the shadows themselves which are produced in each climate, it is proved that the sun does not exceed in size two climates, nay, even that the earth is flat, as the delineation shows, and not spherical."[49] He never considers that positing a spherical earth explains the same phenomena, only better (as Eratosthenes had demonstrated earlier, in the third century B.C.E., in the very same city of Alexandria).

Cosmas next turns his attention to a corollary objection, that if the sun really is smaller than the earth, then the shadows cast should not be conical. In so doing, he recounts a debate that occurs in Alexandria between the proponents of the two views of the earth. At the encounter, Cosmas's supporters conducted an experiment by holding up a wooden globe in the sunlight. No conical shadow was detected, even though the experiment was conducted "at a short distance and at a long distance."[50] He does not state how long the long distance was, but it obviously was not long enough. For if they had continued to hold the globe farther and farther away from the surface on which the shadow fell, they would have noticed that the globe's shadow was indeed conical, and would have reduced to a smaller and smaller size until it disappeared. Nevertheless, those in attendance considered the evidence gathered by the experiment to be in Cosmas's favor. Addressing his mentor, Cosmas triumphantly reports the debates' conclusion: "And it is the truth I speak, O most God-beloved Father, through the power of Christ they went away dumbfounded and sadly crestfallen, having been put to shame by our exposure of their fictions."[51]

At the end of his work, Cosmas takes some parting shots at Philoponus. If anyone doubts that adhering to a round earth does not lead to abandoning the doctrine of creation, then look no further than the philosophers themselves. He asks, "For among the philosophers whether of old or late times who are the most celebrated among the pagans, and have been of the opinion that the heaven is a sphere, has he found one affirming that it is dissoluble? It is a fact that all of them, proceeding on the illative method, have declared it to be indissoluble."[52] Cosmas concludes by saying that the only support Philoponus might find among the church fathers is Origen, who was himself found heretical.[53]

Philoponus's Response to Cosmas

Cosmas's attack goaded Philoponus into writing his first distinctly Christian work; a commentary on Genesis titled *On the Creation of the World*. Philoponus's intent was to demonstrate that what Moses wrote can be harmonized with Ptolemy, and that Cosmas failed to accurately interpret the Bible or correctly understand the physical world.[54]

First, Philoponus responds to Cosmas's handling of the biblical text. He replies to Cosmas's contention that the Bible teaches that the world is tent-shaped by pointing out that such statements are not in conflict with the phenomena and are not intended, at any rate, to teach astronomy. Philoponus demonstrates that, not only does the sun not travel behind a northern mountain range, but neither does Ecclesiastes 1:5-6 teach that it does. Cosmas is not just a bad geographer, but a bad exegete.[55]

Philoponus explains that the purpose of the creation account in Genesis is to direct us to God, not to give a scientific explanation.

> Let no one demand that the work of Moses was intended to be a techni-
> cal account of nature for those who came later: [including] what sort
> of material principles of things there are, whether we must posit one
> or many, and if many, how many and what they are, and if they are
> the same for all or different for different things. . . . Since, then, Moses
> wants to instill the knowledge of God into completely unguided souls
> that know hardly anything of the phenomena, he leads them from the
> well-known and familiar up to the conception of an invisible God.[56]

In other words, Moses is writing to a general audience. Cosmas fails to recognize that the Bible speaks phenomenally.[57]

Second, Philoponus proceeds to give an Aristotelian interpretation of the creation account.[58] The seven days of creation are understood to be seven levels of existence. He locates Aristotle's four elements—earth, air, water, and fire—in the first two verses of Genesis. Moses' threefold division between plant, animal, and human corresponds to Aristotle's tripartite understanding of the soul. In his interpretation of Genesis, Philoponus explicitly depends on Basil of Caesarea (ca. 330–379).[59]

What intrigues historians of science about *On the Creation of the World* is how Philoponus further breaks with Aristotle and lays the groundwork for a new understanding of physics. In his discussion of impetus, he clearly places the heavens under the same laws that govern the earth and presents an all-encompassing explanation of motion. According to Sorabji, Philoponus is the first to establish a unified understanding of dynamics.[60] His Christian belief in creation allows him to view the heavens and the earth as a whole. It is a case where "theology influences scientific theory to an extent paralleled in antiquity only perhaps in Plato's *Timaeus*."[61]

Concluding Observations

First, the debate between Cosmas and Philoponus reminds us of the importance of distinguishing between creation and creationism. For the Christian, creation is the biblical truth that God alone is eternal and that the universe is contingent upon God. Creationism, by contrast, is the attempt to integrate the doctrine of creation and the current understanding of the natural sciences. Philoponus considered Cosmas ignorant and Cosmas saw Philoponus as a traitor, but the disagreement between the two was over which approach was more faithful to their mutual Christian belief. Creation is a doctrine; creationism is an apologetic.

While creation is an unchanging bedrock belief, creationism constantly evolves (if one pardons the expression). This is because the natural sciences, with which creationism interfaces, constantly change and develop. Philoponus and Cosmas engaged with the prevailing views of their day, and now for the most part their attempts seem quaint. Their efforts are dated, and this is the fate of all similar apologetic efforts, due to the very nature of the task. The doctrine of creation and its derived corollary truths—that is, that the universe had a beginning in time and the goodness of the created world— are nonnegotiable, while any particular apologetic should be held much less tightly. One must remember this whether one is trying to reconcile Genesis with the big bang or is making the case for a young earth with the appearance of age hypothesis.

Second, Philoponus wins, Cosmas loses. Not just in the obvious sense that Philoponus is right, but in the sense that his position becomes the prevailing view. Contrary to the claims of some, Cosmas's position was never taken seriously by the Church.[62] Cosmas's objections concerning the spheres were considered answered by Philoponus. The Medieval Church's acceptance of the Ptolemaic system demonstrates this. The Venerable Bede, Roger Bacon, and Thomas Aquinas all accepted a spherical earth.[63]

In fact, Philoponus wins too well. The Church eventually baptized the Ptolemaic system and incorporated it into accepted belief. Ptolemy's model became so entrenched that when Galileo advocated the Copernican model, the Roman Curia perceived it as a threat. Once again, this demonstrates the importance of distinguishing between a doctrine and an apologetic.

Third, Cosmas shows that sometimes it is possible to be right in principle but wrong about the question at hand. He was right in his overall rejection of the Aristotelian-Ptolemaic worldview, but he obviously was wrong about the particular issue of whether the world was round. And it was he who decided to make the shape of the earth a hill on which to die. And die he did. Proponents of using the warfare metaphor to describe the relationship between Christianity and science have a field day with Cosmas. Draper and White both hold him up as exhibit A in their contention that religious faith produces minds closed to intellectual inquiry.[64]

We have seen that Philoponus takes a different tack. He remains committed to the distinctives of a Christian doctrine of creation while accepting as reasonable the overall findings of the natural philosophers of his day. Then, operating within the academic community and engaging with the philosophers, Philoponus challenges that which is antithetical to the Christian faith. In so doing, he intended to present a reasonable faith and provide a benefit to natural philosophy.

Fourth, do any of Cosmas's criticisms of Philoponus have merit? To a certain extent, the answer is yes. Philoponus accepts many of the errant theories of his day. To a certain degree, Cosmas was right in warning about too quickly embracing the current findings of the natural sciences and too readily accepting the worldview that guides their conclusions. After all, even though Philoponus rejects many fundamental tenets of Aristotle's physics, for the most part he accepts the Ptolemaic cosmology that was based upon it.[65]

Cosmas is committed to a universe created in time no matter where it takes him logically. His advocacy of a flat earth seemed absurd to his contemporaries and seems even more ridiculous to us today. But the pagans declared that a round earth is an eternal earth, and Cosmas finds their arguments convincing enough to determine never to accept a spherical world.

As stated before, the Christian doctrine of creation entails four component truths: *creatio ex nihilo* in time, God's freedom from necessity in creating, creation's contingency and dependency upon God, and the original goodness of creation. Cosmas believes that allegiance to the first component requires holding to a flat earth. And it is a commitment to the last component—the original goodness of a fallen creation—that causes many creationists to adhere to a young earth in a way that seems similarly quixotic to detractors.[66] Young-earth creationists are concerned about the age of the universe only to a certain degree; what really matters to them is the denial that creation contained natural evil since the beginning of time. They reject any notion that God created the world "red in tooth and claw." God declared the original creation very good (Gen. 1:31), and if the early world included death, disease, and a multitude of other horrific evils, then it says something very disturbing about the nature and character of God.

Let us remember, however, just how wrong the pagans were in Cosmas's day. They were right about the shape of the earth and not much else. A round earth does not require a round universe, and it certainly does not prove an eternal one. Creationists need to be open to the idea that the similar reasoning of current pagans concerning an ancient earth is just as erroneous.

History demonstrates that it is Philoponus, not Cosmas, who presents a better model for a Christian endeavoring to interact with science. By engagement, Philoponus is able to change things. It is Philoponus who interacts with the Aristotelians on their own terms, and no small part of his success comes from his ability to demonstrate the internal contradictions of the Aristotelian-Ptolemaic paradigm. Therefore, it is Philoponus who chips away at the foundations of Aristotelian physics and sets in motion the eventual collapse of the entire Ptolemaic cosmology. And it is Philoponus, not Cosmas, who provides key concepts (namely that of impetus) that enable the progress of scientific thought. This brings up the final point.

Fifth, Philoponus's insights lead to genuine advances in the field of science. The typical scientist does not care about a sixth-century theological debate, nor probably should he. What makes Philoponus scientifically significant, however, is that, in the realm of physics, he moved the ball forward. Whether or not the advocates of the intelligent design hypothesis can make similar contributions will play a major part in determining its acceptance in the broader scientific community.

Traditional creationists and intelligent design proponents agree about rejecting Darwinism, but often disagree about how Christians should interact with the findings of the natural sciences that are used by Darwinists to make their case. The flat- versus round-earth debate seems to indicate that we should somehow endeavor to follow Philoponus while paying attention to the theological concerns of Cosmas.

Afterword

Faith in God and the World of Nature

Wolfhart Pannenberg

The Christian faith in God the Father, to whom the prayer of Jesus for the advent of his kingdom is addressed, cannot be separated from the belief that he is the creator of the world. Faith in creation was presupposed in the case of Jesus as well as that of the first Christians. It was presupposed by the Old Testament, and without this belief that God is not only the creator of human beings, but also of the entire universe, we could not count on God in our lives, could not trust him in all the contingencies of our lives and abandon ourselves to him. In 1529, Martin Luther in his *Large Catechism*, when he had to account for the belief in God the father, declared: "Except for this one I do not consider anything for God, because except for him there is no one who could have created heaven and earth" (Article 1). This is a very strong affirmation. It says, after all, that there is no other explanation for the existence of the natural world and of its different forms that could seriously compete with the belief in a creator. The plausibility of this affirmation of the Christian faith is at the center of the dialogue between Christian theology and the natural sciences. The description of the world of nature by the sciences and the biblical faith in the creation of the world cannot simply exist in neutrality toward each other. After all, both are concerned for one and the same world. The theological exposition of the Christian faith in creation, in any event, has to relate positively to the world of nature as it is described by the sciences.

This was true already of the biblical report on creation in the first chapter of the Bible. A number of details of that report are indebted to the historical status of knowledge about the world of nature in the late seventh and early sixth centuries before Christ, especially to the Babylonian epic *Enuma Elish* on the origins of the world at large. Specifically, the biblical idea of the origin of the heavens as separate and above the earth is rooted in the Babylonian *epos*. According to this epic, the heavens as well as the earth were built out of a primordial, chaotic sea. According to the biblical report, God the Creator divided the chaotic sea by building a firmament in the midst of the waters that separates the waters above from those below and prevents them from coming down. The mechanical consequence was that the waters below the firmament did not receive supply from above and receded to deeper regions, while dry land emerged between those regions (Gen. 1:9). This was thus the origin of the earth. The palpable conception of this process in the biblical report comes from Babylon, then, and represents the scientific knowledge of that time, the sixth century before Christ. This conception has the rationality of ancient engineering. It also explains the possibility of rain on the earth: in a vault of heaven, the firmament, there are windows, and when they are opened, some of the waters of the upper ocean pour down upon earth. When they are left open, however, a flood occurs on earth like the Bible reports in a later epic.

The biblical report on creation, then, already made use of the knowledge of that time about nature when it intended to describe the creative action of God. The understanding of nature and ideas about the origin of heaven and earth did, of course, undergo fundamental changes since the sixth century before Christ, and the authority of the biblical report on creation with regard to contemporary humanity is not appropriately respected, where the ideas of a firmament and of waters above and below the vault of heaven are preserved. Rather, the biblical report on creation has its authority in its function of providing an example for using the natural science of each period in the task of describing God's action in the creation of the world. If we insist on particular biblical ideas in that report, that represent an obsolete understanding of nature, unnecessary conflicts with contemporary scientific descriptions of nature will result. Unnecessary conflicts of this kind burdened the relationship between theology and science in past centuries. Of course, there have also been genuine differences. Good theology will carefully distinguish between these two types of differences. It is important to avoid unnecessary conflict on the one hand and to clarify and overcome the more profound differences. The aim has to be to make use of our contemporary scientific knowledge of nature in explaining the Christian confession of the creation of the universe by the God of the Bible in a similar way to what the biblical report on creation itself did with the help of the knowledge of that time about the realities of nature.

During the eighteenth and nineteenth centuries, the relationship between belief in creation and natural science was also characterized by sharp differences. They were more or less the result of a mechanistic description and explanation of natural processes by classical physics. This mechanistic description had been inaugurated already by the French philosopher René Descartes, when he interpreted all changes in natural processes as effects of a transfer of movement in the interactions of physical bodies, because God was conceived of as immovable. Therefore, it was impossible that changes in the realm of creation originated with him. All changes of movement were thus retraced solely to the interactions of the creatures, that is, of physical bodies. Isaac Newton was concerned that such a conception of natural processes must end up in atheism, because God would have no place anymore in the understanding of natural processes. Newton attempted to avoid such an outcome by his concept of *force*, which was not only to be understood as mechanical transfer of movement, but also in terms of forces working over distances as in the case of gravitation. Newton considered this type of force as an example of how God can guide the processes of nature as we guide our own bodies through the power of our will. But in the eighteenth century, Newton's doctrine of force and movement was reduced to a mechanistic interpretation; all force was conceived as function of bodies. The consequence was, of course, that God was excluded from any activity in natural processes, because God is certainly not a physical body.

It was only with the introduction of the concept of *field* by Michael Faraday and the consequent ascent of the field concept to that of a fundamental concept of physics in general that the mechanistic conception of physical processes began to be overcome and new possibilities of conceiving a creative influence of God in such processes could be perceived—as Faraday himself actually had in mind—when he conceived of fields of forces not in terms of functions of bodies, but rather tended to a conception of bodies as effects of fields of force. Certainly the scientific concept of field went through many changes on its way from Faraday to Einstein and the quantum field theory. Nevertheless, the British theologian Thomas Torrance, who has significantly contributed to the dialogue between theology and science, turned in 1969 to the field concept in order to describe the efficacy of the divine spirit in natural processes. I shall return to this contribution of Torrance later.

Together with the widely held belief in a world without beginning or end, the mechanistic description of natural processes brought about in the eighteenth and nineteenth centuries a deep alienation between natural science and Christian belief in creation. The pivotal point of this development has been seen by many observers as Darwin's theory of evolution, because here even the origin of living beings and of their species was no longer considered the effect of purposeful action of a divine intelligence, but as resulting from a quasi-mechanical interaction of random variations of life via the mechanism of natural selection and environmental conditions. It is understandable that from early on Darwin's theory was considered the final triumph of a mechanistic description of natural processes. Even in early discussions about Darwin's theory, however, some theologians argued for a different evaluation. They did not consider the theory of evolution as a final triumph of a mechanistic description of natural processes, but as a break-through toward a new image of natural processes in terms of a history of life starting from primitive beginnings all the way to the emergence of the human race. This history of living forms could be seen from the perspective of biblical salvation history in terms of a prehistory of God's history of the salvation of humankind, such that God's incarnation in Jesus Christ could be understood as the culmination of the entire process of an evolution of life. Such a conception was represented as early as 1889 in the volume *Lux Mundi*, edited by Charles Gore. This idea later inspired British theologians of evolu-tion like William Temple and, presently, Arthur Peacocke. Closely related also was the influential work of Teilhard de Chardin. Contributions in the twentieth century to the further development of the doctrine of evolution in the sense of a process of emergence that gives rise to ever new forms of life appeared under names like "emergent evolution" or "organic evolution."

The most effective impulse toward a conception of natural processes in terms of a history of nature came in the twentieth century from physical cos-mology. The observation that there is a process of expansion of the universe because the galaxies increasingly turn to diverge from each other leads to the assumption that the whole universe must have started about fifteen billion years ago with a kind of explosion, a big bang. In the process of expan-sion and of the cooling effect connected with such expansion, solid bodies became possible, beginning with atoms and molecules, but all the way to the formation of stars and galaxies. As early as 1948, the well-known German physicist Carl Friedrich von Weizsäcker, who later became a philosopher, described this process in terms of a history of nature, that began with the big bang and leads toward the origin of life on our planet and, finally, to the origin and history of humanity.

Such a description of nature in terms of a history is a significant depar-ture from the conception of the universe that was presented by the classical physics of earlier centuries. There, the world of nature had been conceived as without beginning and end, and natural processes were thought of as revers-ible in principle and also as always repeatable. That was deeply different from the new scientific cosmology, according to which the universe started its history with a big bang and is characterized by increasing expansion. Here, the process of nature at large is conceived as the unique and irreversible process of history. That implies that each moment in the history of the universe occurs as something more or less new that is comparable with all that went before only to a degree. Even the uniformities of natural processes described by scientific formulas of law can in such a perspective only represent approximations. The element of contingency, the occurrence of novelty in the course of events, became increasingly important in the science of the twentieth century, first in quantum physics, where each individual event is strictly speaking unpredictable, although the course of events overall follows statistical regularities. The German physicist Hans-Peter Dürr, a former student of Heisenberg, captured this situation occasionally with the remark that in a certain sense this world occurs anew in each moment. This importance of contingency is not confined to microphysics. In 1980, Ilya Prigogine demonstrated, together with Isabelle Stengers, that in hydrodynamic processes far from equilibrium, chaotic situations can occur with unpredictable new events that occasionally can provide a new direction for the entire process. The order of natural law is not destroyed by the occurrence of chaotic processes of such a type, but, according to John Polkinghorne, it appears now as much more "elastic" than earlier generations, with their belief in rigid determinism of natural processes, could imagine.

This new conception of a history of nature, and especially the new scientific cosmology with its assumption of an origin of the entire universe at some finite time in the past, sometimes gives the impression of a closer approximation of science to the biblical view of the origin of the world in a divine act of creation than had previously been considered possible. But these new developments in science, and especially the new scientific cosmology, should not be considered confirmation or support for the Christian belief in the creation of the world, as Pope Pius XII seemed to assume in 1951. The Catholic philosopher Ernan McMullin has spoken with more restraint of the fact of a new consonance concerning the relationship between natural science and Christian faith in the creation of the world, in distinction from the situation in earlier centuries. This new consonance not only applies to the question of a beginning of our universe, but also, and more importantly, to the general conception of a history of nature. This new situation enables Christian theologians today once more to illustrate and interpret the biblical affirmation of the creation of the world by the God of the Bible with reference to contemporary knowledge about the world, like the biblical report on its creation used the knowledge about the world that was available at that time. At present, Christian theology should no longer talk about the creation of a vault of heaven, a firmament, in order to separate heaven and earth.

Rather, it will be said that God produced the universe and the multitude of its creatures by way of a cooling process starting from the very hot original condition of the universe and accompanying its expansion. The process of cosmic cooling, then, functions as an instrument that God used in his activity of creating the world. The biblical report on the creation of the world already mentioned that God in some cases made use of the cooperation of already existing creatures. In the biblical report this applies especially to the earth. According to Genesis 1:11, God calls upon the earth to bring forth vegetation. In our contemporary language, this means nothing less than the formation of organic life from inorganic matter such as has been affirmed by recent hypotheses concerning an original formation of organic life by way of self-organization of protein particles. Such ideas do not contradict the biblical report of creation, since the immediacy of God's creation of each of his creatures through the divine word does not exclude the cooperation of already existing creatures. Moreover, the earth is addressed by the creator a second time with a call for cooperation: astonishingly—at least for a modern reader—God calls upon the earth when it comes to the creation of beasts such as cattle and other animals: "Let the earth bring forth living creatures according to their kinds: cattle and creeping things and beasts of the earth according to their kinds" (Gen. 1:24). The Bible is here more audacious than Darwin ever dared to be. Certainly, Darwin taught the origin of species from other, more primitive forms of life, but never directly from inorganic matter. His theory of evolution was more moderate at this point than what the biblical text here suggests. The biblical report did not yet know of the idea of an evolution of the forms of life, of organic species from other more primitive ones, but that idea is less audacious at this point than the biblical report is. Perhaps, then, the passionate battle of some Christians against the theory of evolution all the way to contemporary creationism has been an unnecessary conflict after all, and even the conservative Christian creationists, who still continue the fight against Darwinism, might come to a milder judgment, if they were to consider the literal meaning of the biblical text in its report on the creation of the world concerning the function of the earth with regard to the origin of organic life, of vegetation, and even of the higher animals. Whether or not the theory of evolution is true must remain an empirical question, but it is not an issue of categorical opposition from the perspective of Christian theology.

What I said so far about the use of contemporary scientific assumptions concerning the origin and evolution of the universe, of its stars and galaxies and of the origin and evolution of life on earth in a theological account of the divine action of the creation of the universe presupposes, to be sure, the clarification of a number of further questions concerning the relationship between God and nature. At least two of these questions must be dealt with in the reflections I am offering here. The first of these questions concerns the precise meaning of the term *creation*, while the second asks how the activity of God in natural processes can be conceived without getting into competition with our knowledge about natural forces and their efficacy.

The concept of creation as used in the first chapter of the Bible relates to the primordial origin of the different forms of creatures, to the first origin of heaven and earth, of land and sea, of the stars, of vegetation on earth, of plants and animals according to their different species and, finally, of the human creature. All the affirmations of this report on creation relate to the primordial origin of these creatures, the creation in the beginning, which determines for all subsequent times the forms of created existence. Presupposed is the idea that the order of the world must have been established initially for all subsequent time. This, however, is not the only idea of creation, of God's creative activity, that we have in the Bible. In the Psalms, especially Psalm 104, and in the prophetic writings of the Bible, we have the idea that God is continuously acting as creator in such a way that God brings forth again and again something new, as we read in the book of Isaiah: "Behold, I am doing a new thing" (Isa. 43:19). This conception of God's creative activity in the sense of a continuing creation corresponds more closely to our contemporary understanding of nature and of natural processes than a concept that applies the idea of creation exclusively to the beginning. The idea of a creation in the beginning need not be excluded. It is indeed consonant with contemporary scientific cosmology, and it is also plausible that this beginning remains constitutive in everything that follows. Nevertheless, in the history of the universe, again and again something new originated that was not present in the beginning—the elements with their atoms and molecules, the stars and galaxies, the planets and among them our earth, and after billions of years, organic life on our earth, the world of plants and animals and, finally, the human race. The history of the universe, where new creatures and new forms of creatures occur along the way, is bound up with the nature of its creation, and the Christian faith expects the completion of God's creation not before the final future that God will bring about in the full realization of his kingdom and his creation, a future that according to our Christian faith is already dawned in the resurrection of Christ. In this perspective, creation and consummation of the created world are bound up with each other, and some such perspective is already prefigured in a pre-Christian exposition of the biblical report of creation, where the seventh day of creation, when God rests of God's works, is related to the future completion of the world. This is an idea that is also used in the New Testament, in the epistle to the Hebrews (4:4ff.), where participation in God's rest after his work of creation on the seventh day is said to be the final destination also of creatures.

The intrinsic logic of the concept of creation, of God's intention in creating a world of creatures, aims at providing some form of independent existence for a multitude of creatures, although such independent existence may be limited and perishable. One form of such an independent existence is already the permanence of solid physical bodies in difference to the ephemeral existence of elemental particles. Atoms and molecules and all complex physical bodies such as stars or mountains possess this form of independent existence. A condition for the formation of permanent existence and, therefore, of all higher organized forms of created existence is, of course, the permanent validity of natural law. Without the order of natural law, no permanent existence is conceivable. There are higher, more complex forms of independence because they can to some degree actively influence and shape their own existence. In the highest degree, this applies to human beings. Although they too are perishable, they nevertheless possess a higher degree of independence than mountains and stars because they are called to shape their own lives. In a biblical perspective, the aim of such independent activity of shaping one's own life is to realize it in free submission to their Creator and Father in order to participate in such a way in the relationship of God's Son to the Father and, therefore, in God's eternal life. The future completion of the creation in participation in God's eternal life, like it is described by the apostle Paul in the eighth chapter of his letter to the Romans, will also be the ultimate consummation of God's own action as creator, the completion of God's intention to provide some form of independent existence to creatures in communion with himself.

There remains the question of how the creative action of God in the process of nature can be imagined without competition with the activity of natural forces. The biblical report on the creation of the world talks about the production of creatures by the divine command, but this does not yet answer the question of the mode of their production. Therefore, the biblical report is characterized by a coordination of word and action, which also can include the cooperation of created factors such as the earth. The creative word is always related to the specific nature of what is to be produced. Concerning the creative action itself, one learns more from other texts like Psalm 104, where it is said of the living beings that they are created through the breath of God, through God's Spirit (Ps. 104:30). In the Bible, this Spirit of God is not something like consciousness or self-consciousness, but rather the vital energy of life as it comes to expression in the blowing of wind or storm. It occurs not only in the living creatures, however, but according to the first chapter of the Bible, the blowing of the divine Spirit is the source of all movement. When it is said of the Spirit of God that in the beginning he "was moving over the face of the water" of the primeval ocean (Gen. 1:2), this is the source of all movement.

Earlier in this presentation, I mentioned the Scottish theologian Thomas Torrance, who in 1969 described the activity of the divine Spirit with the help of the physical concept of field in the sense of Faraday's conception of fields of force. At first sight such a comparison may come as a surprise, but the history of the scientific concept of field shows that there exists a substantial relationship between spirit and field. The famous historian of scientific conceptuality, Max Jammer, published an article on the concept of field in 1972 and retraced the scientific concept of field to the ancient, especially stoic, concept of *pneuma*, which meant not only "spirit" in our modern sense, but also "air" and, more precisely, air as filled with tension. This description also applies to the biblical concept of *pneuma* as we find it in the Gospel of John, where it is said of the nature of Spirit, "the wind blows where it wills, and you hear the sound of it, but you do not know whence it comes or whither it goes" (3:8). This corresponds to the Hebrew concept of the divine spirit as *ruah*. In view of these connections in the history of philosophical and scientific conceptuality, it is no longer absurd to explain the biblical conception of the Spirit of God and his activity by the concept of field, especially in its conception by Faraday as field of force. Certainly the activity of the divine Spirit cannot be calculated by counting waves. Nevertheless, as a comprehensive field of force, the Spirit of God may penetrate all creaturely forces and movements and thus be active in his creation. When we read in the Gospel of John that "God is spirit" (4:24), we should not think in the first place of the divine consciousness or self-consciousness, but much more of a field of power that pervades, animates, and holds together the entire world of creation. God confronts creation as Father of the universe, and God is through his *Logos* the origin of all specific formations, but it is through his Spirit that God is creatively sustaining and animating his creatures.

Notes

Preface Notes

1. For a helpful computer visual of the flooding process in the New Orleans area, see www.nola.com/katrina/graphics/flashflood.swf (accessed June 6, 2007).

2. See my introduction.

Introduction Notes

1. Phillip E. Johnson, *Darwin on Trial* (Downers Grove, Ill.: InterVarsity, 1991).

2. Richard Dawkins, *The Blind Watchmaker: Why the Evidence of Evolution Reveals a Universe Without Design* (New York: Norton, 1987).

3. Michael Denton, *Evolution: A Theory in Crisis* (Bethesda, Md.: Adler & Adler, 1986).

4. "I read these books, and I guess almost immediately I thought, This is it. *This is where it all comes down to, the understanding of creation.*" Tim Stafford, "The Making of a Revolution: Law professor Phillip Johnson wants to overturn the scientific establishment's 'creation myth,'" *Christianity Today*, December 8, 1997. www.ctlibrary.com/ct/1997/december8/7te016.html (accessed June 7, 2007).

5. Access Research Network: Origins Research Archive, "An Interview with Michael Denton," vol. 15, no. 2, www.arn.org/docs/orpages/or152/dent.htm (accessed June 7, 2007).

6. William A. Dembski, "Preface," in *Darwin's Nemesis: Phillip Johnson and the Intelligent Design Movement*, ed. William A. Dembski (Downers Grove, Ill.: InterVarsity, 2006),14.

7. I am thinking here primarily of a host of Web sites that caricature and ridicule ID without distinguishing between ID and creation science or presenting accurately its position. For an academic treatment that offers a strong rejection of ID, see Barbara Forrest and Paul R. Gross, *Creationism's Trojan Horse: The Wedge of Intelligent Design* (New York: Oxford University Press, 2004). For an ID perspective, see Angus Menuge, "Who's Afraid of ID? A Survey of the Intelligent Design Movement," in *Debating Design: From Darwin to DNA*, ed. William A. Dembski and Michael Ruse (New York: Cambridge University Press, 2004), 32–51. See also Discovery Institute, "The 'Wedge Document': 'So What?'" at www.discovery.org/scripts/viewDB/filesDB-download.php?id=349 (accessed June 7, 2007). These are just a few of the many sources that could be listed here, but they have useful bibliographies and notes to help the interested reader further investigate this issue.

8. Phillip E. Johnson, *Reason in the Balance: The Case Against Naturalism in Science, Law and Education* (Downers Grove, Ill.: InterVarsity, 1995).

9. The center is presently named The Center for Science and Culture.

10. Michael J. Behe, *Darwin's Black Box: The Biochemical Challenge to Evolution* (New York: The Free Press, 1996).

11. Selected papers from this conference were published in 1998. See William A. Dembski, ed., *Mere Creation: Science, Faith and Intelligent Design* (Downers Grove, Ill.: Inter-Varsity, 1998).

12. Behe, *Darwin's Black Box*, 39.

13. Behe, *Darwin's Black Box*, 65–73.

14. Behe, *Darwin's Black Box*, 75–97.

15. Behe, *Darwin's Black Box*, 98–116.

16. Behe, *Darwin's Black Box*, 117–39.

17. Behe, *Darwin's Black Box*, 140–61.

18. Kenneth R. Miller, *Finding Darwin's God: A Scientist's Search for Common Ground Between God and Evolution* (New York: Cliff Street, 1999), 160. See also Kenneth R. Miller, "The Flagellum Unspun: The Collapse of 'Irreducible Complexity,'" in *Debating Design*, ed. Dembski and Ruse, 81–97.

19. For numerous responses by Behe, see Behe's author's page at Access Research Network, www.arn.org/authors/behe.html (accessed June 7, 2007). Two of Behe's responses to Miller are "Comments on Ken Miller's Reply to My Essays," January 8, 2001, Access Research Network: Michael Behe Files, www.arn.org/docs/behe/mb_responsetokmiller0101.htm (accessed June 7, 2007) and "A True Acid Test: Response to Ken Miller," July 31, 2000, Access Research Network: Michael Behe Files, www.arn.org/docs/behe/mb_trueacidtest.htm (accessed June 7, 2007.) It is worth noting Behe mentions Miller several times in *Darwin's Black Box*, 222–23, 225–26, 227, 228, 239.

20. William A. Dembski, *The Design Inference: Eliminating Chance Through Small Probabilities*, Cambridge Studies in Probability, Induction, and Decision Theory (New York: Cambridge University Press, 1998).

21. William A. Dembski, *The Design Revolution: Answering the Toughest Questions About Intelligent Design* (Downers Grove, Ill.: InterVarsity, 2004), 75.

22. Dembski, *The Design Revolution*, 27.

23. Dembski, *The Design Revolution*, 34.

24. Dembski, *The Design Revolution*, 35.

25. Dembski, *The Design Revolution*, 35.

26. Dembski, *The Design Revolution*, 84–85; Dembski, *No Free Lunch: Why Specified Complexity Cannot Be Purchased without Intelligence* (Lanham, Md.: Rowman and Littlefield, 2002), 22.

27. Dembski, *The Design Revolution*, 83–84. For more on this principle, Dembski points his readers to the Web site "Minimum Description Length on the Web," www.mdl-research.org/ (accessed June 7, 2007).

28. Dembski, *The Design Revolution*, 83–84.

29. Branden Fitelson, Christopher Stephens, and Elliott Sober, "How Not to Detect Design," *Philosophy of Science* 66 (1999): 472–88. Reprinted in James B. Miller, *An Evolving Dialogue: Theological and Scientific Perspectives on Evolution* (Harrisburg, Pa.: Trinity Press International, 2001), 491–507.

30. Dembski, *No Free Lunch* and *The Design Revolution*. See also his Web site, "Design Inference Website: The Writings of William A. Dembski," www.designinference.com/ (accessed June 7, 2007).

31. Forrest and Gross, *Creationism's Trojan Horse*. Cf. Menuge, "Who's Afraid of ID?" 32–51.

32. Stuart Kauffman, "Intelligent Design, Science or Not?" in *Intelligent Thought: Science Versus the Intelligent Design Movement*, ed. John Brockman (New York: Vintage, 2006), 169–78.

33. Dembski, *The Design Revolution*, 280–90.

34. Kauffman, "Intelligent Design, Science or Not?" 169–70.

35. For a brief history of the design argument, see Michael Ruse, "The Argument from Design: A Brief History," in *Debating Design*, ed. Dembski and Ruse, 13–31. For a brief analysis of design arguments with readings and bibliography relevant to our present discussion, see Michael Palmer, *The Question of God: An Introduction and Sourcebook* (New York: Routledge, 2001), 92–169.

36. Dembski, *The Design Revolution*, 77. Critics of ID typically respond that such may be formally true but actually irrelevant because ID proponents do take the next step, that is, reason their way to the existence of God. For example, see Jerry A. Coyne, "Intelligent Design: The Faith That Dare Not Speak Its Name," in *Intelligent Thought*, ed. Brockman, 13. Coyne holds that there is a weak version of ID and a strong version of ID. The weak version is the minimalist depiction given above. The strong version is what ID advocates believe and admit to religious audiences.

37. Behe, *Darwin's Black Box*, 210–21. Behe does agree that the identity of the designer cannot be established by ID.

38. As noted above, Michael Denton is a religious agnostic; David Berlinski, a secular Jew, who professes to have no religious convictions or beliefs. Jonathan Witt, "An Interview with David Berlinski: Part 1," www.idthefuture.com/2006/03/an_interview_with_david_berlin.html (accessed June 7, 2007).

39. Phillip E. Johnson, *Darwin on Trial*, 14.

40. Behe, *Darwin's Black Box*, 5.

41. For instance, see Daniel Dennett, "The Hoax of Intelligent Design and How It Was Perpetrated," in *Intelligent Thought*, ed. Brockman, 33–49. See also Coyne, "Intelligent Design," as well as Forrest and Gross, *Creationism's Trojan Horse*.

42. E.g., see Carl Wieland, "AiG's views on the Intelligent Design Movement," August 30, 2002, www.answersingenesis.org/docs2002/0830_IDM.asp (accessed June 7, 2007).

43. See "Judge: Evolution stickers unconstitutional," January 14, 2005, www.cnn.com/2005/LAW/01/13/evolution.textbooks.ruling/ (accessed June 7, 2007).

44. See press release, "Agreement Ends Textbook Sticker Case," December 19, 2006, www2.ncseweb.org/selman/2006-12-19_Sticker_Agreement.pdf (accessed June 7, 2007).

45. See "Memorandum Opinion," Case 4:04-cv-02688-JEJ, Document 342, Filed 12/20/2005 in the United States District Court for the Middle District of Pennsylvania, December 20, 2005, www.pamd.uscourts.gov/kitzmiller/kitzmiller_342.pdf (accessed June 7, 2007).

46. "Memorandum Opinion."

47. "Memorandum Opinion."

48. David Ray Griffin, *Religion and Scientific Naturalism: Overcoming the Conflicts* (Albany: State University of New York Press, 2000), 287, n.23.

49. Behe, *Darwin's Black Box*, 5.

50. Ted Peters and Martinez Hewlett, *Evolution from Creation to New Creation: Conflict, Conversation, and Convergence* (Nashville: Abingdon, 2003), 114.

Chapter 2 Notes

1. Aage Petersen, "The Philosophy of Niels Bohr," in *Niels Bohr: A Centenary Volume*, ed. A. P. French and P. I. Kennedy (Cambridge: Harvard University Press, 1985), 299.

2. Thomas Kuhn, *The Structure of Scientific Revolutions* (Chicago: Chicago University Press, 1996).

3. John Maynard Smith, "A Darwinian View of Symbiosis," in *Symbiosis as a Source of Evolutionary Innovation: Speciation and Morphogenesis*, ed. L. Margulis and R. Fester (Cambridge: MIT Press, 1991), 26–39.

4. Julian Huxley, *Evolution: The Modern Synthesis* (London: Allen and Unwin, 1942).

5. E. Cullota and E. Pennisi, "Breakthrough of the Year: Evolution in Action," *Science* 310 (2005): 1878–79.

6. Karl Popper, *The Logic of Scientific Discovery* (New York: Basic Books, 1959).

7. Stephen Jay Gould, *The Structure of Evolutionary Theory* (Cambridge, Mass.: Belknap, 2002).

8. "Letter from T. Huxley to C. Darwin," January 30, 1859, located at the Clark University Thomas Huxley Web site: aleph0.clarku.edu/huxley/letters/59.html (accessed June 8, 2007).

9. Julian Huxley, "Evolution and Religion," in *Issues in Evolution*, ed. Sol Tax, (Chicago: University of Chicago Press, 1960), 41.

10. Julian Huxley, "The Coming New Religion of Humanism," *Humanist*, (January/February 1962).

11. Richard Dawkins, *The Blind Watchmaker* (London: Norton, 1986), 6.

12. Herbert Spencer, "The Development Hypothesis," in *Essays: Scientific, Political and Speculative* (London: Williams and Norgate, 1852), 377–83.

13. Charles Darwin, *The Origin of Species by Means of Natural Selection* (New York: Encyclopedia Britannica, 1952), 32.

14. Francis Galton, *Hereditary Genius: An Inquiry into its Laws and Consequences* (London: MacMillan, 1892).

15. Richard Dawkins, *The God Delusion* (London: Norton, 2006).

16. Ted Peters and Martinez Hewlett, *Evolution: From Creation to New Creation* (Nashville: Abingdon, 2003); Peters and Hewlett, *Can You Believe in God and Evolution? A Guide for the Perplexed* (Nashville: Abingdon, 2006).

17. The Web site AntiEvolution.org has a great deal of information about this landmark ruling, including testimony and the text of the ruling itself. See www.antievolution.org/projects/mclean/new_site/index.htm (accessed June 8, 2007).

18. William Paley, *Natural Theology, or Evidences of the Existence and Attributes of the Deity*, new ed. (New York: Oxford University Press, 2006).

19. Dawkins, *The God Delusion*, 77–79.

20. Thomas Aquinas, *Summa Theologica*, Q. 2, Art. 3 (Chicago: Encyclopedia Britannica, 1952), 13.

21. Michael J. Behe, *Darwin's Black Box: The Biochemical Challenge to Evolution* (New York: The Free Press, 1996).

22. William Dembski, *No Free Lunch: Why Specified Complexity Cannot Be Purchased without Intelligence* (Lanham, Md.: Rowman and Littlefield, 2002).

23. Robert John Russell, "Intelligent Design Is Not Science and Does Not Qualify to be Taught in Public School Science Classes," *Theology and Science* 3, no. 2 (July 2005): 131–32.

24. Aquinas, *Summa Theologica*, Q. 2, Art. 3.

25. Dembski, *No Free Lunch*. Intelligent causes occupy much of the discussion of this book.

26. Peters and Hewlett, *Can You Believe in God and Evolution?*

27. John Paul II, "Message of His Holiness Pope John Paul II," in *Physics, Philosophy, and Theology*, ed. R. J. Russell, W. R. Stoeger, and G. V. Coyne (Vatican City: Vatican Observatory Foundation, 1997), M13.

Chapter 3 Notes

1. William Dembski, *The Design Revolution* (Downers Grove, Ill.: InterVarsity, 2004), 21.

2. Dembski, *The Design Revolution*, 21–22.

3. Dembski, *The Design Revolution*, 169.

4. Dembski, *The Design Revolution*, 171–72.

5. Dembski, *The Design Revolution*, 169.

6. Dembski, *The Design Revolution*, 169.

7. Dembski, *The Design Revolution*, 92.

8. Dembski, *The Design Revolution*, 169, 171.

9. Dembski, *The Design Revolution*, 148.

10. Dembski, *The Design Revolution*, 39.

11. Dembski, *The Design Revolution*, 94.

12. Dembski, *The Design Revolution*, 281–82.

13. Dembski, *The Design Revolution*, 170.

14. Dembski, *The Design Revolution*, 170.

15. Dembski, *The Design Revolution*, 172.

16. Dembski, *The Design Revolution*, 177.

17. Dembski, *The Design Revolution*, 170–71.

18. Dembski, *The Design Revolution*, 170.

19. Isaac Newton, *Sir Isaac Newton's 'Mathematical Principles of Natural Philosophy' and his 'System of the World,'* trans. Andrew Motte, rev. with an appendix by Florian Cajori, 2 vols. (Los Angeles: University of California Press, 1966), 1:6.

20. Henri Poincaré, "The Measure of Time," in *The Foundations of Science* (Science Press, 1913; rep. ed., Washington, D.C.: University Press of America, 1982), 228–29; H. A. Lorentz to A. Einstein, January 1915, Boerhaave Museum, cited in Jozsef Illy, "Einstein Teaches Lorentz, Lorentz Teaches Einstein. Their Collaboration in General Relativity, 1913–1920," *Archive for History of Exact Sciences* 39 (1989): 274; Arthur Eddington, *Space, Time and Gravitation*, Cambridge Science Classics (Cambridge: Cambridge University Press, 1920; rep. ed., 1987), 166.

21. Lin Dyson, Matthew Kleban, and Leonard Susskind, "Disturbing Implications of a Cosmological Constant," November 14, 2002, 421, arXiv.org/abs/hep-th/0208013v3 (accessed June 8, 2007).

22. Dyson, Kleban, and Susskind, "Disturbing Implications," 20–21.

23. Dyson, Kleban, and Susskind, "Disturbing Implications," 20–21.

24. Dyson, Kleban, and Susskind, "Disturbing Implications," 2.

25. Dyson, Kleban, and Susskind, "Disturbing Implications," 21.

26. Richard Dawkins, *The God Delusion* (New York: Houghton Mifflin, 2006), p. 2 and throughout the book.

27. Dawkins, *The God Delusion*, p. 156.

28. One is tempted to construe Dawkins' objection as an appeal to simplicity or economy; but that cannot be right, since the inference to natural super-human designers, which Dawkins allows, will also postulate causes as, or even more, complex than the phenomena to be explained. Moreover, such an objection would preclude even archaeologists' inferring human designers of excavated materials or SETI scientists' inferring extra-terrestrial intelligence behind some signal, for in such cases, too, the *explanans* is as complex as the *explanandum*. In any case, the theist could rightly counter that God, as an unembodied mind, is a remarkably simple entity, having no separable parts, so that the *explanans* is vastly simpler than the variegated and contingent universe. Dawkins has apparently confused a mind's ideas, which may indeed, be infinitely complex, with a mind itself, which as a spiritual substance is amazingly simple. Thus, an advance in economy has clearly been made in postulating a divine designer.

So more than mere simplicity must be at issue here. What Dawkins must find objectionable in the hypothesis of divine design is that in this case the designer cannot be explained. But why is that a problem for the adequacy of the explanation? Recall that in this case the *explanandum* is "the appearance of design *in the universe*" (ibid., p. 157, my emphasis). The designer's complexity represents another *explanandum*. It is no indictment of an explanation that it fails to explain some other *explanandum*. If Dawkins insists that in order to infer that some hypothesis is the best explanation, we must have an explanation of the explanation, then we are immediately launched on an infinite regress, so that nothing will be explained. Moreover, as the above examples of the archaeologists and SETI scientists illustrate, we do not need to have an explanation of the explanation to recognize that the explanation is the best. So Dawkins must be objecting in principle to the postulation of casually inexplicable explanatory entities. Earlier in his book he insists that " *any creative intelligence, of sufficient complexity to design anything, comes into existence only as the end product of an extended process of gradual evolution*" (ibid., p. 31). One wonders how Dawkins could possibly know such a thing. It appears to be nothing more than a sweeping and gratuitous metaphysical presupposition, an expression of anti-teleological naturalism. Since this presupposition is assumed by his argument, his objection to positing God as the cosmic designer takes on the appearance of reasoning in a circle.

Chapter 4 Notes

1. P. William Davis, Dean H. Kenyon, and Charles B. Thaxton, *Of Pandas and People: The Central Question of Biological Origins*, 2nd ed. (Dallas: Haughton, 1993). Other authors of portions of the book include Stephen Meyer, Mark Hartwig, Nancy Pearcey, and Michael Behe.

2. Thomas More Law Center, *About Us*, www.thomasmore.org/about.html (accessed June 14, 2007).

3. Laurie Goodstein, "In Intelligent Design Case, a Cause in Search of a Lawsuit," *New York Times*, November 4, 2005.

4. *Kitzmiller v. Dover Area School District*, 400 F.Supp.2d 707 (M.D. Pen. 2005).

5. For example, at the beginning of the trial, William Dembski estimated that there was "less than a 10% probability" that ID would be ruled both unconstitutional and unscientific. William A. Dembski, "Life After Dover," *Uncommon Descent*, September 30, 2005, www.uncommondescent.com/intelligent-design/life-after-dover/ (accessed June 14, 2007).

6. Nicholas J. Matzke, "Am I Psychic or What?" *The Panda's Thumb*, December 20, 2005, www.pandasthumb.org/archives/2005/12/am_i_psychic_or.html (accessed June 14, 2007).

7. *McLean v. Arkansas Board of Education*, 529 F.Supp. 1255 (E.D. Ark. 1982).

8. *Edwards v. Aguillard*, 482 U.S. 578 (S.Ct. 1987).

9. See Nicholas J. Matzke and Paul R. Gross, "Analyzing Critical Analysis: The Fallback Antievolutionist Strategy," in *Not in Our Classrooms: Why Intelligent Design Is Wrong for Our Schools*, ed. Eugenie Carol Scott and Glenn Branch (Boston: Beacon, 2006), 28–56, for a detailed critique of the 2005 Kansas Science Standards. The chapter also rebuts the ID movement's attempt to throw its critics off the scent by claiming that the Kansas Science Standards did not include ID.

10. Kansas' pro-ID science standards were finally repealed by the new board on February 13, 2007.

11. Nicholas J. Matzke, "History and Cobb County," *The Panda's Thumb*, 2006, www.pandasthumb.org/archives/2006/12/history_and_cob.html (accessed June 14, 2007); Matzke, *The Cobb County Anti-Evolution Textbook Disclaimer Case*, 2006, www2.ncseweb.org/selman/ (accessed June 14, 2007).

12. Previously known as the Center for the Renewal of Science and Culture. See NCSE, *Evolving Banners at the Discovery Institute*, August 29, 2002, www.ncseweb.org/resources/articles/8325_evolving_banners_at_the_discov_8_29_2002.asp (accessed June 14, 2007).

13. For some analysis, see Barbara Forrest, *The "Vise Strategy" Undone: Kitzmiller et al. v. Dover Area School District, Committee for the Scientific Investigation of Claims of the Paranormal*, 2006, www.csicop.org/intelligentdesignwatch/kitzmiller.html (accessed June 14, 2007); and Wesley R. Elsberry, "Can I Keep a Witness?" *Reports of the National Center for Science Education* 26, no. 1 (2006).

14. "The Wedge," *Discovery Institute*, 1998, www.seattleweekly.com/2006-02-01/news/the-wedge.php (accessed June 14, 2007).

15. David K. DeWolf, Stephen C. Meyer, and Mark E. DeForrest, *Intelligent Design in Public School Science Curricula: A Legal Guidebook* (Richardson, Tex.: Foundation for Thought and Ethics, 1999).

16. "Discovery Institute and Thomas More Law Center Squabble in AEI Forum," www.ncseweb.org/resources/news/2005/US/98_discovery_institute_and_thomas_10_23_2005.asp (accessed June 14, 2007).

17. For example, Francis J. Beckwith, *Law, Darwinism and Public Education: The Establishment Clause and the Challenge of Intelligent Design* (Lanham, Md.: Rowman & Littlefield, 2003); Beckwith, "Public Education, Religious Establishment, and the Challenge of Intelligent Design," *Notre Dame Journal of Law, Ethics, and Public Policy* 17, no. 2 (2003): 461–519; Beckwith, "Science and Religion Twenty Years after *McLean v. Arkansas*: Evolution, Public Education, and the New Challenge of Intelligent Design," *Harvard Journal of Law and Public Policy* 26, no. 2 (2003): 455–99; David K. DeWolf, "Academic Freedom After Edwards," *Regent University Law Review* 13 (2000): 447–81; DeWolf, Meyer, and DeForrest, *Intelligent Design in Public School Science Curricula*; DeWolf, Meyer, and DeForrest, "Teaching the Origins Controversy: Science, or Religion, or Speech?" *Utah Law Review* 39 (2000): 39–110.

18. Stephen C. Meyer, Scott Minnich, Jonathan Moneymaker, Paul A. Nelson, and Ralph Seelke, *Explore Evolution: The Arguments for and against Neo-Darwinism* (Melbourne & London: Hill House, 2007).

19. David K. DeWolf, John G. West, and Casey Luskin, "Intelligent Design Will Survive *Kitzmiller v. Dover*," *Montana Law Review* 63, no. 1 (2007): 7–57. See also the response to the article in the same issue: Peter Irons, "Disaster in Dover: The Trials (and Tribulations) of Intelligent Design," *Montana Law Review* 63, no. 1 (2007): 59–87.

20. Edward J. Larson, *Trial and Error: The American Controversy over Creation and Evolution*, 3d ed. (New York: Oxford University Press, 2003).

21. Nicholas J. Matzke, "But Isn't It Creationism? The Beginnings of 'Intelligent Design' in the Midst of the Arkansas and Louisiana Litigation," in *But Is It Science?*, ed. Michael Ruse and Robert T. Pennock, (Buffalo, N.Y.: Prometheus Books, 2007); Eugenie C. Scott and Nicholas J. Matzke, "Biological Design in Science Classrooms," *Proceedings of the National Academy of Sciences* 104, no. suppl. 1 (2007): 8669–676.

22. *Epperson v. Arkansas*, 393 U.S. 97 (S.Ct. 1968).

23. Ronald L. Numbers, *The Creationists: From Scientific Creationism to Intelligent Design*, exp. ed. (Cambridge: Harvard University Press, 2006).

24. Numbers, *The Creationists*.

25. Roger Lewin, "Creationism on the Defensive in Arkansas," *Science* 215, no. 4528 (1982): 33–34.

26. Rebecca Salner, "Professor teaches a supernatural creation of world," *San Francisco Examiner*, December 17, 1980, A9.

27. Lewin, "Creationism on the Defensive in Arkansas."

28. Wendell L. Bird, "Freedom of Religion and Science Instruction in Public Schools," *Yale Law Journal* 87, no. 3 (1978): 515–70; Bird, "Freedom from Establishment and Unneutrality in Public School Instruction and Religious School Regulation," *Harvard Journal of Law and Public Policy* 2 (1979): 125–205.

29. Jack Weatherly, "Creationists Lose in Arkansas: Missing Witnesses and a Divided Defense Muddled the Issue," *Christianity Today*, 22 January 1982, 28–29.

30. Contrary to regular creationist complaining in subsequent decades, faithfully repeated by ID advocates, McLean's Judge Overton did not arbitrarily employ against creationism a dubious definition of science contrived by Michael Ruse for legal purposes. Overton received testimony from Ruse as well as numerous leading scientists and reached a workable layman's understanding of what constitutes science, and found that "creation science" didn't fit. Contrary to popular belief, a judge's job is not to achieve philosophical perfection that settles every conceivable issue for all times and places; rather, it is to use the evidence presented in the form of sworn testimony to reach a reasonably good decision in a short period of time. This is all a judge is required to do, as was pointed out to Larry Laudan and other critics of Overton and Ruse at the time: Barry R. Gross, "Philosophers at the Bar—Some Reasons for Restraint," *Science, Technology, and Human Values* 8, no. 4 (1983): 30–38. See also a forthcoming article by Robert Pennock in *But Is It Science?* that reviews McLean and its critics in the light of his experience in *Kitzmiller*.

31. Martin Mawyer, "Arkansas: Where Creationism Lost Its Shirt," *Moody Monthly* 82, no. 9 (1982): 10–14.

32. Beckwith, "Science and Religion Twenty Years after *McLean v. Arkansas*."

33. Wendell Bird (1982), "Plaintiffs' Summaries of Expert Testimony," *Keith v. Louisiana Department of Education*, Plaintiffs; Walter Bradley, "Foreword," in *Origin Science: A Proposal for the Creation-Evolution Controversy* (Grand Rapids: Baker, 1987), 7–9.

34. Dean H. Kenyon (1984), "Affidavit of Dean Kenyon," *Edwards v. Aguillard*, Expert, Eastern District of Louisiana: Civil Action No. 81-4787. (Emphasis added.)

35. *Edwards v. Aguillard*, 482 U.S. 578 (1987).

36. *Edwards v. Aguillard*.

37. *Edwards v. Aguillard*.

38. Reviewed by Beckwith, *Law, Darwinism, and Public Education*.

39. Davis, Kenyon, and Thaxton, *Of Pandas and People*.

40. Jon Buell, "Preface," in *The Design of Life: Discovering Signs of Intelligence in Biological Systems*, ed. Michael J. Behe, Percival Davis, William A. Dembski, Dean H. Kenyon, Jonathan Wells (Richardson, Tex.: Foundation for Thought and Ethics, 2004), iv–vi. The third edition of *Pandas* is to be titled *The Design of Life*. It was to be published in 2004; however, as of this writing, it is not out. Currently, it is expected to be published in summer 2007. The preface and several other sections of the book were available on William Dembski's Web site, www.designinference.com, for much of 2004.

41. Richard Thompson, Robert J. Muise, Patrick T. Gillen, and Ron Turo (2005), "Answer," *Kitzmiller v. Dover*, Defendants, Middle District of Pennsylvania: 04-CV-2688.

42. Robert J. Muise, Richard Thompson, Patrick T. Gillen, Edward L. White III, and Ron Turo (2005), "Defendants' Brief in Support of Motion for Summary Judgment," *Kitzmiller v. Dover*.

43. Patrick T. Gillen, Richard Thompson, Robert J. Muise, and Ron Turo (2005), "Defendants' Proposed Findings of Fact and Conclusions of Law," *Kitzmiller v. Dover*. The word *scientist* is a typo; it was meant to read scientists.

44. Gillen, Thompson, Muise, and Turo, "Defendants' Proposed Findings."

45. Galatians 6:7. In fact, it is clear that the Discovery Institute legal scholars don't even believe their own arguments in this area, as they continue to invoke the "teaching a variety of scientific theories" language from Edwards as justification for getting ID and other forms of creationism taught in the public schools.

46. David K. DeWolf, Leonard G. Brown, III, and Randall L. Wenger (2005), "(Revised) Brief of Amicus Curiae, The Discovery Institute, Appendix A: Documentation showing that the scientific theory of intelligent design makes no claims about the identity or nature of the intelligent cause responsible for life." *Kitzmiller v. Dover*, Discovery Institute (Amicus).

47. *Kitzmiller v. Dover*, 400 F.Supp.2d 707.

48. *Kitzmiller v. Dover*, 400 F.Supp.2d 707.

49. Scott and Matzke, "Biological Design in Science Classrooms."

50. *Kitzmiller v. Dover*, 400 F.Supp.2d 707. See especially the section on "Whether ID is Science."

51. Nicholas J. Matzke, "Design on Trial: How NCSE Helped Win the Kitzmiller Case," *Reports of the National Center for Science Education* 26, no. 1 (2006): 37–44.

52. *Kitzmiller v. Dover*, 400 F.Supp.2d 707.

53. Davis, Kenyon, and Thaxton, *Of Pandas and People*, 99–100.

54. Davis, Kenyon, and Thaxton, *Of Pandas and People*, 99–100.

55. Davis, Kenyon, and Thaxton, *Of Pandas and People*, 99–100.

56. Matzke, "But Isn't It Creationism?"

57. Anonymous, "Unbiased Biology Textbook Planned," *Origins Research* 4, no. 2 (1981): 1.

58. *Kitzmiller v. Dover*, P-562, 2-14, 2-15 (emphasis added). Similar versions of this sentence appear in all drafts except the 1983 *Creation Biology*.

59. Scott and Matzke, "Biological Design in Science Classrooms."

60. For more detailed analysis, see Matzke, "But Isn't It Creationism?"; and Scott and Matzke, "Biological Design in Science Classrooms."

61. Meyer, Minnich, Moneymaker, Nelson, and Seelke, *Explore Evolution*.

Chapter 5 Notes

1. *Kitzmiller v. Dover Area School District*, 400 F. Supp. 2d 707.

2. See Edward J. Larson, *Trial and Error: The American Controversy Over Creation and Evolution* 58-72 (New York: Oxford University Press, 1985).

3. *Epperson v. Arkansas*, 393 U.S. 97 (1968).

4. *Epperson v. Arkansas*, 103.

5. *McLean v. Ark. Bd. of Educ.*, 529 F. Supp. 1255 (E.D. Ark. 1982).

6. *Edwards v. Aguillard*, 482 U.S. 578 (1987).

7. Robert T. Pennock ("Reply to Plantinga's 'Modest Proposal,'" in *Intelligent Design Creationism and Its Critics: Philosophical, Theological, and Scientific Perspectives*, ed. Robert T. Pennock [Cambridge: M.I.T. Press, 2001], 795) writes: "Rational agents . . . would assent, I believe, to something very similar to our current system, along the lines I mentioned above—a separation of the public and the private. They would require that public institutions, like the public schools, not teach views based on 'private epistemologies' such as special revelation, because one cannot rationally adjudicate among beliefs that different persons purport 'to know' simply 'as a Christian' or a Hindu, a Raelian, a Pagan, or whatever."

8. What I mean by the "knowledge class" are those in our most influential cultural-shaping institutions such as academia, the mainstream media, and the federal judiciary.

9. Pennock ("Reply to Plantinga's 'Modest Proposal,'"), *Intelligent Design Creationism and Its Critics*, 593.

10. Pennock ("Reply to Plantinga's 'Modest Proposal,'"), *Intelligent Design Creationism and Its Critics*, 594.

11. Pennock ("Reply to Plantinga's 'Modest Proposal,'"), *Intelligent Design Creationism and Its Critics*, 605, see *Harris v. McRae*, 448 U.S. 297, 319 (1980), *McGowan v. Md.*, 366 U.S. 420, 442 (1961) (Powell, J., concurring).

12. According to the Court, Louisiana's Balanced-Treatment Act did not give teachers any more academic freedom than what they already had in supplanting "the present science curriculum with the presentation of theories, besides evolution, about the origin of life" (*Edwards*, 482 U.S., 587). Because "the Act provides Louisiana school teachers with no new authority[,] . . . the stated purpose is not furthered by it" (*Edwards*, 482 U.S., 587). The Court of Appeals made a similar observation; see *Aguillard v. Edwards*, 765 F.2d 1251, 1257 (5th Cir. 1985).

13. The Wright Center for Science Education (Tufts University), *Cosmic Evolution: An Interdisciplinary Approach*, from the Web site *Cosmic Evolution—From the Big Bang to Humankind*, www.tufts.edu/as/wright_center/cosmic_evolution/docs/fr_1/fr_1_site_summary. html (accessed June 8, 2007).

14. It's not clear whether Judge Jones is saying that ID in any version is identical to creationism or only the version offered by the Dover school board is creationism. In *Kitzmiller*, 400 F. Supp. 2d, 824, he writes: "The disclaimer's plain language, the legislative history, and the historical context in which the ID Policy arose, all inevitably lead to the conclusion that Defendants consciously chose to change Dover's biology curriculum to advance religion. We have been presented with a wealth of evidence which reveals that the District's purpose was to advance creationism, an inherently religious view, both by introducing it directly under the label ID and by disparaging the scientific theory of evolution, so that creationism would gain credence by default as the only apparent alternative to evolution. . . ."

15. See Francis J. Beckwith, *Law, Darwinism, and Public Education: The Establishment Clause and the Challenge of Intelligent Design* (Lanham, Md.: Rowman & Littlefield, 2003), chaps. 1 and 2; and Francis J. Beckwith, "Rawls' Dangerous Idea: Political Liberalism,

Naturalistic Evolution, and The Requirements of Legal Neutrality in Shaping Public School Curricula." *Journal of Law & Religion* 20, no. 2 (2004–05): 423–58.

16. *Kitzmiller*, 400 F. Supp. 2d, at 709.

17. *Kitzmiller*, 869–72.

18. In *McLean*, 529 F. Supp., 1264, the federal district court took motive into consideration, though it was not dispositive: "The unusual circumstances surrounding the passage of Act 590, as well as the substantive law of the First Amendment, warrant an inquiry into the stated legislative purposes. The author of the Act had publicly proclaimed the sectarian purpose of the proposal. The Arkansas residents who sought legislative sponsorship of the bill did so for a purely sectarian purpose. These circumstances alone may not be particularly persuasive, but when considered with the publicly announced *motives* of the legislative sponsor made contemporaneously with the legislative process; the lack of any legislative investigation, debate or consultation with any educators or scientists; the unprecedented intrusion in school curriculum; and official history of the State of Arkansas on the subject, it is obvious that the statement of purposes has little, if any, support in fact" (footnote omitted; emphasis added).

19. The Court writes in *Edwards*, 482 U.S., 593 n.13: "Besides Senator Keith, several of the most vocal legislators also revealed their religious motives for supporting the bill in the official legislative history. See, *e.g., id.*, at E-441, E-443 (Sen. Saunders noting that bill was amended so that teachers could refer to the Bible and other religious texts to support the creation-science theory); 2 App. E-561—E-562, E-610 (Rep. Jenkins contending that the existence of God was a scientific fact)."

20. For example, Barbara Forrest writes: "At heart, proponents of intelligent design are not motivated to improve science but to transform it into a theistic enterprise that supports religious faith." Barbara Forrest, *The Newest Evolution of Creationism: Intelligent Design is About Politics and Religion, Not Science*, 111.3 Nat. History 80 (Apr. 2002).

21. Much of what follows in the chapter is adapted from my article, "The Court of Disbelief: The Constitution's Article VI Religious Test Prohibition and the Judiciary's Religious Motive Analysis," *Hastings Constitutional Law Quarterly* 33, no. 2 (2006): 337–60.

22. Derek H. Davis, "Thomas Jefferson and the 'Wall Of Separation' Metaphor," *Journal of Church & State* 5, no. 10 (Winter 2003): 45.

23. Davis, "Thomas Jefferson and the 'Wall Of Separation' Metaphor."

24. Thomas Jefferson, "Jefferson's Letter to the Danbury Baptists" (Jan. 1, 1802), *The Library of Congress Information Bulletin* 6 (June 1998): 57, available at www.loc.gov/loc/lcib/9806/danpre.html (accessed June 8, 2007).

25. *McDaniel v. Paty*, 435 U.S. 618, 626 (1978) (emphasis added).

26. *Reynolds v. U.S.*, 98 U.S. 145, 166 (1878). The Court did say in *Wisconsin v. Yoder*, 406 U.S. 205, 220 (1972) that "this case [*Yoder*], therefore, does not become easier because respondents were convicted for their 'actions' in refusing to send their children to the public high school; in this context belief and action cannot be neatly confined in logic-tight compartments." However, I do not believe the general principle in Reynolds is jettisoned, for in *Yoder* the concern was whether the state's prohibition of the religious action in question (the free exercise right of Amish parents to be exempted from the compulsory education laws) could be rejected on the grounds that their actions and not their beliefs were being prohibited by the state in a case in which belief and action overlapped at

points. But it was clear the Court did not touch the long-held principle that mere belief could not be proscribed by government.

27. *Torcaso v. Watkins*, 367 U.S. 488 (1961).

28· *Torcaso v. Watkins*, 495.

29. *Everson*, 330 U.S. 1 (1947).

30· *Everson*, 15–16.

31. *West Virginia Board of Education v. Barnette*, 319 U.S. 624, 642 (1943).

32· *West Virginia Board of Education v. Barnette*, at 642.

33. Although a minority view at the time of the American founding, Thomas Jefferson articulates it well in his "A Bill for Establishing Religious Freedom" (1786), as reprinted in Michael W. McConnell, Thomas Berg, and Garvey, *Religion & The Constitution* (New York: Aspen Books, 2002), 70: "That our civil rights have no dependence on our religious opinions, any more than our opinions in physics or geometry; that, therefore, the proscribing of any citizen as unworthy of the public confidence by laying upon him an incapacity of being called to offices of trust and emolument, unless he profess or renounce this or that religious opinion, is depriving him injuriously of those privileges and advantages to which in common with his fellow-citizens he has a natural right."

James Madison's defense of freedom of conscience ["Memorial and Remonstrance Against Religious Assessments (1785)," in *The Complete Madison* (S. Padover ed. 1953), 299–301, as quoted in *Wallace v. Jaffree*, 472 U.S. 38, 53 n.38 (1985)] is more explicit than Jefferson's. Madison writes:

> Because we hold it for a fundamental and undeniable truth, 'that Religion or the duty which we owe to our Creator and the [Manner of discharging it, can be directed only by reason and] conviction, not by force or violence.' The Religion then of every man must be left to the conviction and conscience of every man; and it is the right of every man to exercise it as these may dictate. This right is in its nature an unalienable right. It is unalienable; because the opinions of men, depending only on the evidence contemplated by their own minds, cannot follow the dictates of other men: It is unalienable also; because what is here a right towards men, is a duty towards the Creator. It is the duty of every man to render to the Creator such homage, and such only, as he believes to be acceptable to him. . . . We maintain therefore that in matters of Religion, no man's right is abridged by the institution of Civil Society, and that Religion is wholly exempt from its cognizance. . . . .

> Because, it is proper to take alarm at the first experiment on our liberties. We hold this prudent jealousy to be the first duty of citizens, and one of [the] noblest characteristics of the late Revolution. The freemen of America did not wait till usurped power had strengthened itself by exercise, and entangled the question in precedents. They saw all the consequences in the principle, and they avoided the consequences by denying the principle. We reverse this lesson too much, soon to forget it. Who does not see that the same authority which can establish Christianity, in exclusion of all other Religions, may establish with the same ease any particular sect of Christians, in exclusion of all other Sects?

34. The Court writes in *McDaniel*, 435 U.S. at 626: "If the Tennessee disqualification provision were viewed as depriving the clergy of a civil right solely because of their religious beliefs, our inquiry would be at an end. The Free Exercise Clause categorically prohibits government from regulating, prohibiting, or rewarding religious beliefs as such . . ." (references omitted). In *Torcaso v. Watkins*, 367 U.S. 488 (1961), the Court reviewed the Maryland constitutional requirement that all holders of "any office of profit or trust in this State" declare their belief in the existence of God. In striking down the Maryland requirement, the Court did not evaluate the interests assertedly justifying it but rather held that it violated freedom of religious belief.

Chapter 6 Notes

1. Richard Dawkins, *The God Delusion* (Boston: Houghton Mifflin, 2006). For a response to this highly aggressive book, see Alister E. McGrath and Joanna Collicutt McGrath, *The Dawkins Delusion? Atheist Fundamentalism and the Denial of the Divine* (Downers Grove, Ill.: InterVarsity, 2007).

2. For example, in November 2005, *Prospect* magazine declared Dawkins to be one of the three greatest living intellectuals. The same magazine was decidedly unimpressed by *The God Delusion*, which it described (October 2006) as an "incurious, dogmatic, rambling, and self-contradictory" book. The title given to the review was "Dawkins the dogmatist."

3. See, for example, Antony Kenny's observations concerning its dogmatism, especially in the chapter titled "Why I Am Not an Atheist" in his *What I Believe* (London: Continuum, 2006).

4. The use of this religious imagery is entirely appropriate. Dawkins is widely revered and regarded as lying beyond criticism in many atheist circles today, being invested with an intellectual and spiritual authority directly paralleling that directed toward the Pope by traditionalist Roman Catholics.

5. Readers who would value an extended engagement with Dawkins' views on religion will find the most comprehensive critical analysis to date in Alister E. McGrath, *Dawkins' God: Genes, Memes and the Meaning of Life* (Malden, Mass.: Blackwell, 2004).

6. Daniel C. Dennett, *Breaking the Spell: Religion as a Natural Phenomenon* (New York: Viking, 2006). For an earlier work of relevance, see Daniel C. Dennett, *Darwin's Dangerous Idea: Evolution and the Meaning of Life* (New York: Simon & Schuster, 1995). Other works of relevance include David Sloan Wilson, *Darwin's Cathedral : Evolution, Religion, and the Nature of Society* (Chicago: University of Chicago Press, 2002).

7. *Oxford University Calendar 2003–4* (Oxford: Oxford University Press, 2003), 77.

8. For an assessment of Dawkins's distinctive approach, see Kim Sterelny, *Dawkins vs. Gould: Survival of the Fittest* (Cambridge: Icon Books, 2001); Alan Grafen and Mark Ridley, eds., *Richard Dawkins: How a Scientist Changed the Way We Think—Reflections by Scientists, Writers, and Philosophers* (New York: Oxford University Press, 2006).

9. Richard Dawkins, *River Out of Eden: A Darwinian View of Life* (New York: Basic Books, 1995), 19.

10. Dawkins, *River Out of Eden*, 133.

11. Dawkins, *The God Delusion*, 67.

12. A point made by Luke Davidson, "Fragilities of Scientism: Richard Dawkins and the Paranoid Idealization of Science," *Science as Culture* 9 (2000): 167–99. Dawkins is often singled out as a leading representative of "scientism": see, for example, Mikael Stenmark, *Scientism: Science, Ethics and Religion* (Aldershot, UK: Ashgate, 2001). For leading critiques of the naïve approaches to rationalism that seem to underlie Dawkins's worldview, see Alasdair MacIntyre, *Whose Justice? Which Rationality?* (London: Duckworth, 1988).

13. These criticisms are developed especially in Richard Dawkins, *Unweaving the Rainbow: Science, Delusion and the Appetite for Wonder* (London: Penguin, 1998).

14. Richard Dawkins, "A Survival Machine," in *The Third Culture*, ed. John Brockman (New York: Simon & Schuster, 1996), 75–95.

15. The point here is that nature does not designate an epistemologically autonomous entity: for a detailed analysis, see Alister E. McGrath, *A Scientific Theology: 1- Nature* (Grand Rapids: Eerdmans, 2003), 81–133.

16. Francis S. Collins, *The Language of God: A Scientist Presents Evidence for Belief* (New York: Basic, 2006).

17. For the historical aspect of this question, see James R. Moore, *The Post-Darwinian Controversies: A Study of the Protestant Struggle to come to terms with Darwin in Great Britain and America, 1870–1900* (Cambridge: Cambridge University Press, 1979).

18. The best study of this aspect of Miller's thought is John Hedley Brooke, "Like Minds: The God of Hugh Miller," in *Hugh Miller and the Controversies of Victorian Science*, ed. Michael Shortland (Oxford: Clarendon, 1996), 171–86.

19. Dawkins, *The God Delusion*, 188.

20. Richard Dawkins, *The Selfish Gene*, 2nd ed. (Oxford: Oxford University Press, 1989), 21.

21. Denis Noble, *The Music of Life: Biology beyond the Genome* (Oxford: Oxford University Press, 2006), 11–15.

22. Noble, *The Music of Life*, 13; see also Richard Dawkins, *The Extended Phenotype: The Gene as the Unit of Selection* (New York: Oxford University Press, 1982), 1.

23. A much more satisfactory account may be found in John Hedley Brooke, "The Relations between Darwin's Science and His Religion," in *Darwinism and Divinity*, ed. John Durant (Oxford: Blackwell, 1985), 40–75.

24. Edward Aveling, *The Religious Views of Charles Darwin* (London: Freethought, 1883).

25. For the best analysis of this point, see Frank Burch Brown, *The Evolution of Darwin's Religious Views* (Macon, Ga.: Mercer University Press, 1986).

26. Richard Dawkins, "Universal Darwinism," in *Evolution from Molecules to Men*, ed. D. S. Bendall (Cambridge: Cambridge University Press, 1983), 403–25.

27. For an exhaustive analysis of the problems encountered with the approach, see Alister E. McGrath, "The Evolution of Doctrine? A Critical Examination of the Theological Validity of Biological Models of Doctrinal Development," in *The Order of Things: Explorations in Scientific Theology* (Oxford: Blackwell, 2006), 117–68.

28. Peter B. Medawar, *The Limits of Science* (Oxford: Oxford University Press, 1985), 66.

29. There is a vast literature. On the basic issue of "underdetermination of theory by evidence," see Larry Laudan and Jarrett Leplin, "Empirical Equivalence and

Underdetermination," *Journal of Philosophy* 88 (1991): 449–72. On theory change, see Sylvia Culp and Philip Kitcher, "Theory Structure and Theory Change in Contemporary Molecular Biology," *British Journal for the Philosophy of Science* 40 (1989): 459–83.

30. For the development of Polanyi's views on this issue, see William Taussig Scott and Martin X. Moleski, S.J., *Michael Polanyi: Scientist and Philosopher* (Oxford: Oxford University Press, 2005), 211–36.

31. Richard Dawkins, *A Devil's Chaplain: Selected Writings* (London: Weidenfield & Nicholson, 2003), 81.

32. Timothy Shanahan, "Methodological and Contextual Factors in the Dawkins/Gould Dispute over Evolutionary Progress," *Studies in History and Philosophy of Science* 31 (2001): 127–51.

33. For this point in Max Weber's analysis of the sociology of leadership, see Christopher Adair-Toteff, "Max Weber's Charisma," *Journal of Classical Sociology* 5 (2005): 189–204.

Chapter 7 Notes

1. J. P. Moreland, *Christianity and the Nature of Science* (Grand Rapids: Baker, 1989), chap. 6; and Larry Laudin, *Progress and Its Problems* (Berkeley: University of California Press, 1977), chap. 3.

2. J. P. Moreland, *The Creation Hypothesis* (Downers Grove, Ill.: InterVarsity, 1994); and William Lane Craig, *Reasonable Faith* (Wheaton: Crossway, 1994), chap. 3.

3. Jaegwon Kim, *Physicalism or Something Near Enough* (Princeton: Princeton University Press, 2005), chap. 3.

4. This informal characterization of agent causal versions of libertarian freedom may be stated more precisely and formally. In general, person P exercises libertarian agent causation, and freely and intentionally brings about some event e just in case (1) P is a substance that has the active power to bring about e; (2) P exerted his power as a first mover/first cause (an "originator" of change) to bring about e; (3) P had the categorical ability to refrain from exerting his power to bring about e; (4) P acted for the sake of a reason that served as the final cause or teleological goal for which P acted. Taken alone, 1–3 state necessary and sufficient conditions for a pure voluntary act. Propositions 1–4 state necessary and sufficient conditions for an intentional act. In this sense, teleology is a fundamental form of (final) causality and it cannot be reduced to or replaced by efficient causality. A final cause is a teleological end, purpose, or goal for the sake of which something happens. An efficient cause is that by means of which something happens. See J. P. Moreland, "Naturalism and Libertarian Agency," *Philosophy and Theology* 10 (1997): 351–81.

5. J. P. Moreland and Scott Rae, *Body & Soul: Human Nature and the Crisis in Ethics* (Downers Grove, Ill.: InterVarsity, 2000); William Hasker, *The Emergent Self* (Ithaca, N.Y.: Cornell University Press; 1999); Richard Swinburne, *The Evolution of the Soul* (Oxford: Clarendon Press, 1997).

6. Dallas Willard, *Logic and the Objectivity of Knowledge* (Athens: Ohio University Press, 1984), 166–86.

7. Swinburne, *Evolution of the Soul*, chap. 4.

8. William A. Dembski, *Intelligent Design: The Bridge Between Science and Theology* (Downers Grove, Ill.: InterVarsity, 1999), chaps. 5, 6; Michael Behe, *Darwin's Black Box: The Biochemical Challenge to Evolution* (New York: The Free Press, 1996).

9. Dembski, *Intelligent Design*, 183.

10. More formally, two structures, S_1 and S_2, are isomorphic just in case:

(i) For every non-relational part of S_1, there is precisely one nonrelational part of S_2, and conversely;

(ii) For every relation of S_1, there is precisely one relation of S_2, and conversely;

(iii) the parts of S_1 that correspond to S_2 stand in the relations of S_1 to each other, which correspond to the relations of S_2, and conversely.

See Reinhardt Grossmann, *The Existence of the World* (London: Routledge, 1992), 48–51.

11. Knowledge gained by studying the brain and body movements of humans will never exhaust what can be known about them and, methodologically, the information gained from such third-person approaches will be subject to first-person reports for their validation and interpretation, even if those reports derive not from the subjects of a study, but from the first-person knowledge of the researcher. See Geoffrey Madell, *The Identity of the Self* (Edinburgh: University of Edinburgh Press, 1981).

12. Frank Jackson, *From Metaphysics to Ethics* (Oxford: Clarendon Press, 1998).

13. Jackson, *From Metaphysics to Ethics*, chap. 1.

14. J. P. Moreland, "The Explanatory Relevance of Libertarian Agency as a Model of Theistic Design," in *Mere Creation: Science, Faith, & Intelligent Design*, ed. William Dembski (Downers Grove, Ill.: InterVarsity, 1998), 265–88; Richard Swinburne, *Evolution of the Soul*, chap. 10.

15. J. P. Moreland, "Theistic Science and Methodological Naturalism," in *The Creation Hypothesis: Scientific Evidence for an Intelligent Designer*, ed. J. P. Moreland (Downers Grove, Ill.: InterVarsity, 1994), 41–66.

16. Moreland, "The Explanatory Relevance"; Nancy Duvall, "From Soul to Self and Back Again," *Journal of Psychology and Theology* 26 (1998): 6–15; W. W. Meisner, "Can Psychoanalysis Find It's Self?" *Journal of the American Psychoanalytic Association* 34 (1986): 379–400; Meisner, "Self-as-Agent in Psychoanalysis," *Psychoanalysis and Contemporary Thought*, 16 (1993): 459–95.

17. William Lane Craig and J. P. Moreland, eds., *Naturalism: A Critical Analysis* (London: Routledge, 2000).

18. David Buss, "Evolutionary Psychology," in *Encyclopedia of Psychology* (New York: Oxford University Press, 2000), 277–78.

19. Jackson, *From Metaphysics to Ethics*, chap. 1.

20. David Papineau, *Philosophical Naturalism* (Oxford: Blackwell, 1993), 16.

21. Jaegwon Kim, *Philosophy of Mind* (Boulder: Westview, 1996), 9–13.

22. Geoffrey Madell, *Mind & Materialism* (Edinburgh: University of Edinburgh Press, 1988), 7.

23. Leda Cosmides and John Tooby, *Evolutionary Psychology: A Primer*, www.psych.ucsb.edu/research/cep/primer.html (accessed June 11, 2007), 3.

24. John Bishop, *Natural Agency* (Cambridge: Cambridge University Press, 1989), 1.

25. Thomas Nagel, *The View from Nowhere* (New York: Oxford University Press, 1986), 110.

26. Hasker, *The Emergent Self*, chap. three; John Bishop, *Natural Agency*, 32–38.

27. Joshua Hoffman and Gary S. Rosenkrantz, *Substance: Its Nature and Existence* (London: Routledge, 1997), 98–99.

28. E. Mayr, *Populations, Species, and Evolution* (Cambridge: Harvard University Press, 1970), 4.

29. David Hull, *The Metaphysics of Evolution* (Albany: State University of New York Press, 1989), 4.

30. Paul Churchland, *Matter and Consciousness* (Cambridge: MIT Press, 1984), 21.

31. Jaegwon Kim, *Mind in a Physical World* (Cambridge: MIT Press, 1998), 37–56.

32. Cosmides and Tooby, *Evolutionary Psychology: A Primer* (see n. 23).

33. Alvin Plantinga, *Warrant and Proper Function* (New York: Oxford University Press, 1993), chaps. 11–12.

34. Michael Ruse, "Evolutionary Theory and Christian Ethics," in *The Darwinian Paradigm: Essays on Its History, Philosophy, and Religious Implications* (London: Routledge, 1989), 262–69.

35. Swinburne, *The Evolution of the Soul*, 208; cf. chaps. 11, 12.

36. John E. Post, *Metaphysics: An Introduction* (New York: Paragon House, 1991), 121.

37. Nagel, *The View from Nowhere*, 27.

38. Cosmides and Tooby, *Evolutionary Psychology: A Primer* (see n. 23).

39. Churchland, *Matter and Consciousness*.

40. Kim, *Mind in a Physical World*, 29–37.

41. Geoffrey Madell, *Mind & Materialism* (Edinburgh: Edinburgh University Press, 1988), 6.

42. John Searle, *The Rediscovery of the Mind* (Cambridge: MIT Press, 1992), chaps. 1, 2.

43. Buss, "Evolutionary Psychology," 280.

Chapter 8 Notes

1. Referred to hereafter as the WAP and the SAP.

2. John D. Barrow and Frank J. Tipler, *The Anthropic Cosmological Principle* (New York: Oxford University Press, 1986), 16, 21.

3. More simply, the weak version of the ACP may be construed simply as the pure variables, the straight numbers that seem to carry extremely improbable coincidental relations to the observed properties of the universe. In contrast, the strong version may be denoted as an organizing principle for why the fundamental constants and parameters of the universe *must* exist as they do. It is as if the principle takes on the accouterments of a deeper physical mechanism, the purpose of which is to fix the values of the constants and parameters so that human beings can exist within the cosmos. With journalistic flair, Dennis Overbye writes: "The features in question are mysterious numbers in the equations of physics and

cosmology, denoting, say, the amount of matter in the universe or the number of dimensions, which don't seem predictable by any known theory yet. They are like the knobs on God's control console, and they seem almost miraculously tuned to allow life." "Zillions of Universes? Or Did Ours Get Lucky?" *The New York Times*, October 28, 2003.

4. Reinhard Breuer, *The Anthropic Principle: Man as the Focal Point of Nature*, trans. Harry Newman and Mark Lowery (Boston: Birkhäuser, 1991), 238–44. Cf. Walter L. Bradley, "The 'Just So' Universe: The Fine-Tuning of Constants & Conditions in the Cosmos," *Touchstone: A Journal of Mere Christianity* (July/August 1999): 70–75.

5. Stanley L. Jaki, *Cosmos and Creator* (Edinburgh: Scottish Academic Press, 1980), 48. The only proviso to this, he continues, is that it may be impossible to achieve a definitional package large enough to accommodate the input of each and every interested party. Although Jaki does not specifically utilize the term *quantum cosmocausality*, he is at least calling for an *a priori* explanatory framework of cosmic cause.

6. The Greek philosopher Aristotle (384–322 BCE) was the first to analyze carefully at least four of six of these versions of cause but only after distinguishing their different emphases in the teachings of his philosophical predecessors: Plato, Socrates, and a few of the pre-Socratics. Found in his *Metaphysics* I. 3, Aristotle divided causality/causation into four categories: material cause, formal cause, efficient cause, and final cause. See Paul Edwards, ed., *The Encyclopedia of Philosophy* (New York: Macmillan, 1972), vol.1, s.v. "Aristotle," by G. B. Kerferd. Others, however, find two other kinds of cause in his works: instrumental cause and sufficient cause. See R. C. Sproul, *Not a Chance: The Myth of Chance in Modern Science and Cosmology* (Grand Rapids: Baker, 1994), 195–97. Whether these two particular kinds of cause and effect are actually located within the Aristotelian corpus is debated. Some researchers see them as more properly derived from later philosophers such as René Descartes, Nicolas de Malebranche, Göttfried Wilhelm Leibniz, Baruch Spinoza, David Hume, and J. S. Mill; also Edwards, *The Encyclopedia of Philosophy*, vol. 2, s.v. "Causality," by Richard Taylor.

7. Nicola Dallaporta, "Metaphysical Outlooks in Physics and the Anthropic Principle," in *The Anthropic Principle: Proceedings of the Second Venice Conference on Cosmology and Philosophy, November 18–19, 1988*, ed. Francesco Bertola and Umberto Curi (New York: Cambridge University Press, 1989), 164.

8. For example, Ian Barbour states that "the cosmos seems to be balanced on a knife edge" ("Creation and Cosmology," in *Cosmos as Creation: Theology and Science in Consonance*, ed. Ted Peters [Nashville: Abingdon, 1989], 130). Freeman Dyson infers more openly, "The more I examine the universe and the details of its architecture, the more evidence I find that the universe in some sense must have known we were coming" (*Disturbing the Universe* [New York: Harper & Row, 1979], 250). Another respected astrophysicist, George F. R. Ellis, believes that "the existence of life in general, and intelligent life in particular, is an incredibly unlikely eventuality, both in terms of the possibility of its existence (that is, the compatibility of the possible structures of intelligent life with the local laws of physics) and of the probability of its evolution" (cited in Breuer, *The Anthropic Principle*, 12). And more explicitly yet with regard to divine cause, George Greenstein examines the evidences for a theologically engineered universe only to deduce that "as we survey all the evidence, the thought insistently arises that some supernatural agency—or, rather, Agency—must be involved. Is it possible that suddenly, without intending to, we have stumbled upon scientific proof of the existence of a Supreme Being? Was it God who stepped in and so providentially crafted the cosmos for our benefit?" (*The Symbiotic Universe: Life and Mind in the Cosmos* [New York: William Morrow, 1988], 27).

9. Charles B. Thaxton, Walter L. Bradley, and Roger L. Olsen, *The Mystery of Life's Origin: Reassessing Current Theories* (New York: Philosophical Library, 1984), 201. The authors confirm their point by citing J. W. N. Sullivan, a one-time science writer for *Time* magazine, who wrote as far back as 1933 that "[creation] carries with it what are felt to be, in the present mental climate, undesirable philosophic implications, and it is opposed to the scientific desire for continuity. It introduces an unaccountable break in the chain of causation, and therefore cannot be admitted as part of science unless it is quite impossible to reject it. For that reason most scientific men prefer to believe that life arose, in accordance with the laws of physics and chemistry." J. W. N. Sullivan, *The Limitations of Science* (New York: Viking, 1933), 94.

10. See Michael Denton, *Evolution: A Theory in Crisis* (Bethesda, Md.: Adler & Adler, 1986), 353: "The idea that life might be fundamentally a discontinuous phenomenon runs counter to the whole thrust of modern biological thought. The infusion with the spirit of continuity has been so prolonged and so deeply imbibed that for most biologists it has become quite literally inconceivable that life might not be a continuous phenomenon."

11. A strong view of cosmic necessity would say that "no genuine form of contingency would have ever *really* existed in the universe, because all outcomes would have been both foreseen and predetermined by God beforehand," whereas a weaker view of cosmic necessity would posit that the development of the universe was "only necessary in fact. . . , and *not* logically necessary *per se*," a view that would preserve a weak form of contingency (i.e., freedom) in the universe while simultaneously avoiding the spectre of absolute determinism." M. A. Corey, *God and the New Cosmology: The Anthropic Design Argument* (Lanham, Md.: Rowman & Littlefield, 1993), 225–26. Livio Gratton, however, wants to dispense with these categories completely in relation to the anthropic potentialities of the cosmos. Preferring the role of agnostic, he states: "It is impossible to say whether a series of events has been produced by a chance process, . . . [T]he only thing we can say is that a series of events satisfies or does not satisfy the tests which we have tried on it. . . . [I]nnumerable pointless discussions upon determinism and indeterminism were caused by forgetting this simple argument" ("Metaphysical Outlooks," in *The Anthropic Principle: Proceedings*, ed. Bertola and Curi, 166).

12. While it is true that the general definition of *empiricism* has received different emphases and refinements historically, it is defined here as the epistemological theory that experience alone rather than reason is the source of knowledge. See Edwards, ed., *Encyclopedia of Philosophy*, vol. 2, s.v. "Empiricism," by D. W. Hamlyn. Philosopher of science Lawrence Sklar characterizes empiricism by the following description: "The observational/nonobservational distinction bears a heavy burden in empiricist approaches to theories. That such a distinction exists and that its existence is not overly context-relative seem essential if observationality is to play as distinguished a role in our account of the sources of knowledge and of meaning as the empiricist demands. . . . In realms of epistemic warrant, observations are, for the empiricist, foundational. All knowledge of reasonable belief . . . begins with our knowledge of the contents of observation. For some empiricists observational facts can be known with certainty. For the more modest they are the only facts of the world that bear intrinsic, noninferential warrant for belief" (*Philosophy and Spacetime Physics* [Berkeley: University of California Press, 1985], 168).

13. A number of biblical materials/science harmonization schemas could be introduced here in order to argue for the existence and justification of metascientific viewpoints, especially those attempting to overcome empiricism's deficiencies. But this would

go beyond the intent of the present study. Suffice it to say that although the Gen. 1:1-2:4 account of creation (as well as other passages relating to creation) should not be understood hermeneutically as scientific reference material, it does in fact depict a metacosmology of sorts. Whether it is interpretationally consistent or nonconflicting with reference to scientific facts is the provocative hermeneutical issue. According to Robert John Russell: "*Any* scientific cosmology must in *some* sense be consistent with the doctrine of creation since it ought not contain within it and proper to it a metascientific counterpart to the concept of God." In context, Russell is saying that created reality is not to be equated with God himself so that pantheistic interpretations of reality may be avoided, but metascientific/metaempirical concerns are nonetheless intrinsic to creation texts. Robert John Russell, "Cosmology, Creation, and Contingency," in *Cosmos as Creation*, ed. Peters, 205.

14. Philosopher David Hume's interpretation of causal relations basically states that it is impossible to see "causes" in and of themselves, but it *is* possible to observe successions of events. In his own words: "We may define a cause to be *an object, followed by another, and where all the objects similar to the first are followed by objects similar to the second. Or in other words where, if the first object had not been, the second never had existed.* The appearance of a cause always conveys the mind, by a customary transition, to the idea of the effect. We may, therefore, suitably to this experience, form another definition of cause, and call it, *an object followed by another, and whose appearance always conveys the thought to that other*" (*Enquiries Concerning Human Understanding and Concerning the Principles of Morals*, ed. L. A. Selby-Bigge, 3d ed. [Oxford: Clarendon Press, 1975], 76–77). Cf. Colin Brown, *Miracles and the Critical Mind* (Grand Rapids: Eerdmans, 1984), 82–83.

15. Philip Gasper, "Causation and Explanation," in Richard Boyd, Philip Gasper, and J. D. Trout, ed., *The Philosophy of Science* (Cambridge: MIT Press, 1991), 290–91.

16. Gasper, "Causation and Explanation," 291–92.

17. Nancy Cartwright, "The Reality of Causes in a World of Instrumental Laws" in *The Philosophy of Science*, 379–80. Note the approach of Henry J. Folse: "The metaphysical task of reconstructing the scientists' world-view in whatever way is necessary. . . demands to be dealt with from a perspective that accepts at least the *possibility* of constructing a philosophy of nature. For this reason the opponent to the scientific realist cannot be a Humean skeptic" ("What Does Quantum Theory Tell Us about the World?" *Soundings* 72, no. 1 [Spring 1989]: 183).

18. Norman D. Newell, *Creation and Evolution: Myth or Reality?* (New York: Columbia University Press, 1982), 155.

19. "In saying that God is, and that God is Creator, we do not affirm that he . . . is any ordinary 'cause' in the physical nexus of the universe itself-otherwise God would be neither explanation nor possible meaning." Arthur R. Peacocke, *Creation and the World of Science* (Oxford: Clarendon Press, 1979), 77–78.

20. William P. Alston argues for the philosophical integrity of "causal determinism" in that universal divine agency may be said to follow logically from it as an inevitable feature of the universe. See "God's Action in the World," in Ernan McMullin, ed., *Evolution and Creation* (Notre Dame: University of Notre Dame Press, 1985), 200–01.

21. "I would like to argue that to exclude intelligent design *a priori* as a working hypothesis . . . is both gratuitous and anti-intellectual. . . . Indeed, it must be acknowledged that it is at least logically possible that a personal agent existed before the appearance of the first life on earth. It is therefore at least logically possible that such an agent

(whether visible or invisible) designed or influenced the origin of life on earth." Stephen C. Meyer, "Laws, Causes and Facts: Response to Michael Ruse," in Jon Buell and Virginia Hearn, eds., *Darwinism, Science or Philosophy? Proceedings of a Symposium Entitled "Darwinism: Scientific Inference or Philosophical Preference?"* (Richardson, Tex.: Foundation for Thought and Ethics, 1994), 33–34.

22. The second law of thermodynamics states that "the entropy of the universe tends to a maximum," where entropy is defined as "the measure of the total disorder, randomness, or chaos in a system," with the effect of increased entropy being that "things progress from a state of relative order to one of disorder." Richard P. Brennan, *Dictionary of Scientific Literacy* (New York: John Wiley & Sons, 1992), 296. Cf. Ervin Laszlo, *Evolution: The Grand Synthesis* (Boston: New Science Library, 1987), 15, 21–22; and George Murphy, "Time, Thermodynamics, and Theology," *Zygon: Journal of Religion and Science* 26, no. 3 (September 1991): 363–66.

23. See F. David Peat, *The Philosopher's Stone: Chaos, Synchronicity, and the Hidden Order of the World* (New York: Bantam Books, 1991), 204–31. Peat further states that his doctrine of gentle action explains why a system that appears superficially chaotic may be correlated at a deeper level in such a way that its distant parts are ordered nonlocally. What appears to be a simple increase in entropy, or disorder, then, could conceal a more subtle form of order. Microworld chaos, he believes, "may conceal a rich and infinitely complex degree of order that lies beyond conventional description" Ibid. (228).

24. Ilya Prigogine and Isabelle Stengers, *Order out of Chaos: Man's New Dialogue with Nature* (New York: Bantam, 1984), 286–87. Officially known as "nonequilibrium thermodynamics," Prigogine and his associates work under the stated assumption that further research in the area will eventually yield results as unusual as those of relativity and quantum mechanics. See Prigogine's two volumes, *From Being to Becoming* (San Francisco: W. H. Freeman, 1980) and *Thermodynamics of Irreversible Processes*, 3d ed. (New York: Interscience, 1967).

25. Ibid., 288–90. For a briefer treatment of Prigogine's views, see Ilya Prigogine, "Man's New Dialogue with Nature," *Perkins Journal of Theology* 36, no. 4 (Summer 1983): 4–14.

26. Friedrich Cramer, for instance, opts for an evolutional field theory to explain the entropy problem: "There exists an evolutional field, in which matter organizes itself. Self-organization or the evolutional field cannot be separated from matter" ("The Entropic versus the Anthropic Principle: On the Self-Organization of Life," in *The Anthropic Principle: Proceedings*, ed. Bertola and Curi, 137.

27. In March 1994, I spoke briefly with William Klink, a professor of physics at the University of Iowa, about the possibility of the existence of such a metalevel below the quantum world. Dr. Klink was kind enough not only to provide an answer, but also to recommend his then yet-to-be-published journal article, now in *Zygon*, in which he touches upon the subject in a roundabout way. His response to my question was that, if such a realm exists, we will never be able to locate it apart from another "in-breaking" of God into human science, *an "in-breaking" equivalent to or surpassing the ones God has already given us through relativity and quantum theories!* Dr. Klink's thoughts about these "in-breakings" are found in his "Ecology and Eschatology: Science and Theological Modeling," *Zygon: Journal of Religion and Science* 29, no. 4 (December 1994): 529–45 (emphasis mine).

28. Interestingly, William Alston reverses the usual way of looking at the quantum world's state of "irregularity" in order to favor its "regularity" aspects. In building a case

for quantum causal determinism, pending as it may be, Alston surmises: "Many thinkers today hold that the results of quantum mechanics show that no physical events are strictly causally determined though for macroscopic events the chances of things having come out differently are negligible. It would be interesting to explore the bearing of a quantum mechanical point of view on the case for universal divine agency. Could we think of God as having . . . used means that are only very, very, very likely to bring [a quantum action] about? I would think so" ("God's Action in the World," 202). Alston, 203, also subsumes the free actions of human beings under the rubric of God's causal determinism: "Free autonomous created agents, as much as other creatures, exist and exercise their powers only because God continuously sustains them in existence. And the divine omnipotence extends to them as much as to other creatures. . . . In allowing some created agents a say in what they do, God is also giving them a share in causally determining other sorts of events. Human voluntary actions themselves have effects as much as any other worldly happenings."

29. J. H. Lambert asks: "How would you connect . . . time and space with one another, so that all this would be governed by one universal law? . . . I can never imagine that, when each part has the most perfect order, this order should be missing in the whole. The world-edifice is a whole and ought therefore to be necessarily interconnected through universal laws" (*Cosmological Letter on the Arrangement of the World-Edifice*, trans. Stanley L. Jaki [Edinburgh: Scottish Academic Press, 1976], 107).

30. Ted Peters, "Cosmos as Creation," in *Cosmos as Creation: Theology and Science in Consonance* (Nashville: Abingdon, 1989), 101. In addition, the well-respected philosopher R. B. Braithewaite deliberates about "ontology of law," indicating that "scientific" explanations of things never seem to live up to expectations whenever deductive systems of natural law fail to ground themselves in a higher, more comprehensive level of laws, which, in turn, must appeal to still higher premises. As Braithewaite puts its, "At each stage of explanation a 'Why?' question can significantly be asked of the explanatory hypotheses; there is no ultimate end to the hierarchy of scientific explanation, and thus no completely final explanations" (*Scientific Explanation* [Cambridge: Cambridge University Press, 1953], 347). In other words, if science alone tries to explain the "lawful" behavior of created reality, the "lawfulness" of natural laws will never be sufficiently finalized with respect to its beingness, its ontological status. Along these lines, R. Nobili sees the counterfactual difficulty posed by an ontologically deprived quantum world: "The basic difficulty in understanding the biological character of the universe lies in the difficulty to understand the ontological status of the physical world as stated by quantum mechanics" ("Metaphysical Outlooks," in *The Anthropic Principle: Proceedings*, ed. Bertola and Curi, 166).

31. According to Howard Van Till, some scientists are "guilty of the common error of thinking that the 'laws of nature' govern the behavior of the universe. They do no such thing. . . . The 'laws of nature' are only our finite and fallible attempts at describing the regular patterns of behavior that we observe in the world around us. The identity of the ultimate power that governs those patterns must be determined on extra-scientific grounds." Howard J. Van Till, Clarence Menninga, and Davis A. Young, *Science Held Hostage: What's Wrong with Creation Science AND Evolutionism* (Downers Grove, Ill.: InterVarsity, 1988), 132.

32. Howard J. Van Till, "When Faith and Reason Meet," in Michael Bauman, ed., *Man and Creation: Perspectives on Science and Theology* (Hillsdale, Mich.: Hillsdale College Press, 1993), 155–56. Despite the value of Van Till's efforts, I wish to interject a disclaimer here

against any personal belief in Van Till's concept of a "fully gifted creation," a detailed account of which is found in J. P. Moreland and John Mark Reynolds, eds., *Three Views on Creation and Evolution* (Grand Rapids: Zondervan, 1999).

33. "Our understanding of a structure depends largely on the discovery of its *telos*, its purpose or end: In other words, what is it good for? . . . One comes to understand the structure or order via a discovery of finality, while mechanism divorced from finality is in some sense unintelligible." William N. Shea, *The Naturalists and the Supernatural: Studies in Horizon and an American Philosophy of Religion* (Macon, Ga.: Mercer University Press, 1984), 148.

34. Cramer, "The Entropic versus the Anthropic Principle: On the Self-Organization of Life," 135.

35. George N. Schlesinger, "The Anthropic Principle," *Tradition: A Journal of Orthodox Jewish Thought* 23, no. 3 (Spring 1988): 8. Similarly, "Here is the cosmological proof of the existence of God—the design argument of Paley updated and refurbished. The fine tuning of the universe provides prima facie evidence of deistic design." Edward R. Harrison, *Masks of the Universe* (New York: Macmillan, 1985), 248.

36. This is not to say that skeptical inquiries are to be rejected entirely; in epistemological moderation they may ultimately prove helpful, but metaempiricist concerns are not without warrant. Theologian Karl Rahner, while acknowledging the role that healthy skepticism plays in science, nevertheless exhorts naturalistic scientists not "to extrapolate in an all too facile way a total world view based on the conclusions of natural science" (*Theological Investigations*, vol. XXI, *Science and Christian Faith*, trans. Hugh M. Riley [New York: Crossroad, 1983], 17).

37. For a fascinating examination of these "connections and resonances" within nature, many of which may be described without appealing to anthropic parameters at all, see Frank Wilczek and Betsy Devine, *Longing for the Harmonies: Themes and Variations from Modern Physics* (New York: Norton, 1988). But these other kind of natural cosmic harmonies in no way detract from the weightiness of the cosmic coincidences. As anthropic theorist Joseph M. Zycinski declares: "Now when the period of fascination with empiricism has ended in science, reflection on the puzzling manifestation of the harmony of nature is necessary, a harmony which is revealed by, among other things, cosmological coincidences" ("The Anthropic Principle and Teleological Interpretations of Nature," *Review of Metaphysics* 41, no. 2 [December 1987]: 332).

38. John Polkinghorne, *Science and Creation: The Search for Understanding* (London: SPCK, 1988), 30.

39. Brandon Carter, "Anthropic Selection Principle and the Ultra-Darwinian Synthesis," in *The Anthropic Principle: Proceedings*, ed. Bertola and Curi, 50–51.

40. Gratton, "Metaphysical Outlooks," 103.

41. G. F. R. Ellis, "The Anthropic Principle: Laws and Environments," in *The Anthropic Principle: Proceedings*, ed. Bertola and Curi, 29.

42. Paul Davies, *The Cosmic Blueprint: New Discoveries in Nature's Creative Ability to Order the Universe* (New York: Simon & Schuster, 1988), 163.

43. When the universe is described in these terms, anthropic theorists often characterize the ACP as being too anthropocentric in character. On the other hand, some seem to glory in its anthropocentricity by virtue of its cosmic *telos*, a teleology that thankfully produced human beings. As Oddone Longo states: "There is no doubt that the anthropic

principle implies axioms of the teleological and anthropocentric type, and may in a certain sense be defined as the scientific formulation of an anthropocentric teleology" ("The Anthropic Principle and Ancient Science," in *The Anthropic Principle: Proceedings*, ed. Bertola and Curi, 18).

44. Along these lines, M. A. Corey is not advocating such a position, but his ideas about God's creative intellect and power are thought-provoking. As Corey relates: "The truly unfathomable degree of complexity found at all levels of universal reality also seems to be explicable only in terms of an all-knowing Intelligence. It just doesn't seem to be possible for a mindless product of chance to consistently produce instances of complexity that completely overwhelm our ability to understand them. It would thus seem that the origin of any complex process requires at least as much intelligence as it takes for that process to be understood by other intelligent beings. As long as we assume this to be true, it follows that the universe had to have been created by a universal power that is *infinitely* more advanced than we are at the present time, since the underlying details of the physical universe appear to be infinitely complex. The only being who is capable of such infinitely advanced creative tasks is God *by definition*." Corey, *God and the New Cosmology*, 257.

45. "Why should it not be claimed that reason and experience at present confirm the hypothesis that some event of the past was due to the direct (primary) causality of God rather then to any derivative (secondary) cause or causes?" Hugo A. Meynell, *The Intelligible Universe: A Cosmological Argument* (Totowa, N.J.: Barnes & Noble, 1982), 109. With some revision of what primary and secondary causal sources involve, Arthur Peacocke writes similarly: "We must conceive of God as creating within the whole process from beginning to end, through and through, or he cannot be involved at all. It is not so much a question of primary and secondary causes, as classically expounded by Thomas Aquinas, but rather the natural causal creative nexus of events *is* itself God's creative action. It is this that the attribution of immanence to God in the creation of his world must be taken to convey. . . . We wish to say that all that is in its actual processes is God manifest in his mode as continuous creator" ("Theology and Science Today," in *Cosmos as Creation*, ed. Peters, 34).

46. At the volitional level, not every theologian, philosopher, or scientist will champion the ACP as fertile ground for theistic ways and means. In the context of twenty thought-provoking questions concerning fine tuning arguments as a whole, Jay W. Richards states that "if someone does not think it possible that the universe is fine-tuned, or does not think any observation or inference from, say, physics, could provide evidence or grounds for believing the same, then no argument is going to matter" ("Some Preliminary Questions to Any Future Fine-Tuning Argument," *Philosophia Christi* 7, no. 2 [2005]: 375).

47. Gerhard Staguhn, *God's Laughter: Man and His Cosmos*, trans. Steve Lake and Caroline Mähl (New York: HarperCollins, 1992), 155.

48. "One of the main reasons it is so tempting to supplant the [naturalistic] anthropic principle with its theistic interpretation is that this interpretation provides a much more coherent view. . . . The proposed anthropic process at work in the universe can be seen, not as some mysterious, unjustifiably proposed tendency, but as just another intentional product of the Creator's actions." Patrick A. Wilson, "The Anthropic Cosmological Principle," Ph.D. diss. (University of Notre Dame, 1989), 191.

49. *Canonical* is used here to mean "approved," because it is difficult to imagine another authorized used of the word *cause* beyond the six discussed, and *conjugates* is used to mean words that have related meanings.

50. Jaki, *Cosmos and Creator*, 97.

51. Definitions provided by Sproul, *Not a Chance*, 197.

52. As cited in Barrow and Tipler, *The Anthropic Cosmological Principle*, 49.

53. See Robert Audi, ed., *The Cambridge Dictionary of Philosophy*, 2d ed. (New York: Cambridge University Press, 1999), 125, s.v. "Causation," by Jaegwon Kim.

54. Jaki, *Cosmos and Creator*, 107–08.

55. Ernan McMullin, in Robert John Russell, William R. Stoeger, and George V. Coyne, eds., *Physics, Philosophy, and Theology: A Common Quest for Understanding* (Notre Dame: University of Notre Dame Press, 1988), 74 (emphasis original).

56. The present article is an abridged and amended version of chapter 3 of my doctoral dissertation: *A Christian Analysis of the Anthropic Cosmological Principle as the Basis for a Constructive Theistic Quantum Cosmology* (Fort Worth: Southwestern Baptist Theological Seminary, 1995).

Chapter 9 Notes

1. See Bas C. van Fraassen, *Laws and Symmetry* (Oxford: Clarendon Press, 1989), 1–14.

2. René Descartes, *Principles of Philosophy* (1644), part II, xxxvi.

3. Charles Hodge, *Systematic Theology*, 3 vols. (New York: Scribner's Sons, 1871; quotations from 1891 edition), 1:618.

4. Hodge, *Systematic Theology*, 1:607.

5. See Owen Thomas, ed., *God's Activity in the World: The Contemporary Problem* (Chico, Calif.: Scholars Press, 1983), 3.

6. Friedrich Schleiermacher, *The Christian Faith* (Edinburgh: T&T Clark, 1928), secs. 46 and 47.

7. Gordon Kaufman, "On the Meaning of 'Act of God,'" *Harvard Theological Review* 61 (1968): 175–201. Reprinted in Thomas, ed., *God's Activity in the World* (Note: page references are to the reprint), 153.

8. Kaufman, "On the Meaning," 148.

9. Kaufman, "On the Meaning," 156.

10. Kaufman, "On the Meaning," 157.

11. Owen Gingrich, "Where in the World is God?" in Michael Bauman, ed., *Man and Creation: Perspectives on Science and Theology* (Hillsdale, Mich.: Hillsdale College Press, 1993), 209–29; quotations on 220–21, 222.

12. Gingrich, "Where in the World is God?" 223.

13. Robert T. Pennock, *Tower of Babel: The Evidence against the New Creationism* (Cambridge: MIT Press, 1999), 30–31.

14. Phillip E. Johnson, *Darwin on Trial* (Downers Grove, Ill.: InterVarsity, 1991), 127.

15. See Carl Hempel, *Aspects of Scientific Explanation* (New York: Free Press, 1965).

16. Jaegwon Kim, "Causation," in Robert Audi, ed., *The Cambridge Dictionary of Philosophy* (Cambridge, Cambridge University Press, 1995), 110–12: 112.

17. John Hedley Brooke, *Science and Religion: Some Historical Perspectives* (Cambridge: Cambridge University Press, 1991), 313.

18. Aubrey Moore, quoted by Arthur Peacocke in "Biological Evolution and Christian Theology—Yesterday and Today," in John Durant, ed., *Darwinism and Divinity* (Oxford: Oxford University Press, 1985), 111.

19. Karl Heim, *The Transformation of the Scientific World* (London: SCM, 1953).

20. The first five conferences resulted in volumes edited by Robert J. Russell, et al., with the subtitle *Scientific Perspectives on Divine Action*. The titles and respective dates are: *Quantum Cosmology and the Laws of Nature; Chaos and Complexity; Evolutionary and Molecular Biology; Neuroscience and the Person;* and *Quantum Mechanics* (Vatican City State and Berkeley: Vatican Observatory Press and Center for Theology and the Natural Sciences, 1993, 1995, 1998, 1999, 2001). The final volume is *Scientific Perspectives on Divine Action: Twenty Years of Problems and Progress* (2007).

21. See *inter alia* Arthur Peacocke, "The Sound of Sheer Silence: How Does God Communicate with Humanity?" in Russell, et al., eds., *Neuroscience and the Person*, 215–48.

22. John Polkinghorne, "The Metaphysics of Divine Action," in Robert J. Russell, Nancey Murphy, and Arthur R. Peacocke, eds., *Chaos and Complexity*, 147–56.

23. My theory is spelled out in detail in "Divine Action in the Natural Order: Buridan's Ass and Schrödinger's Cat," in Russell, et al., eds., *Chaos and Complexity*, 325–58. For complementary accounts, in the same volume see Thomas F. Tracy, "Particular Providence and the God of the Gaps"; and George F. R. Ellis, "Ordinary and Extraordinary Divine Action: The Nexus of Interaction." See also references to Russell's work in the next section.

24. See Robert J. Russell, "Quantum Physics in Philosophical and Theological Perspective," in Russell, William R. Stoeger, S.J., and George V. Coyne, S.J., eds., *Physics, Philosophy, and Theology: A Common Quest for Understanding* (Vatican City State: Vatican Observatory Press, 1988), 343–74.

25. In Robert J. Russell, William R. Stoeger, S.J., and Francisco J. Ayala, eds., *Evolution and Molecular Biology*, 191–223; 192. For his most detailed discussion of quantum mechanics in relation to what he calls "non-interventionist objective divine action" (NIODA), see Robert John Russell, "Divine Action and Quantum Mechanics: A Fresh Assessment," in *Quantum Mechanics*, 293–328. Note that what Russell means by NIODA is equivalent to what I mean by "noninterventionist special divine action."

26. Russell, et al., *Evolution and Molecular Biology*, 203.

27. Russell, et al., *Evolution and Molecular Biology*, 203.

28. Russell, et al., *Evolution and Molecular Biology*, 206.

29. Russell, et al., *Evolution and Molecular Biology*, 193.

Chapter 10 Notes

1. See John C. Polkinghorne, *Exploring Reality* (London and New Haven: SPCK/Yale University Press, 2005), chap. 3.

2. For quantum ideas, see for example, John C. Polkinghorne, *Quantum Theory: A Very Short Introduction* (Oxford: Oxford University Press, 2002).

3. David Bohm and Basil J. Hiley, *The Undivided Universe: An Ontological Interpretation of Quantum Theory* (London: Routledge, 1993).

4. John C. Polkinghorne, *Exploring Reality*, chap. 2.

5. John C. Polkinghorne, *Belief in God in an Age of Science* (New Haven: Yale University Press, 1998), chap. 3.

6. See Philip Clayton, *Mind and Emergence: From Quantum to Consciousness* (Oxford: Oxford University Press, 2004).

7. Stuart A. Kauffman, *The Origins of Order: Self-Organization and Selection in Evolution* (Oxford: Oxford University Press, 1993).

8. John D. Barrow and Frank J. Tipler, *The Anthropic Cosmological Principle* (Oxford: Oxford University Press, 1986); John Leslie, *Universes* (London: Routledge, 1989).

9. See John C. Polkinghorne, ed., *The Work of Love* (London and Grand Rapids: SPCK/Eerdmans, 2001).

10. See Robert J. Russell, Nancey Murphy, and Arthur R. Peacocke, eds., *Chaos and Complexity* (Vatican City State and Berkeley: Vatican Observatory Press and Center for Theology and the Natural Sciences, 1995); Robert J. Russell, Philip Clayton, Kirk Wegter-McNelly, and John C. Polkinghorne, eds., *Quantum Mechanics* (Vatican City State and Berkeley: Vatican Observatory Press and Center for Theology and the Natural Sciences, 2001); and n. 5, above.

11. John C. Polkinghorne, *Science and Providence: God's Interaction with the World* (London: SPCK, 1989), chap. 4.

12. William A. Dembski, *Intelligent Design: The Bridge Between Science and Theology* (Downers Grove, Ill.: InterVarsity, 1999).

13. Michael J. Behe, *Darwin's Black Box: The Biochemical Challenge to Evolution* (New York: The Free Press, 1996), 39.

14. Arthur R. Peacocke, *God and the New Biology* (San Francisco: Harper & Row, 1986), 97–99.

15. For a clear discussion, see David J. Bartholomew, *God of Chance* (London: SCM, 1984), chap. 4.

Chapter 11 Notes

1. Richard Dawkins, *The God Delusion* (New York: Houghton Mifflin, 2006).

2. Francis Collins, *The Language of God: A Scientist Presents Evidence for Belief* (New York: Free Press, 2006).

3. John Brooke, *Science and Religion: Some Historical Perspectives* (Cambridge: Cambridge University Press, 1991).

4. I do not intend to suggest that theism and atheism are the only worldviews, only that they are, historically, the main views involved in the debate.

5. Note that "creationism" is another example of a shift in the meaning of terminology. It no longer simply means belief in a Creator but also commitment to a whole raft of additional ideas, the most dominant of which, based on a particular interpretation of Genesis, is that the earth is only a few thousand years old.

6. The *Oxford Companion to Science and Religion* (Oxford: Oxford University Press, 2006).

7. William A. Dembski and Michael Ruse, "General Introduction," in *Debating Design*, ed. William A. Dembski and Michael Ruse (Cambridge: Cambridge University Press, 2004), 3.

8. My worldview is Christian.

9. Indeed, this is just the kind of thing that understandably goads Richard Dawkins into using his lance.

10. We might also note that Socrates and Plato used design arguments, but their designing intelligence was not the God of Christianity.

11. William A. Dembski, *The Design Inference: Eliminating Chance Through Small Probabilities*, Cambridge Studies in Probability, Induction, and Decision Theory (New York: Cambridge University Press, 1998).

12. E. O. Wilson, "Intelligent Evolution: The consequences of Charles Darwin's 'one long argument'," *Harvard Magazine* (November-December 2005), 29–30.

13. Romans 1:20.

14. Albert Einstein, *Letters to Solovine: 1906–1955*, ed. Peter Kensington (New York: Philosophical Library, 1987), 131.

15. Roger Penrose, *The Emperor's New Mind: Concerning Computers, Minds, and the Laws of Physics* (London: Vintage, 1991), 430.

16. John Polkinghorne, *Reason and Reality* (London: SPCK, 1991), 76.

17. Melvin Calvin, *Chemical Evolution* (Oxford: Clarendon, 1969), 258.

18. Peter Harrison, *The Bible, Protestantism and the Rise of Natural Science* (Cambridge: Cambridge University Press, 1998).

19. Thomas F. Torrance, *Theological Science* (Edinburgh: T&T Clark, 1996), 57.

20. Richard Swinburne, *Is There a God?* (Oxford: Oxford University Press, 1996), 68.

21. Francis Crick, *The Astonishing Hypothesis—The Scientific Search for the Soul* (London: Simon and Schuster, 1994), 3.

22. Such ontological reductionism must be distinguished from the methodological reductionism on which science (and much else) thrives: take a complex problem and split it into smaller more manageable problems to see if their solution gives insight into how to solve the big problem.

23. John C. Polkinghorne, *One World: The Interaction of Science and Theology* (London: SPCK, 1986), 93.

24. John Houghton, *The Search for God—Can Science Help?* (Oxford: Lion, 1995), 59.

25. See, for example, John C. Polkinghorne, "The Inbuilt Potentiality of Creation," in Dembski and Ruse, eds., *Debating Design*, 246–60; or John Barrow and Frank Tipler, *The Anthropic Cosmological Principle* (Oxford: Oxford University Press, 1986).

26. Arno Penzias, "Creation is Supported by All the Data So Far," in *Cosmos, Bios, and Theos: Scientists Reflect on Science, God, and the Origins of the Universe, Life, and Homo Sapiens*, ed. Henry Margenau and Roy Abraham Varghese (La Salle, Ill.: Open Court, 1992), 83.

27. The author is well aware that the idea of a beginning is being challenged, but it is still fair to say that the standard model has majority support.

28. See Malcolm Browne, "Clues to the Universe's Origin Expected," *New York Times*, March 12, 1978, 1.

29. Dawkins, *The God Delusion*.

30. Daniel C. Dennett, *Darwin's Dangerous Idea: Evolution and the Meanings of Life* (New York: Simon & Schuster, 1995), 203.

31. Houghton, *The Search for God—Can Science Help?*, 54

32. Keith Ward, "Theistic Evolution," in Dembski and Ruse, eds., *Debating Design*, 262.

33. Polkinghorne, "The Inbuilt Potentiality of Creation," in Dembski and Ruse, eds., *Debating Design*, 257.

34. Darwin's staunchest supporter in the United States.

35. For example, Collins, *The Language of God*; Denis Alexander, *Rebuilding the Matrix* (Oxford: Lion, 2001), 291; Kenneth R. Miller, *Finding Darwin's God: A Scientist's Search for Common Ground Between God and Evolution* (New York: Cliff Street, 1999).

36. Stephen J. Gould, "Impeaching a Self-appointed Judge," *Scientific American*, 267, no.1 (1992): 118–21.

37. Dennett, *Darwin's Dangerous Idea*, 50.

38. Dennett, *Darwin's Dangerous Idea*, 76.

39. Richard Dawkins, *The Blind Watchmaker: Why the Evidence of Evolution Reveals a Universe Without Design* (London: Longmans, 1986), 14.

40. For the issue is not whether the evolutionary mechanism does something, since explanation in terms of mutation and natural selection of, say, the variations observed by Darwin himself, is surely uncontroversial. This, of course, implies for a theist that theistic evolution is at least true in the sense that God has created and maintains a world in which mutation and natural selection occur.

41. Richard N. Ostling, "Atheist Philosopher, 81, Now Believes in God," Associated Press Report, December 10, 2004, www.livescience.com/strangenews/atheist_philosopher_041210.html (accessed June 13, 2007).

42. Robert Laughlin, *A Different Universe: Reinventing Physics from the Bottom Down* (New York: Basic Books, 2005), 168–69.

43. C. S. Lewis, *Miracles* (New York: Macmillan, 1947).

44. Alvin Plantinga, "Should Methodological Naturalism Constrain Science" in *Science: Christian Perspectives for the New Millenium*, ed. Scott B Luley, Paul Copan and Stan W Wallace (Addison, Tex.: CLM/RZIM, 2003), 130–31.

45. See Clive Cookson, "Scientists who glimpsed God," *Financial Times*, April 29, 1995, 20.

46. Lewis, *Miracles*.

47. Ephesians 1:19-20.

48. The word *emergent* is used in many ways and can mask hidden presuppositions and beg the question of whether the "emergence" involves additional inputs of energy or intelligence or both.

49. Paul Davies, *The Fifth Miracle: The Search for the Origin and Meaning of Life* (New York: Simon & Schuster, 2000), 122.

50. We do not, of course, mean that there could be a full proof in the mathematical sense since that kind of proof is only to be found in mathematics, what we mean by "provably" here is compelling evidence of the sort that scientists accept.

51. Leonard Brillouin, *Science and Information Theory*, 2d. ed. (New York: Academic, 1962).

52. Kurt Gödel, "On 'Computabilism' and Physicalism: Some Subproblems," in *Nature's Imagination: The Frontiers of Scientific Vision*, ed. John Cornwell and Freeman Dyson (Oxford: Oxford University Press, 1995), 173.

53. Peter B. Medawar, *The Limits of Science* (Oxford: Oxford University Press, 1984).

54. William A. Dembski, "Intelligent Design as a Theory of Information," *Perspectives on Science and Christian Faith* 49, no. 3 (1997): 180–90; see also Dembski, *No Free Lunch: Why Specified Complexity Cannot Be Purchased without Intelligence* (Lanham, Md.: Rowman and Littlefield, 2002).

55. See John C. Lennox, *God's Undertaker—Has Science Buried God?* (Oxford: Lion Hudson, 2007).

56. The Laws of Nature and the Laws of Physics," in *Quantum Cosmology and the Laws of Nature: Scientific Perspectives on Divine Action*, 2d ed., ed. Robert John Russell, Nancey Murphy, and C. J. Isham (Vatican City and Berkeley: The Vatican Observatory and The Center for Theology and Natural Sciences, 1999), 438. Note that Polkinghorne's view is that the nature of God's interaction is "not energetic but informational," which we find somewhat puzzling in light of the Christian doctrines of creation and resurrection. Surely energy must also be involved?

57. Michael Polanyi, *Tacit Dimension* (New York, Doubleday, 1966).

58. Some might argue that, although the semiotics of the letters cannot be given an explanation in terms of physics and chemistry *directly*, nevertheless the argument fails since, in the end, the human authors of the writing can ultimately be explained in terms of physics and chemistry. However, this simply begs the question that lies at the heart of our consideration: Does such a reductionist explanation for human beings actually exist?

59. Paul Davies, "Bit Before It," *New Scientist,* January 30, 1999, 3. See also Hans Christian von Baeyer, "In the Beginning was the Bit," *New Scientist*, February 17, 2001, p. 24.

Chapter 12 Notes

1. Rob Moll, "The Other ID Opponents: Traditional creationists see Intelligent Design as an attack on the Bible," in *Christianity Today*, April 25, 2006, www.ctlibrary. com/ct/2006/aprilweb-only/117-22.0.html (accessed June 13, 2007).

2. Proclus, *On the Eternity of the World*, trans. Helen S. Lang and A. D. Marco (Berkeley: University of California Press, 2002). Not all neo-Platonists were equally antagonistic toward Christianity. In fact, neo-Platonism had a significant impact on the theology of the early church.

3. Richard Sorabji, *Philoponus and the Rejection of Aristotelian Science* (Ithaca, N.Y.: Cornell University Press, 1987), vii, 7–10; Carol William Pearson, "Scripture as Cosmology: Natural Philosophical Debate in John Philoponus's Alexandria," Ph.D. diss., Harvard University, 1999, 225–27; c.f. Thomas Kuhn, *The Structure of Scientific Revolutions* (Chicago: University of Chicago Press, 1962), 120.

4. Sorabji, *Philoponus and the Rejection of Aristotelian Science*, 34. In addition, Galileo will credit Philoponus for providing crucial solutions to the question of motion in a vacuum. See *Philoponus*, 13–14.

5. Sorabji, *Philoponus*, vii; Kuhn, *The Structure of Scientific Revolutions*, 120.

6. Philoponus's *Against Aristotle* has been lost and fragments are reconstructed from Simplicius's rejoinder.

7. Pearson, "Scripture as Cosmology," 147.

8. Comas Indicopleustes, *Christian Topography*, trans. J. W. McCrindle (New York: Burt Franklin, 1967), 8–10.

9. John Philoponus, *On the Creation of the World*, 3.8, quoted in Pearson, "Scripture as Cosmology," 160.

10. John Philoponus, *Against Aristotle on the Eternity of the World* (frag. 1.18-32, 4.92-93), trans. Christian Wildberg (Ithaca, N.Y.: Cornell University Press, 1987), 52–55, 104–06. I wish to express my thanks to Gary Harris, a student at Southeastern, for his assistance in researching Philoponus's works.

11. Philoponus, *Against Aristotle* (4.62-72), 78–81.

12. Philoponus, *Against Aristotle* (6.108-32), 12446.

13. Sorabji, *Philoponus*, 7–8.

14. Sorabji, *Philoponus*, 8. cf. Kuhn, *The Structure of Scientific Revolutions*, 120.

15. Sorabji, *Philoponus*, 24.

16. Philoponus, *Against Aristotle* (4.77-80), 88–89.

17. Philoponus, *Against Aristotle* (3.52-55), 70–72.

18. Philoponus, *Against Aristotle* (1.9-17), 47.

19. Philoponus, *Against Aristotle* (1.18-32), 50–52.

20. Sorabji, *Philoponus*, 9.

21. Cosmas, *Christian Topography*, 135.

22. Cosmas, *Christian Topography*, 136.

23. Cosmas, *Christian Topography*, 30–31.

24. Cosmas, *Christian Topography*, 130–31. The four navigable gulfs are the Roman, Arabian, Persian, and Caspian seas.

25. Cosmas, *Christian Topography*, 110–11.

26. Cosmas, *Christian Topography*, 39–40.

27. Cosmas, *Christian Topography*, 146, 267. Cosmas has particular trouble explaining Paul's use of the term "third heaven" in 2 Corinthians 12.

28. Cosmas, *Christian Topography*, 76–77. Cosmas argues that the angels were created to move the elements located in the heavens—the stars, sun, moon, and even the air. The angels received this commission on the fourth day, and on that day some of them rebelled because they resented their servile existence. He understands "the creature" in Rom. 8:19 to be referring to the angels.

29. Cosmas, *Christian Topography*, 30–41; 130–31. Cosmas cites expressions such as, "He that hath established the heaven as a vaulted chamber," and "having stretched it out as a tent to dwell in" (Isa. 40:22; cf. Isa. 49:2). Other passages to which he appeals

are "stretching out the heaven as a curtain" (Ps. 104:2-3); "who layeth the beams of his chambers in the waters" (Isa. 40:22); "He that made the earth and pitched it" (Isa. 42:5); "and he inclined heaven to earth, and the earth is poured out as dust, and I have fastened it as a square block to a stone" (Job 38:38); "He that hath founded the earth upon its own stability" (Ps. 104:5). Cosmas uses the LXX exclusively.

30. Cosmas, *Christian Topography*, 52, 251.

31. Cosmas, *Christian Topography*, 42.

32. Cosmas, *Christian Topography*, 42, 84, 131–32. "The sun riseth and the sun goeth down, and draweth to his own place. On his rising he goeth then to the south and wheeleth his circles, and turneth around the air upon his circles" (Eccl. 1:6-7 LXX).

33. Cosmas, *Christian Topography*, 86–87.

34. Cosmas, *Christian Topography*, 259–60.

35. Cosmas, *Christian Topography*, 299.

36. Cosmas, *Christian Topography*, 133–34.

37. Cosmas, *Christian Topography*, 134.

38. Cosmas, *Christian Topography*, 300.

39. Cosmas, *Christian Topography*, 136.

40. Cosmas, *Christian Topography*, 130–31.

41. Cosmas, *Christian Topography*, 146–47.

42. Cosmas, *Christian Topography*, 31–51.

43. Cosmas, *Christian Topography*, 149–52.

44. Cosmas, *Christian Topography*, 33-37.

45. Cosmas, *Christian Topography*, 66–74.

46. Cosmas, *Christian Topography*, 67.

47. Cosmas, *Christian Topography*, 49, 67.

48. Cosmas, *Christian Topography*, 244–45.

49. Cosmas, *Christian Topography*, 252.

50. Cosmas, *Christian Topography*, 250.

51. Cosmas, *Christian Topography*, 250.

52. Cosmas, *Christian Topography*, 263–64. Again speaking to his mentor, Cosmas states, "For you have informed me that one of those who glory in being Christians, when wishing to speak against the pagans, unconsciously agreed with them in their opinion, that heaven is a sphere which is always revolving; and yet that in the same work he proclaimed it to be dissoluble. I know not what induced him to make this assertion, and I could not but wonder that the wisdom of a man so great learning should be blinded by his craving for distinction. For if, as a Christian, he had in view to refute the view of the pagans, he ought first to have overthrown from the foundation their principles relating to the sphere and its revolution, just as we ourselves, by the will of God, have done in the other work, which as requested we composed. But if he admits their foundation and their principles, from which their demonstrations of eternal duration proceed, why does that wise man indulge to no purpose in idle talk, basing his nonsense not on a rock, but upon the sand?"

53. Cosmas, *Christian Topography*, 302.

54. Pearson, "Scripture as Cosmology," 30, 42–43.

55. Pearson, "Scripture as Cosmology," 173.

56. John Philoponus, quoted by Pearson, "Scripture as Cosmology," 100.

57. Pearson, "Scripture as Cosmology," 172.

58. Pearson, "Scripture as Cosmology," 40–41.

59. Pearson, "Scripture as Cosmology," 120.

60. Sorabji, *Philoponus and the Rejection of Aristotelian Science*, 7–10.

61. Sorabji, *Philoponus*, 30.

62. See Stephen Jay Gould, "The Late Birth of a Flat Earth," in *Dinosaur in a Haystack* (New York: Harmony, 1995), 38–52.

63. Russell demonstrates that proponents of the "warfare metaphor," such as John William Draper and Andrew Dickson White, are inconsistent in their respective portrayals of the Medieval Church's position on the shape of the earth. On the one hand, they claim that the clergy opposed Columbus because they believed the earth was flat, and then on the other hand, they claim that the clergy opposed Galileo because they held to the Ptolemaic system. The Church might have done one or the other, but it cannot have done both. Russell demonstrates that it is the latter. See Jeffrey Burton Russell, *Inventing the Flat Earth: Columbus and Modern Historians* (New York: Praeger, 1991).

64. See John William Draper, *History of the Conflict between Religion and Science* (London: C. Kegan Paul, 1878), 152–81; and Andrew Dickson White, *A History of the Warfare of Science with Theology*, vol. 1 (New York: Dover [1896], 1960), 93–98.

65. Philoponus's commitment to rationalism will lead him astray in the theological realm. Late in life, Philoponus advocates three heterodox doctrines—monophysiticism (a rejection of the orthodox doctrine of the two natures of Christ), tritheism (the three Persons of the Trinity are three beings), and the discontinuity of the resurrected body. After his death, Philoponus is condemned by the Council of Constantinople (680) for heresy. As a result, Islamic and Jewish scholars utilize his scientific breakthroughs centuries before his contributions are entirely appreciated in the Christian West.

66. A recent *Time* magazine article records a debate between Richard Dawkins and Francis Collins, both of whom accept the evolutionary hypothesis. Dawkins is famous for his militant atheism while Collins, who directed the Human Genome Project, converted at age twenty-seven from atheism to an evangelical faith. When they begin to discuss creationists, Dawkins dismisses them by asking Collins, "Why bother with these clowns?" See David Van Biema, "God vs. Science," *Time*, Nov. 2, 2006, www.time.com/time/magazine/article/0,9171,1555132,00.html (accessed June 13, 2007).

Index